PROPERTY RIGHTS IN THE DEFENCE OF NATURE

PROPERTY RIGHTS IN THE DEFENCE OF NATURE

ELIZABETH BRUBAKER

Environment Probe

EARTHSCAN
London ■ Toronto

First edition published simultaneously in the United Kingdom by Earthscan
Publications Ltd., 120 Pentonville Road, London N1 9JN; and in Canada by
Earthscan Canada, 225 Brunswick Avenue, Toronto, Ontario M5S 2M6

A catalog record for this book is available from the British Library.

Canadian Cataloguing in Publication Data

Brubaker, Elizabeth, 1958-
    Property rights in the defence of nature

Includes bibliographical references and index.
ISBN 0-919849-24-5

1. Right of property.   2. Land use – Government policy.
3. Land use – Environmental policy.   I. Environment
Probe (Organization).   II. Title.

K721.5.B78 1995   333.3   C95-930955-1

Earthscan Publications Ltd. is an editorially independent subsidiary of Kogan
Page Ltd. and publishes in association with the International Institute for
Environment and Development and the World Wide Fund for Nature.

Environment Probe is a division of EPRF Energy Probe Research Foundation.

Book design and layout by Elizabeth Rentzelos
Printed in Canada by Webcom

ISBN Summary
1-85383-278-2   Softcover UK
0-919849-24-5   Softcover Canada

Contents

Foreword

This book does not simply reiterate the present orthodoxy about protecting nature. Its approach goes much further.

Today most environmentalists have abandoned the early approach of targeting bad-guy polluters. Instead they work on politicians to enact ever more regulations, controls, and standards. Profoundly dissatisfied with laggard government, they strain ever harder to whip it on, their urgency leaving them little time to wonder whether there may not be a better way. Uncritical of the fundamental basis of existing laws, they find it simplest to maintain the dislike of property rights inherited from earlier movements that fought against feudal proprietors, serfdom, slavery, enclosures, clearances, absentee ownership, share cropping, speculative reserves, and exploitative rents.

More recently, interest in an ecosystem approach has drawn some to the *deep ecology* principle that humans have no right to interfere with the richness and the diversity of life forms, which have inherent value. Because landed property rights (to manage, to profit from, and to sell or exchange) do confer rights to interfere with nature, deep ecology gives activists another reason to oppose property rights.

But most activists and anti-pollution workers are more pragmatic. True, they may one week attack a firm whose human greed and foreign capital combine with its "entrenched property" to motivate it to dangerous pollution. But the next week, the worker sees property in a new guise. No longer villains, property holders are now "local citizens" protecting their homes and families against outside polluters. The worker's casual pragmatism admits that in disputes about pollution, property is often the victim's ally.

Here this book is refreshing and precise. Property *can* be a weapon that victims use in their own defence. Those who care more about nature than about the glorification or vilification of government will find property protects it better than government does.

Protection by property tends to avoid courtrooms as well as legislatures. Although legal professors too often forget it, property law does its job best when land is held and exchanged in an orderly way without litigation. A good standard property right works regularly and informally to keep disputes out of the courts; indeed knowledge of it prevents disputes from even arising.

Millions and millions of registered holders of land, woods, water rights and minerals, many of them overlapping, knowing and accepting their rights and responsibilities, never see a court. A good foundation of property rights allows neighbours to routinely tailor their boundary fences, views, noise, trees, crops, gates or roaming livestock to suit their particular circumstances.

Of course Elizabeth Brubaker, in clearly displaying property's defensive powers, is not quite alone. She has on her side small camps of environmental lawyers and environmental economists who invoke property. We need her book because, surprisingly, they are not whole-hearted allies.

Consider environmental lawyers. Sometimes they even seem hostile to Brubaker's approach. They seem too concerned with *laws*, not *Law*: with government statutes, standards controls, and enforcement. They deal with politicians and regulators, in strategies and policies. This is easy to understand. Because the lawyers for polluters and developers spend their time trying to get environmental rules defeated, weakened, ignored, or set aside, environmental lawyers spend their time defending the rules, rarely considering whether, instead of trying to supply governments with backbone, they could be developing the common-law concepts illustrated here.

If we look into the various camps of economists, we again find few who actively support a property approach. Property, if thought about at all, is considered the shield of parties who create environmental problems. Consequently environmental economists join teams that, with environmental lawyers, attack that shield, doing duty somewhere in the enforcement procedure— making either demand projections, input-output estimates, benefit-cost analyses, environmental impact statements, contingent valuations, or searches for alternative technologies. Sadly, this long list of procedural studies offers a career to many economic researchers. Indeed, the demand for their research is greatest for problems where property rights are weakest, biasing them against property.

In another camp, where both lawyers and economists dwell, property has adherents. A few of them, often academics, have long favoured pricing: taxes, charges, graded penalties, and fines set at rates that make pollution a costly alternative, in order to harness the cost-conscious attitudes of polluters and developers. Such proposals win automatic support from other academics and textbooks, but never from real decision makers. In still another camp, members have long and consistently backed a property-and-market approach to environmentalism. Political and economic conservatives by inclination, they tend to see an increase in private property primarily as a means of narrowing the domain of government.

These latter two groups are sometimes confused with a more truly environmentally oriented school whose members like property rights because they can produce better environmental results, both alone and in property markets, than any tax or charge gimmick. This school's increasing influence can be seen in the modern design of emission or pollution rights. Emission rights can work within the structure of old common-law rights described in this book, having the right abstract characteristics to make them exclusive, secure before the courts, and tradable in the market. The book's chapter on the new individual fishing quotas, now being adopted all over the world, from New Zealand to Iceland, also illustrates the modern creation of property in the defence of nature. However, this book does not focus on such new creations. Instead it concentrates on the power in the common law and old kinds of property interest that many busy environmentalists, lawyers, and economists have come to neglect. I'm all for it.

The recognition of property in defence of nature is well rooted. The conservation movement, under way in Canada and the U.S. around 1900, thought very hard about property. An impressively active group in Ontario worried about dangers to the forest from fire and disease, but also from over-cutting and waste, and about dangers to soil, fisheries and mine lands. What united its members was the conservation goal, something like today's sustainable-development goal: to preserve natural resources for future generations.

To this end they favoured long-term ownership, either private or public. Permanent government ownership was more or less acceptable, if only government would show any sign of resolute forest policy. Short-term timber licences, which gave lumbermen no incentive to ensure a second crop, were criticized. Such weakness of government forest management provoked these early conservationists into a decade of discussion and complaint, from which many of them emerged favouring long-term private rights of various kinds, for loggers, settlers, summer people and miners. Early conservationists concentrated on preserving natural resources from over-harvesting. Today, the principles they embraced can also be used to fight air and water pollution.

The author's loyalty to the property-rights approach is courageously consistent. When her outline brings her face to face with the 1980s litmus-paper test, whether to entrench property in the Constitution along with other items in the Charter, she does not blink. Many of the pragmatic lawyers, economists and nature protectors failed that test. They argued that property would confer the right to pollute. Not so, Brubaker answers. Property, such as riparian water rights, give potential victims power to fight polluters, independently of the government's programs.

Two characteristics of property rights—their exclusivity and security—have made them powerful environmental protection tools. But property rights have a third characteristic: transferability. The fuller a holder's powers of ownership, the wider the rights to dispose of them in whatever way, and to whomever, the holder wishes. Ordinarily they get transferred to heirs or traded to the highest bidder. By being the highest bidder, a polluting firm can pay off its victims. In particular it can buy the riparian rights of landowners along a river. River-law history shows that it need not actually buy their lands: it need merely contract informally with them not to object to its pollution. Should such pollution-permitting transfers be allowed? Do they not convey rights to the wrong people? If so, should not a revived property regime prohibit sales of rights to certain parties? (This is sometimes recommended for fishing quota rights. Even now not everyone can buy his way into becoming a holder.)

While transferability does not directly or invariably protect nature, Brubaker argues that the transferability in a property right works indirectly to do so, through the setting of a price which not only tempts its owner but also deters the polluter. When the defence of nature is left to a property owner, he will abandon the defence only when paid enough to do so: he will transfer to a polluter the right to use nature only if the price fully compensates for his loss. Conversely, a firm can pollute only if it can induce the victim to trade or transfer to it his property right or his right to enforce an injunction. Collectively, property owners can be regarded as sellers in a market. Their willingness or reluctance to sell reflects their own valuation of nature.

Just as important, the market brings each of them knowledge of what property like theirs is worth to the keenest enthusiast for nature, whether conservation groups in the business of acquiring environmentally valuable properties, wilderness outfitters whose business depends on pristine attractions, or individuals seeking a private refuge. Potential offers from these parties free owners, even owners with personal reasons for a quick sale, from selling for a song to the first comer. With a market price, mortgage financing becomes available, raising the price and also enabling some owners to hold on, or to lease instead of selling. These influences establish a money cost to the polluter of disposing of its wastes in the natural environment. The extent of this cost depends on how many owners it must buy or rent rights from, the cost of finding and bargaining with each of them, the penalty for cancellation if its wastes change, the future costs of renegotiation when rights expire, and other legal, inspection, and enforcement costs. Will the polluter pay this price? Brubaker argues that the cost of buying owners' rights will often be prohibitively higher than the cost of the next-best alternative or opportunity. Instead of acquiring rights to pollute, a firm can change its location, its product, its process, or its recycling policy. It will choose these alternatives or make an informed choice combining pollution abatement costs with the costs of damaging nature.

The argument is convincing, at least insofar as it applies to resources sought by a limited number of users. But it raises questions about a forest or body of water used for multiple purposes, be they recreational, aesthetic, scientific, commercial, or industrial. Each *purpose* depends upon a site's particular group of *attributes* and their value to a specific group of *users*. Where property rights have been assigned, owners may typically use or enjoy a particular attribute, often in conjunction with other users of other attributes. But there are gaps in the spectrum of property: rights to attributes that are useful for some purposes—say fishing rights downstream of a potential dam-site—may not have been granted to any group of users. Where missing rights produce conflict government arbitrarily decides, rationing some uses, protecting some attributes, promoting some purposes. Although environmentalists have been urging governments for years to plan river basins as "multiple-use resources," they have not done so, and show no sign of doing so in the future. Even if governments did, the chance that they would get it right would be vanishingly small.

Could a market, and property rights, prevent governments from enforcing their uninformed priorities? When overlap turns into conflict, promoters of one use can buy out one or more of the others. Their ownership of physical attributes expands in the process, requiring them to deal with owners or holders of still other rights, easements, licences, permits, and privileges. The market prices of the various kinds of rights would guide a dominant user to devise a compromise mixture of uses, to bring about a multiple-purpose regime. Users of an attribute for which there is no specialized right generally get a free ride on the compromise plans to protect or provide other attributes; canoeists, for example, may benefit from water flows protected or enhanced for fisheries.

This book, in suggesting that owners of transferable property rights can do better than governments, questions whether the current property system is up to the job. Does a sufficient variety of rights and entitlements exist? Will the government allow them to be traded? Can representative holders be found for attributes that are widely valued by scattered users? Today government agencies often deliberately *prevent* their resource and environmental licences and permits from becoming rights in the hands of their holders. Because rights to use resources lack useful property characteristics, their security is reduced (they are not satisfactorily recorded or registered), their exclusivity is unknown (not even the agencies know or tell how many are to be issued), their transferability is denied, their duration is bafflingly short, and they cannot be divided or modified by negotiation. Change is needed for property rights holders to protect the environment: we will have to assign exclusive and transferable rights to resources, and we will have to ensure their security against threats from other resource users and governments alike.

Exclusive, transferable property rights are also needed at the global level, where they can play a central role in resolving resource-use conflicts and in reducing international pollution. Today the diplomats who negotiate environmental treaties are far removed from those whom the treaties will affect. Limited knowledge foils their attempts to speak for all. Their negotiations, excluding resource owners and users, often ignore the agreements' net costs to them. The resulting agreements may be inefficient, ineffective, difficult to enforce, and subject to lobbying for change.

The expansion of the domain of property rights is changing all this. In some international fisheries the individual fishermen have their own quotas. Now their governments are not free to offer more fish to other nations at the expense of their own propertied fishermen. Indeed, fishermen may soon, as a matter of private international law, agree together without government intervention. Property rights may also curb international air pollution. Under U.S. acid rain law, polluters hold property rights to limited emissions. Not so in Canada or the U.K. If in the future it were to be decided that the balance of greenhouse gas emissions between countries should be revised, governments would have to act. But if in various countries the emitters held rights like the present U.S. acid rain rights, government participation would hardly be needed. Parties in the countries that wanted more rights could buy them from parties in the others. The governments could confine themselves to buying rights on the market, screwing down the total emissions allowed to parties in the two countries combined. Directly or indirectly the market and the market price would determine which country undertook most of the joint physical effort to clean up to protect nature on a global scale.

Wherever large commons can be found—be they oceans or the atmosphere, Crown lands or public waterways—we will also find our worst pollution problems. Wherever would-be waste dumpers find that rights are held by private owners, pollution and degradation are rare events. Brubaker would assign property rights to these commons, eliminating them as cheap dumping grounds. Her clear and vigorous argument is convincing: everywhere, property rights have had and will continue to have unmatched power for the defence of nature.

ANTHONY SCOTT
DEPARTMENT OF ECONOMICS
THE UNIVERSITY OF BRITISH COLUMBIA

Preface

From the Canadian widow whose farm has been targeted for a natural gas pipeline to the one million Chinese who will be forced off their land by the Three Gorges dam, individuals and communities the world over are fighting projects that threaten their homes, health and livelihoods. Some don't want to lose their fish or forests. Others fear magnetic fields from transmission lines, air pollution from incinerators, or groundwater contamination from waste dumps. Others worry about aesthetic losses or decreased property values. Still others—particularly indigenous people—believe that existing and proposed projects threaten their very way of life.

Rarely does a week go by without some development's victims contacting Environment Probe, Probe International, or the other sister organizations that operate under the public interest umbrella of Energy Probe Research Foundation. These citizens seek information—often desperately—about the risks they face; they wonder how the decisions affecting them were made, and whether they can save themselves by proposing alternatives to the projects. We who receive their pleas can generally provide accurate—but discouraging—information about the industries confronting them and about their rights; on rare occasions, when shockingly severe injustices would translate into public outrage or when legal arguments might sway the day, we intervene on their behalf.

Our experiences over a quarter century have taught us the value that ordinary citizens place on their land, water, and other resources and their natural roles as environmental stewards. Individuals and communities who depend on resources understand their workings and know their limits. Since they would have to live with changes, their self-interest motivates them to protect their resources. But they need tools with which to do so. We have come to understand that their traditional tools—property rights, be they individual or communal—are the most effective.

Property rights—rules including both permissions and responsibilities—determine how decisions are made, how wealth is secured, and how income is distributed. Property rights govern who has the right to use the environment in which ways, and who has the duty to respect others' rights. They establish who must pay whom in order to exploit or protect resources, influencing the costs that polluters and their victims must take into account before making decisions.

Our foundation's research has spanned a variety of property rights regimes, some of which have benefited the environment and those who depend on it and others of which have done considerable environmental, economic and social harm. Some, such as the customary forestry management schemes in Guatemala or the collective water use systems in Thailand, vest decision-making in local communities. At the opposite end of the spectrum are others, such as those established to promote mining in medieval Germany, that have empowered privileged industries to use resources—even public streams and timber belonging to others—as they please. This book concentrates on the property rights regime developed under the English common law, a system of exclusive, transferable rights that has vested decision-making authority in individuals and firms who own or occupy land.

Empowering those most directly affected by pollution, common law property rights protect powerfully, preventing polluters from arbitrarily fouling streams or spewing poisons onto neighbouring property. No longer victims, the property rights holders set the rules, having veto power over developments. When projects do proceed, the property holders can ensure mutual benefit by negotiating effective mitigation measures and extracting compensation of their choosing for any damages suffered.

Many environmental groups prefer regulatory solutions to environmental problems. But regulations are made by remote governments who, driven by the need to create jobs or some undefined "public good," are often the least responsible stewards of natural resources. Governments of all political stripes have given us thousands of reasons not to trust them to protect the environment: they've licensed—and bankrolled—polluters, turned forests into wastelands, emptied oceans of fish, and dammed rivers that were once magnificent.

The overwhelming number of abuses that developments' victims have brought to our foundation have persuaded us that governments more often than not make unwise decisions about the environment. The plight of British Columbia's Cheslatta Carrier Indians illustrates the disastrous results of entrusting decisions to governments. In 1952, following the provincial government's offers of cheap land and water rights, Alcan Aluminum erected a massive dam on the Nechako River to divert water to a powerhouse at Kemano. A spillway would raise water levels in Cheslatta Lake, drowning the Cheslatta's village and washing away its graveyards. The federal government kept the project secret from the Cheslatta, only informing them two days before the dam's completion that they would be flooded off their land and forced to abandon their homes, farms and traplines. The government, the Cheslatta charge, negotiated compensation amounting to only one-tenth that paid to whites displaced by the project, and ultimately forged signatures on documents surrendering their land.

Three decades later, although many band members had returned to their traditional lands, the powers that be again excluded the Cheslatta from decisions about Cheslatta Lake and the Nechako River. In 1987, the federal and provincial governments quietly approved phase two of the Kemano hydroelectric project, further threatening not only a rich salmon fishery but also the Cheslatta culture and economy. Three years later, the federal government exempted the project from a federal environmental review.

The provincial government's abrupt cancellation of the half-completed project in 1995 signalled a reprieve for the Cheslatta. But their battle was by no means over. Rather than leaving their future security in the hands of capricious legislators whose positions change with economic conditions and the party in power, they continued their fight for the return, restoration and protection of their lands and resources. They continued their fight, in short, for secure property rights.

Forty-five years of government decision making have made losers of all parties. It is impossible not to conclude that both the Cheslatta and the environment on which they depend would have fared far better had the Cheslatta had strong property rights—had they owned their traditional lands with the power to make decisions regarding them. The rest of the province, too, would have benefited from a system based on property rights rather than on the arbitrary exercise of government power. Alcan wouldn't have invested a half billion dollars in now useless infrastructure, and wouldn't have suffered violations of its own rights. Taxpayers wouldn't face huge damage claims resulting from the tangle of conflicting rights and obligations. And British Columbia wouldn't have earned a reputation as an insecure place to invest—a reputation sure to destroy far more jobs than the Kemano project ever created.

The story of the Cheslatta is just one among the hundreds that our foundation has grappled with over the years. Some of the others appear in the following pages. Far more remain unrecorded. But the lessons drawn from them became the seeds from which this book has grown.

ELIZABETH BRUBAKER
EXECUTIVE DIRECTOR
ENVIRONMENT PROBE

Acknowledgements

This book owes much to Larry Solomon, who has long promoted property rights in the defence of nature, who first suggested writing a book on the subject and who edited successive versions of the manuscript.

For invaluable research assistance, I am grateful to Rachel Szymanski, whose research into the common law headed me in the right direction, and to Geoffrey Patridge, whose weekly library visits unearthed enough raw material for several books. For information on specific issues, I thank Charles Ficner, Darwin Hamilton, Jill McColl, Al Mussell, Peter Schleifenbaum and Keith Symington.

I am indebted—albeit grudgingly—to Margaret Barber, Peggy Hallward, Leslie Owens, Stephen Owens and Fiona Peterson, whose comments on early drafts of the first chapters persuaded me to revise my approach and helped me develop a more accessible style. There is nothing grudging about my thanks to Bill Hyde for his most encouraging comment, upon reading the same early drafts, that I had made him feel confident that law was indeed made for people.

I am particularly grateful to friends and colleagues who read and criticized the entire manuscript. Pat Adams, Tom Adams, Rick Archbold, Roy Hughes, Sheila Malcolmson and John Thibodeau were all very generous with their time and expertise.

A number of economists and lawyers reviewed drafts of the manuscript or of individual chapters. For their economic insights and advice—both that which I followed and that which I did not—I thank John Dales, Donald Dewees, Glenn Fox, Peter Pearse and Anthony Scott. For their legal wisdom and thoughtful suggestions I thank Douglas Adams, Thomas Berger, Donald Dewees (again), Patrick Macklem, Philippe Sands, Robert Sharpe and especially my husband Richard Owens, who provided ongoing assistance with legal theory and more practical matters, whose critical eye improved the manuscript and whose interest in the project enlivened many a dinner.

I have been privileged to work with an excellent editing and production crew including Norman Houghton, whose professional eye has spared me much embarrassment, and Marcia Ryan, whose commitment to getting things right begins with em dashes and seems never to end. My special thanks to Margaret Barber for taking on the most thankless of all tasks—editing legal citations—

with energy and good humour. And I deeply appreciate the weeks
of hard work by Elizabeth Rentzelos, whose artistry transformed
a mere manuscript into a book.

Finally, I owe my heartfelt thanks to the following Environment Probe supporters—and others wishing to remain anony-
mous—who directed their generous donations to this book.
Production would not have been possible without their financial
assistance.

Friends:

Martin Alford
George and Catherine Ascroft
Robert and Birgit Bateman
Mrs. P. L. Bentz
Erling Bjarnason
Paul E. Boeda
Mrs. E. Davidson
Antonia Dominato
Jacqueline J. Eccles
John Gingrich
William C. Hamilton
William Harmer

E. M. Hughes
Harold Jones
W. B. McCartney
Robert B. McIntyre
Pierre Perron
Lloyd Peterson
J. A. Rainer
R. Guy C. Smith
J. M. Spina
John Williams
Brian Wood

Sponsors:

Frank I. Algar
David A. Apramian
F. B. Athersych
H. M. Barker
Dexter Beach
J. Beauchamp
John E. Beswick
Stanley C. Biggs
Jennifer Bigler

Pamela Block
Carol S. Butcher
Trevor and Sarah Chandler
G. Joseph Cooper
Frances A. Cornish
Clarence Cross
Jack Davidchuk
Richard Dawe
Henry Dumouchel

J. Elliott
Murray W. Etty
J. Fitch
Jeff Floyd
Robert P. Forshaw
David Hughes
John Hughes
Graham Hurley
Rohan Jayasekera
William Jeffery
Charles F. Johnston
Kenneth and Betty Killick
Georgina Lapointe
Mrs. W. J. Latchem
Irene Lund
A. Malcolmson
J. S. Marwick
Sandra Masse
E. Matthews
Edward E. McCullough
H. McLeod
G. D. Mitchell
F. C. Moore
Griffith Morgan
Tom Morley

Murray Paton and June Leong
Trevor Plestid
W. Powlesland
Stephen and Olga Pychyl
Karen E. Robicheau
G. L. Robinson
Howard Russo
Joan E. Scott
Karl D. Simmerling
Hazel Skuce
Phyllis Stewart
Diana A. Stott
U. P. Thomas
Ronald Thompson and
    Madelene Rutski
Mark A. Voysey
Frank G. Wadge
Frances Walbridge
Bruce Wells
Norman and Shiela West
J. R. and S. J. Williams
Josephine Williams
Joshua Wolfe
Robert K. Zimmerman

Part I

The Golden Age of Common Law Property Rights

1

Thou Shalt Not Trespass

The law bounds every man's property, and is his fence.
The Court of the King's Bench, 1711[1]

Under our law every invasion of private property, be it ever so minute,
is a trespass.

Mr. Justice Galt, 1921[2]

Abram and Marie Friesen were picking fiddleheads near a brook
on their New Brunswick farm when three Grumman Avengers
passed directly overhead, engulfing them in a cloud of spray that
burned their cheeks and eyes and made them cough. The Friesens,
organic farmers who shunned pesticides, were furious. They
knew that, as part of its spruce budworm control program, the
New Brunswick government had contracted Forest Protection

Limited to spray forest lands with a pesticide containing a highly toxic agent called fenitrothion. Just one week earlier, Dr. Friesen had asked the company not to spray his property.

That evening, the Friesens discovered several hundred dead bees in front of their hives. Their 12-year-old son, who had inhaled the drifting spray, suffered a protracted asthma attack. During the following weeks Dr. and Mrs. Friesen experienced a variety of physical ailments, which they attributed to fenitrothion poisoning. Two of their cows, a pony, and two sheep died; no evidence, however, linked these deaths to the spraying.

The Friesens sued Forest Protection Limited for damages. Among other things, they argued that the company had trespassed on their property. The judge that heard the case ruled against the company, requiring it to pay $1,328.20 in damages. In finding that the spraying did indeed constitute a trespass, the judge explained the law as follows:

> To throw a foreign substance on the property of another, and particularly in doing so to disturb his enjoyment of his property, is an unlawful act. . . . This of course does not involve any question of whether or not the spray may have been toxic or non-toxic, because even to have thrown water, or garbage, or snow, or earth tippings, or any substance on the property would equally have amounted to an act of trespass.[3]

That was in 1978. But the law that the Friesens relied upon can be traced back many centuries, to the English common law—the unwritten or customary law that from medieval times has governed the rights and responsibilities of property owners. English settlers brought the common law to what is now Canada, first to Newfoundland in the sixteenth century, later to the West (via the Hudson's Bay Company) in the seventeenth century, and still later to Ontario (then Upper Canada) in the eighteenth century. Common law continues to apply in most of Canada, except when it has been overridden by statutes and regulations. Quebec, governed by its civil code, has remained outside the common law system.[4]

Rather than being written in statutes (by being passed as laws by legislatures), common law property rights have evolved in the courts through the ages. The doctrines of precedent and *stare decisis* (from a Latin phrase meaning "to stand by decisions and not to disturb settled matters") have governed the evolution of the common law, requiring judges to follow previous relevant court decisions and establishing a hierarchy of precedents. These doctrines have helped ensure that property rights' traditional importance continues to inform the common law to this day.[5]

Many provisions of the common law function as environmental protection laws.[6] For example, under the common law it is a trespass to place anything upon someone else's property, or to cause anything to be placed there by wind, water or other means. *Any* invasion of another's land—whether by people, flood-waters, structures, or pollutants—constitutes a trespass.[7]

In its early days, trespass law helped people combat the divers environmental problems of an agrarian society, from straying livestock to seeping privies. One 1703 ruling included the following discussion of trespass: "[E]very one must so use his own, as not to do damage to another. And as every man is bound so to look to his cattle, as to keep them out of his neighbour's ground, that so he may receive no damage; so he must keep in the filth of his house of office [his privy], that it may not flow in upon and damnify his neighbour."[8]

Even trespasses that cause no damage are, under the common law, unacceptable. A trespass is a trespass, regardless of its consequences. A 1765 decision, for example, noted that a man could be subject to an action for trespass, "though the damage be nothing," for merely "bruising the grass and even treading upon the soil."[9]

In this century, people have adapted the law of trespass, using it to protect themselves or their land against encroachment by industry. The Alberta Supreme Court held in 1976 that fly ash and sawdust from a lumber company constituted a trespass against a nearby motel. In a decision that should have sweeping implications for air pollution of all kinds, the court explained that it is a trespass to cause any noxious substance to cross the boundary of another's land.[10]

In another Alberta case, the Court of Appeal ruled that the cross-arms and wires of a transmission line belonging to an electric utility trespassed over the airspace of a neighbouring farm. The court noted that early common law cases had determined that signs, telegraph wires, eaves, or any other structures that hang over another's land should be forbidden as trespasses. That the owner was not using his land, and was therefore not damaged by the trespass, was irrelevant: "[A] landowner is entitled to freedom from permanent structures which in any way impinge upon the actual or potential use and enjoyment of his land."[11]

Trespass law has also been used to stem water pollution. (More frequently, people have relied upon a branch of the common law called riparian law to protect lakes and rivers.) In one turn-of-the-century case, a New York court issued an injunction against a town's sewage disposal practices: in emptying sewers into a creek that flowed through a farmer's land, causing filth to accumulate on the creek's bed and along its banks, the town had trespassed against the farmer. This violation of the farmer's property rights could not be permitted, regardless of the public necessity of the sewage works or the great inconvenience that could result from shutting them down.[12]

Even unwanted mail has been the target of at least one trespass case. In 1993 an Ontario court ruled that a record club, by continuing to send mail despite a man's repeated requests to be removed from its mailing list, committed a trespass.[13]

Trespass law has had to evolve to suit modern industrial society. Courts have wrestled with the question of how far property rights extend above and below the land. The thirteenth-century maxim, "a landowner owns everything from the sky to the depths" (in Latin, *cujus est solum, ejus est usque ad coelum et ad inferos*), guided early common law cases. Some recent cases, on the other hand, have narrowed the scope of ownership and determined that airspace is public domain; air traffic far above the ground which is transient and does not directly interfere with the use of people's property does not constitute a trespass. As one judge noted, however, a low-flying aircraft might indeed commit a trespass.[14] As a general rule, rights to airspace extend only as far as is necessary to protect the use and enjoyment of one's land and structures.[15]

Another question facing the courts, as ancient trespass laws evolve to suit contemporary circumstances, is whether an invasion need be tangible to constitute a trespass, and if so, how to define tangibility. Traditionally, courts restrained only sensible, visible invasions—invasions by a tangible mass that could be seen by them in evidence. But modern science, enabling courts to verify the presence of invisible pollutants, has vastly expanded potential applications of trespass laws. Some courts, relaxing traditional requirements, have found invisible gases and microscopic particulates to be trespasses.[16]

In the most frequently cited cases, the invisible trespasses have damaged property.[17] But traditional trespass law allows a landowner or tenant to sue whether or not he has suffered any harm. Conceivably, then, courts could define trespass to include any measurable invasion, any scientifically detectable emission, regardless of its effect.[18]

It is impossible to know what balance the courts will strike in their efforts to preserve common law principles while preventing scientific advances from pushing trespass law to unworkable extremes. At a minimum, trespass law will remain a powerful tool for protecting oneself against visible encroachments. And where it fails as a remedy for environmental wrongs, nuisance law, which has traditionally dealt with less material infractions, may succeed.

Notes

For bibliographic information on references, please see Works Cited.

1. *Star* v. *Rookesby* (1711), 1 Salk. 335, 91 E.R. 295 (K.B.).

2. *Boyle* v. *Rogers*, [1921] 2 W.W.R. 704 (Man. K.B.).
    Although not mentioned in the judgment, this and the passage that follows echo, virtually word for word, the 1765 decision in *Entick* v. *Carrington*. See note #9.

3. *Friesen et al.* v. *Forest Protection Limited* (1978), 22 N.B.R. (2d) 146 at 162 (S.C.Q.B.).

4. The formal reception of the common law varied from province to province. After its creation by the Constitution Act of 1791, Upper Canada enacted a statute adopting the English law: "In all matters of controversy relative to property and civil rights, resort shall be had to the Laws of England as the rule for the decision of the same" (Risk, "The Law and the Economy in Mid-Nineteenth-Century Ontario," 107). Thus Ontario courts, like those elsewhere in Canada, became legally obligated to follow the laws as revealed by the English courts.

    The Canadian courts gradually gained independence from their British counterparts. The 1931 Statute of Westminster eliminated Britain's capacity to legislate for Canada, unless Canada so requested. And in 1949, the Supreme Court of Canada replaced the Judicial

Committee of the Privy Council in England as the highest court of appeal for Canadian cases. Canadian courts, however, often continue to look to English precedents when deciding cases.

American judicial decisions have also, although to a lesser degree, influenced Canadian courts. While, like their Canadian counterparts, American courts adopted English law, they occasionally interpreted it differently. Loyalists settling in Upper Canada, bringing with them an understanding of American law, may have influenced the early Canadian legal system (Flaherty, "Writing Canadian Legal History," 22, 26). Of greater influence was the similarity of the legal challenges facing the two countries. Canadian judges could look to American cases without violating their obligation to follow English precedent if no English cases applied to the situation at hand (Risk, *op. cit.*, 108).

Because both English and American cases helped form Canadian property law, and continue to influence its development, this book will discuss cases from all three countries.

For more information on the evolution of property rights, see Hogue, *Origins of the Common Law*; Blackstone, *The Commentaries on the Laws of England*, Volume 1, Introduction and Chapter 1; Horwitz, *The Transformation of American Law 1780-1860*; Pollot, *Grand Theft and Petit Larceny*, Chapter 3; and Gall, *The Canadian Legal System*, 25-46.

5. Gall, *op. cit.*, 179-180.

According to Blackstone, "precedents and rules must be followed, unless flatly absurd or unjust" (*op. cit.*, Volume 1, 48).

6. The cases presented in Part One and the Appendices, emphasizing the strengths of the common law, illustrate the ways in which plaintiffs have used their property rights to protect the environment. Cases presented in Part Two illustrate situations in which plaintiffs have lost their bids to protect the environment.

7. A trespass occurs against the person in possession of the invaded land. If a tenant is in possession of the land at the time of the trespass, it is normally he rather than the owner who should sue. See *Halsbury's Laws of England*, Volume 45, 637, 639.

According to Fridman, even a wrongful possessor of land, such as a squatter, can sue for trespass as long as he claims immediate and exclusive possession of the land and as long as the alleged trespasser is not the true owner or is not acting on the true owner's behalf (*Introduction to the Law of Torts*, 190).

See Appendix A for summaries of a number of trespass cases.

8. *Tenant* v. *Goldwin* (1703), 2 Ld. Raym. 1090, 92 E.R. 222 at 224 (K.B.).

Harvey, in "Riparian Water Rights," provided the translation of "house of office."

9. *Entick* v. *Carrington* (1765), 19 St. Tr. 1030 at 1066 (C.P.).

10. *Kerr et al.* v. *Revelstoke Building Materials Ltd.* (1976), 71 D.L.R. (3d) 134 (Alta. S.C.).

Unfortunately for the environment, the decision, which awarded damages instead of an injunction, did not shut down the sawmill. For reasons that he did not explain, the justice decided that "in these circumstances an injunction would not be an appropriate remedy." He may have been influenced by the fact that the motel had been closed for five years. Or he may have been sensitive to the federal government's efforts to encourage industry to locate in this depressed economic area—something he commented on in his judgment.

11. *Didow et al.* v. *Alberta Power Limited*, [1988] 5 W.W.R. 606 at 616 (Alta. C.A.).

12. *Sammons* v. *City of Gloversville*, 34 Misc. Rep. 459, 70 N.Y. Supp. 284 (Sup. Ct. 1901), aff'd 67 App. Div. 628, 74 N.Y. Supp. 1145, 175 N.Y. 346, 67 N.E. 622 (1903).

The court specified that the injunction restraining Gloversville from fouling Mr. Sammons' premises would not become operative for a year, and retained the right to extend it further if it took longer than a year for the city to establish a different sewage system or to obtain legislative relief.

13. *Mather* v. *Columbia House* (6 August 1992), 10315/91 (Ont. Ct. Gen. Div.).

14. *Didow et al.* v. *Alberta Power Limited, op. cit.*

15. *Halsbury's Laws of England, op. cit.*, 632.

See, for example, *Lacroix* v. *The Queen*, in which the court found that "the owner of land has a limited right in the air space over his property; it is limited by what he can possess or occupy for the use and enjoyment of his land. . . . [T]he owner of land is not and cannot be the owner of the unlimited air space over his land, because air and space fall in the category of *res omnium communis*." [1954] 4 D.L.R. 470 (Ex.).

For a more extensive discussion of this issue see Estrin and Swaigen, *Environment on Trial*, 116-7, and Prosser, *Handbook of the Law of Torts*, 69-73.

16. Prosser, *ibid.*, discusses this issue on 66. Also see Heuston, *Salmond and Heuston on the Law of Torts*, 46; "Deposit of Gaseous and Invisible Solid Industrial Wastes," 879-80; and Clover, "Torts," 117 ff.

For a discussion of this issue in the context of nuisance law, see *Walker* v. *McKinnon Industries Ltd.*, [1949] 4 D.L.R. 739 (Ont. H.C.), aff'd [1950] 3 D.L.R. 159 (Ont. C.A.), aff'd [1951] 3 D.L.R. 577 (P.C.).

17. *Fairview Farms Inc.* v. *Reynolds Metals Co.*, 176 F. Supp. 178 (D. Or. 1959); *Martin* v. *Reynolds Metals Co.*, 342 P. 2d 790 (Or. 1959), cert. denied, 362 U.S. 918 (1960).

Also see *McDonald et al.* v. *Associated Fuels Ltd. et al.*, [1954] 3 D.L.R. 775 (B.C.S.C.), in which a justice of the British Columbia Supreme Court suggested that carbon monoxide could constitute a trespass.

18. For further discussion of this problem and a possible solution, see Rothbard, "Law, Property Rights, and Air Pollution," 250-4. Rothbard suggests that if trespass is defined as an interference with one's exclusive use of one's property, many intangible invasions—which would not so interfere—would not constitute trespasses.

Magnet suggests that contemporary courts may be less willing than their traditional counterparts to treat trifling interferences as trespasses ("Intentional Interference with Land," 291).

2

So As Not to Harm Another

If one erects a smelting house for lead so near the land of another, that the vapour and smoke kills his corn and grass, and damages his cattle therein, this is held to be a nuisance. And by consequence it follows, that if one does any other act, in itself lawful, which yet being done in that place necessarily tends to the damage of another's property, it is a nuisance: for it is incumbent on him to find some other place to do that act, where it will be less offensive.

Sir William Blackstone, 1768[1]

Pollution is always unlawful and, in itself, constitutes a nuisance.

Mr. Justice Rinfret, 1928[2]

Soon after Huron Steel Products installed an 800-tonne press at its Windsor, Ontario, stamping plant in 1979, Douglas Kenney complained to both the company and the Ministry of the Environment. As president of the corporation that owned an apartment building near the plant, he objected to noise and vibrations from the press's operation, which were driving his tenants away.

But Mr. Kenney could not get the government to enforce its

own regulations. Although Ministry of the Environment tests indicated that the press exceeded provincial noise guidelines, and despite assurances from Huron Steel that it would improve the situation, the plant continued its noisy operations. Frustrated by the lack of progress, Mr. Kenney's company launched a nuisance case seeking damages and an injunction.

At the trial before the High Court of Justice in 1990, former and current residents of the neighbourhood testified that the press's noise made falling asleep difficult, and that its vibrations shook furniture, disturbed pictures, and rattled dishes. This testimony, along with that of expert witnesses who described the degree to which the plant exceeded provincial noise guidelines, convinced Mr. Justice Potts that the press's noise and vibration were excessive.

The judge determined that the Environmental Protection Act required the press to have a certificate of approval from the Ministry of the Environment. "I do not know why this process was not strictly adhered to by the Ministry for the #1 press," he mused. "Possibly the Ministry was trying to persuade rather than compel Huron Steel and other existing industries to comply with the guideline levels."[3]

The court acted where the government would not. Mr. Justice Potts found that Huron Steel's operations unreasonably interfered with its neighbour's use and enjoyment of its property, thus constituting a nuisance. He awarded $71,427 damages for lost rental revenue and reduction in the value of the apartment building. He also prohibited Huron Steel from operating its press if it failed to complete remedial work within four and a half months.

At the heart of the Huron Steel decision, like the decisions in many other nuisance cases, is the maxim "use your own property so as not to harm another's" (in Latin, *sic utere tuo, ut alienum non laedas*). The maxim reflects a balance under the common law between the rights of neighbours to both *use* and *enjoy* their property; in using one's property, another's enjoyment must not be compromised.[4]

The principle behind the maxim dates back to the English law of the mid-thirteenth century. Henry of Bracton, a judge and prominent legal scholar of that era, stated that "no one may do in his own estate any thing whereby damage or nuisance may happen to his neighbour." Bracton, whose writings provide a foundation for later nuisance law, noted that a landowner could not, in raising a pond, flood his neighbour's land; nor could he divert a watercourse and deprive his neighbour of water.[5]

The maxim's current form is thought to have been coined by an English court in 1611, a time when air pollution was a growing problem in England.[6] Construction of the naval fleet had largely depleted the country's forests, and coal had replaced wood as the common fuel. Being noxious and dangerous, coal use resulted in a number of nuisance actions. The Latin maxim was one of the important legal concepts developed and applied in those seventeenth-century air pollution cases.

By the eighteenth century, the famous jurist Sir William Blackstone cited the maxim as "the rule" in English law. According to Blackstone, "anything that works hurt, inconvenience, or damage" qualified as a nuisance. One such forbidden activity, Blackstone noted, would be the corruption of air, be it by a hoghouse, a tannery, or a tallowchandler. Offensive trades, he explained, should be carried on in remote places, so as not to deprive anyone of the use and benefit of his property.[7]

Nineteenth-century courts continued to accept the maxim as a given. One British law lord summarized the law as it stood in 1885:

> *Prima facie* no man has a right to use his own land in such a way as to be a nuisance to his neighbour, and whether the nuisance is effected by sending filth on to his neighbour's land,

or by putting poisonous matter on his own land and allowing it to escape on his neighbour's land, or whether the nuisance is effected by poisoning the air which his neighbour breathes, or the water which he drinks, appears to me wholly immaterial.

If a man chooses to put filth on his own land he must take care not to let it escape on to his neighbour's land.[8]

The maxim also applied in Britain's North American colonies, where courts have invoked it throughout the centuries.[9] Deeply ingrained in our legal history, it influences the courts to this day in situations where governments have not overridden the common law with statutes and regulations.

Blackstone broadly defined nuisance as "anything done to the hurt or annoyance of the lands, tenements, or hereditaments of another."[10] Two centuries later, where the common law still applies, an interference with the use or enjoyment of property remains a nuisance, for which an owner or tenant can sue.[11]

Blackstone's definition was overly inclusive: successfully stopping a nuisance, unlike a trespass, requires proof of harm. And unlike trespass law, which covers even the most minute invasions, nuisance law does not deal with trivial matters. Courts are generally reluctant to address minor infractions necessarily resulting from everyday practices; they are guided by the notion that everyone benefits from relaxing standards to allow people to carry on common activities. Although some may suffer if their neighbours cook pungent foods or make noisy repairs to their homes, they are equally likely to benefit from their freedom to act similarly; they thus receive compensation in kind for their losses. As an English judge explained in 1862, "It is as much for the advantage of one owner as of another; for the very nuisance the one complains of, as the result of the ordinary use of his neighbour's land, he himself will create in the ordinary use of his own, and the reciprocal nuisances are of a comparatively trifling character. The convenience of such a rule may be indicated by calling it a rule of give and take, live and let live."[12]

Nuisance law nonetheless prohibits an endless variety of environmental harms. People have used it to protect themselves from pesticide sprays, smoke, soot, steam, dust, fumes and other air pollutants. Road salt has been successfully challenged under nuisance law, as have leaking oil tanks and seeping privies. Foul smells are often found to be nuisances, as are noise and vibrations from commercial and industrial operations.[13]

Courts have also found less tangible interferences, as varied as aesthetic blight and the casting or obstruction of light, to be nuisances. In one 1978 case, a cable television company in Atikokan, Ontario, successfully sued Ontario Hydro for locating an electrical transformer and transmission line near its receiving tower, interfering with the transmission and reception of TV broadcast signals. The court found that "in Canada today television viewing is an important incident of ordinary enjoyment of property and should be protected as such."[14] People have invoked nuisance law to keep countless other undesirable commercial operations, from gas stations to houses of prostitution, out of their neighbourhoods.[15]

Industry has long characterized its nuisances as being in the public interest. Manufacturers reiterate the number of people employed, and utilities cite the essential services provided. Although no longer always the case, courts have traditionally refused to consider such social factors. They have instead stressed the sanctity of minority rights and refused to condone activities, whatever their presumed value, that would override them. As Blackstone explained, "So great . . . is the regard of the law for private property that it will not authorize the least violation of it; no, not even for the general good of the whole community."[16]

One early case from Birmingham, England, dealt with a large public sewer built in 1851 that disgorged into the Tame River.

The owner of a downstream estate sued, complaining that the resulting pollution aggravated disease, killed fish, and prevented cattle from drinking from the river and sheep from being washed in it.

The town of Birmingham did not deny that dumping sewage was highly offensive. It argued, however, that the court should allow continued pollution in the name of the public good. "[T]he evil that must ensue if the Court should interfere would be incalculable," it maintained. "The deluge of filth will cause a plague, which will not be confined to the 250,000 inhabitants of Birmingham, but will spread over the entire valley and become a national calamity. The increase of population, inseparable from the progress of a nation in industry and wealth, is attended of necessity by inconvenience to individuals against which it is in vain to struggle. In such cases private interests must bend to those of the country at large."[17]

The judge who heard the case dismissed the argument as an "extreme position . . . of remarkable novelty." He was not, he explained, a public safety committee; his function was simply to interpret the law and to define who has what rights. Once the plaintiff's right to enjoy a clean river was established, the court should grant an injunction, regardless of its consequences: "[I]t is a matter of almost absolute indifference whether the decision will affect a population of 25,000, or a single individual carrying on a manufactory for his own benefit." The judge added that if an injunction would produce considerable injury, the court would, "by way of indulgence," give Birmingham an opportunity to stop its nuisance before restraining its activity. But if the city failed to stop the nuisance, it would be up to Parliament—rather than the court—to allow it to continue: "If, after all possible experiments, they cannot drain Birmingham without invading the Plaintiff's private rights, they must apply to Parliament for power to invade his rights."[18]

In the following century, the courts returned time and again to the themes that informed the Birmingham case: the sanctity of individuals' property rights and the inappropriateness of over-riding them. The courts, it was said, should not weigh a nuisance's cost to an individual against the social costs of shutting down a polluting industry. They should simply determine where property rights lie and enforce them. Any balancing of interests should be done—if at all—by government.

When an electric company protested in 1894 that restraining its steamy, noisy, vibrating generating station would leave London's streets and buildings in darkness, the court refused to sacrifice an individual's rights for the public's convenience: "Neither has the circumstance that the wrongdoer is in some sense a public benefactor (*e.g.*, a gas or water company or a sewer authority) ever been considered a sufficient reason for refusing to protect by injunction an individual whose rights are being persistently infringed." Consideration of the public good, the court explained, would be better left to Parliament: "Courts of Justice are not like Parliament, which considers whether proposed works will be so beneficial to the public as to justify exceptional legislation, and the deprivation of people of their rights with or without compensation."[19]

In an 1899 case regarding the effects of asphalt excavation on neighbouring property, the British Privy Council granted a restraining injunction despite its possible impact on the commu-nity. It rejected the defence of the public good with the following comments: "It was said that digging for pitch was the common industry of La Brea, and that if an injunction were granted the industry would be stopped altogether. . . . Whatever the result may be, rights of property must be respected, even when they conflict, or seem to conflict, with the interests of the community." Any overriding of property rights, the court explained, would be up to the government rather than the court: "If private property is to be sacrificed for the benefit of the public, it must be done under the sanction of the Legislature."[20]

Polluting industries also frequently try to defend themselves by claiming that their actions are reasonable. The "defence of reasonable use" seems to mean something different to every polluter. It can mean that the disputed activity is ordinary and lawful, or, given the location, appropriate. It can mean that a business has taken great care and caution, having installed the most modern machinery available and having operated it responsibly. Or it can be industry's way of urging the courts to balance competing interests and find reasonable compromises among them. Although contemporary courts will occasionally heed the defence, they have traditionally refused to consider whether a disputed activity is reasonable.

A 1915 case in which a Toronto resident claimed that a blacksmith's operation in his neighbourhood constituted a nuisance exemplifies the courts' reluctance to consider the reasonableness of an activity. The fact that the smith did his work "in a usual and reasonable fashion" did not influence the trial judge: "If the defendant has caused a nuisance to the plaintiff, it is of course no defence to say that he is making a reasonable use of his premises in the carrying on of a lawful occupation." On appeal, a higher court judge agreed. "It is," he said, "of no importance."[21]

The defence of reasonable use again failed in a 1952 nuisance case against a foundry whose emissions damaged the finish on cars in a nearby lot. Citing an authoritative legal text, the judge explained, "He who causes a nuisance cannot avail himself of the defence that he is merely making a reasonable use of his own property. No use of property is reasonable which causes substantial discomfort to others or is a source of damage to their property."[22]

The issue also arose in the Huron Steel case discussed earlier. The steel company had argued that its operations were reasonable in its particular neighbourhood. The judge responded that other industrial activity in the mixed use neighbourhood could not justify the nuisance, which would offend the typical resident: "'Unreasonableness' in nuisance law is when the interference in question would not be tolerated by the ordinary occupier."[23] To support his opinion, the judge relied on, among other sources, a respected law text: "It is not enough to ask: Is the defendant using his property in what would be a reasonable manner if he had no neighbour? The question is, Is he using it reasonably, having regard to the fact that he has a neighbour?"[24]

Courts have also rejected two other defences that industries have put forward time and again: that either their responsibility for small fractions of greater environmental problems or their operations' long histories justify continued pollution. The existence of numerous sources of pollution has not prevented courts from ruling against one particular source. An early example can be found in an 1851 English case regarding a brickmaker's pollution. The defendant tried without success to excuse his brick burning on the grounds that others also polluted the local air. But, the judge responded, the plaintiffs had not objected to these more remote operations. And even if they were nuisances, they would "not form a reason why the defendant should set up an additional nuisance. There is no ground, I think, for inferring a licence to him."[25]

Almost one hundred years later, when a foundry in St. Catharines, Ontario, tried to defend itself against a florist's nuisance suit on the grounds that other industries contributed to the offending pollution, the court would not be moved. Other pollution, the Chief Justice explained, is no defence: "[E]ven if others are in some degree polluting the air, that is no defence if the defendant contributes to the pollution so that the plaintiff is materially injured. It is no defence even if the act of the defendant would not amount to a nuisance were it not for others acting independently of it doing the same thing at the same time."[26]

Nuisances can be stopped even when they predate the people complaining of them. For example, in an 1896 case concerning a stable in a residential neighbourhood of Montreal, the defendant objected that since the plaintiff had acquired the neighbouring property after the stable's construction, he had no right to complain. The court dismissed this argument: "This circumstance as to the date of the respondent's acquisition of title can make no difference in his rights to object to the nuisance."[27]

Even a long-established operation may lose its right to pollute if a new neighbour complains about it. Although the Ontario Malleable Iron Co. had been doing business since 1907, and its predecessors had operated a foundry on the property since 1876, a court restrained its harmful emissions in 1952. The Chief Justice refused to consider that the plaintiff company had chosen to locate beside the foundry. He noted that only after two years in business had it become aware of the damage. And regardless, "It is no defence that the plaintiffs themselves came to the nuisance."[28] On this subject the Chief Justice cited a much earlier decision: "whether the man went to the nuisance or the nuisance came to the man, the rights are the same."[29]

The simple rule that one may not harm his neighbour's property, or interfere with his enjoyment of it, has protected the environment from an infinite variety of insults for over seven hundred years. People have relied on nuisance law to prevent or clean up the pollution of their land and the air above it. From nuisance law has evolved a separate branch of the common law, called riparian law, that people can enlist to protect the water flowing past their property.

Notes

1.   Blackstone, *Commentaries on the Laws of England*, Volume 3, 191.

2.   *Malcolm Forbes Groat and Walter S. Groat* v. *The Mayor, Aldermen and Burgesses, being the Corporation of the City of Edmonton*, [1928] S.C.R. 522 at 532.

3.   *340909 Ontario Ltd.* v. *Huron Steel Products (Windsor) Inc. and Huron Steel Products* (1990), 73 O.R. (2d) 641 at 648 (H.C.J.), aff'd (1992), 10 O.R. (3d) 95 (Ont. C.A.).

4.   For further discussion of this issue see Horwitz, *The Transformation of American Law 1780-1860*, 36, 99; Risk, "The Law and the Economy in Mid-Nineteenth-Century Ontario," 100; and Sharpe, *Injunctions and Specific Performance*, 201.
     For one example of the maxim's application, see the 1936 case, *Hollywood Silver Fox Farm, Limited* v. *Emmett*, [1936] 1 All E.R. 825 (K.B.), in which Mr. Justice MacNaghten cited earlier court decisions regarding offensive noises: "'No proprietor has an absolute right to create noises upon his own land, because any right which the law gives him is qualified by the condition that it must not be exercised to the nuisance of his neighbours or of the public.'"

5.   Lauer, "The Common Law Background of the Riparian Doctrine," 65-8. For more on Henry of Bracton see Hogue, *Origins of the Common Law*, 159-60, 185, 200.

6.   *Alfred's Case* (1611), 9 Coke Rep. f. 59a. Cited by Harvey, "Riparian Water Rights," 518. I have relied on Harvey for information on the early development of nuisance law.

7.   Blackstone, *op. cit.*, Volume 3, 191.

8.   From Lord Lindley's decision in *Ballard* v. *Tomlinson* (1885), 29 Ch.D. 115 at 126, cited by Mr. Justice Lamont in *Malcolm Forbes Groat*

and Walter S. Groat v. *The Mayor, Aldermen and Burgesses, being the Corporation of the City of Edmonton, op. cit.* at 537-8.

9.   See, for example, the following cases in Appendix B: *Imperial Gas Light and Coke* v. *Broadbent*; *St. Helen's Smelting* v. *Tipping*; and *Drysdale* v. *Dugas*.

See Horwitz, *op. cit.*, 32 and 102, for a discussion of the frequency with which eighteenth-century American courts invoked the maxim, and its decline in the nineteenth century.

10.   Blackstone, *op. cit.*, Volume 3, 190.

11.   For more information see Wright and Linden, *Canadian Tort Law*, 17-1. Also see Estrin and Swaigen, *Environment on Trial*, 110-2; Scarman, *English Law*, 59; and Nedelsky, "Judicial Conservatism in an Age of Innovation," 286, 315.

12.   *Bamford* v. *Turnley* (1862), 3 B. & S. 66, 122 E.R. 27 at 33 (K.B.). Epstein describes the live and let live rule in *Takings*, 231-2.

13.   Appendix B summarizes a number of such cases.

14.   *Nor-Video Services Ltd.* v. *Ontario Hydro* (1978), 4 C.C.L.T. 244 (Ont. S.C.).

15.   Ellickson, "Alternatives to Zoning," 719, 721, 734.

See *Thompson Schwab* v. *Costaki*, [1956] 1 All E.R. 652 (C.A.), in which London residents obtained an injunction against the use of an adjoining house for prostitution on the grounds that its solicitations interfered with their comfortable enjoyment of their homes.

Also see *Everett* v. *Paschall*, 61 Wash. 47, 111 P. 879, (1910), in which the court issued an injunction against the operation of a tuberculosis sanitarium in a residential district. Although the sanitarium did not endanger its neighbours, fear of tuberculosis caused local properties to depreciate in value. According to the court, "The question is, not whether the fear is founded in science, but whether it exists; nor whether it is imaginary, but whether it is real, in that it affects the movements and conduct of men. Such fears are actual, and must be recognized by the courts as other emotions of the human mind."

16. Blackstone, *op. cit.*, Volume 1, 109-10.

17. *The Attorney-General* v. *The Council of the Borough of Birmingham* (1858), 4 K. &. J. 528, 70 E.R. 220 at 224 (V.Ch.).

18. *Ibid.* at 225-6.

19. *Shelfer* v. *City of London Electric Lighting Company* (1894) and *Meux's Brewery Company* v. *City of London Electric Lighting Company* (1894), [1895] 1 Ch. 287 at 316.

20. *Trinidad Asphalt Co.* v. *Ambard*, [1899] A.C. 594 at 602-3 (P.C.).

21. *Beamish* v. *Glenn* (1916), 36 O.L.R. 10 at 13, 18.

22. Salmond on *Torts*, cited in *Russell Transport Ltd. et al.* v. *Ontario Malleable Iron Co. Ltd.* (1952), 4 D.L.R. 719 at 728 (Ont. H.C.).

23. *340909 Ontario Ltd.* v. *Huron Steel Products (Windsor) Inc. and Huron Steel Products*, *op. cit.* at 645.

24. *Ibid.* at 644, citing Fleming's *The Law of Torts*.

25. *Walter* v. *Selfe* (1851), 4 De G. & S. 315, 20 L.J. Ch. 433 at 435.

26. *Walker* v. *McKinnon Industries Ltd.*, [1949] 4 D.L.R. 739 at 767 (Ont. H.C.), aff'd [1950] 3 D.L.R. 159 (Ont. C.A.), aff'd [1951] 3 D.L.R. 577 (P.C.).

27. *William Drysdale* v. *C.A. Dugas* (1896), 26 SCR 20 at 25.
    Although this case originated in Quebec, the Chief Justice of the Supreme Court of Canada cited another justice's observation that "the

English and French law on the subject of nuisance are exactly alike" (at 23).

28. *Russell Transport Ltd. et al.* v. *Ontario Malleable Iron Co. Ltd.*, *op. cit.* at 728, citing *Salmond on Torts* (10th ed., pp. 228-31).

29. *Ibid.* at 729, citing *Fleming* v. *Hislop* (1886), 11 App. Cas. 686 at 696-7.

3

Without Obstruction, Diversion or Corruption

It is a nuisance to stop or divert water that used to run to another's meadow or mill; to corrupt or poison a water-course, by erecting a dye-house or a lime-pit, for the use of trade, in the upper part of the stream; . . . or in short to do any act in common property, that in its consequences must necessarily tend to the prejudice of one's neighbour. So closely does the law of England enforce that excellent rule of gospel-morality, of 'doing to others, as we would they should do unto ourselves.'

Sir William Blackstone, 1768[1]

Hazen Gauthier read the news in the local paper: Sudbury's Parks and Recreation Commission had approved the use of Bell Park for the 1970 Ontario Outboard Championships. The speed boat regatta, sponsored by the Rotary Club, was to be held on Lake Ramsay—Sudbury's principal source of water.

Mr. Gauthier, concerned that the 60 hydroplane motorboats competing in the regatta would contaminate the small lake, knew he had to act quickly. The races were scheduled for September 12th and 13th—just a month away. On August 14th he had his lawyer contact the Rotary Club, which refused his request to cancel the event. Four days later his lawyer asked the Ontario Water Resources Commission to intervene. But Ontario's Minister of Energy and Resources Management turned down the request, explaining that "the local authorities had made the decision to hold the regatta and no interference by the Commission seemed warranted."[2]

On September 4th, Mr. Gauthier, along with three other Sudbury residents, launched a court action for a restraining order. Six days later, Judge Frank Dunlap forbade the Rotary Club to hold speed boat races on Lake Ramsay.

Judge Dunlap based his decision on a branch of the common law called riparian law. Under the common law, riparians—people who own or occupy land beside lakes and rivers—have the right to the natural flow of water beside or through their property, unchanged in quantity or quality.[3] One of the plaintiffs, Rita Dixon, owned land on Lake Ramsay. It was to protect her riparian rights that the judge issued the injunction.

Mrs. Dixon's riparian rights, Judge Dunlap explained, entitled her "to the flow of water through or by her land in its natural state."[4] By polluting Lake Ramsay—regardless of whether the pollution caused any harm—the planned races would violate Mrs. Dixon's property rights. In such a case, said the judge, the court should grant an injunction as a matter of course.

In his decision, Judge Dunlap reviewed riparian cases from 1859 to 1949, a period when riparian rights played a crucial role in cleaning up lakes and rivers. During those years, riparians—including farmers, mill-owners, manufacturers, absentee landlords, fishermen, and titled aristocrats—exercised their legal rights to protect themselves and the environment from coal mine discharges, pulp and paper mill wastes, sanitary sewage, storm-water runoff, salt, oil and other pollutants.[5]

Riparian rights evolved from nuisance law.[6] Many early nuisance cases concerned water pollution; neighbours would counter tanners or butchers who disposed of their wastes in rivers, or the owners of privies that hung over streams. The industrial revolution and the introduction of piped municipal sewage systems changed the scope of the water pollution problem and the law surrounding it. Mills and factories were dumping their noxious wastes into Britain's rivers, causing an unprecedented and dramatic deterioration of water quality across the country.[7] People fought back, taking their cases to the courts, which gradually honed the law into a finely-tuned system of rights and responsibilities. By the 1850s, when the courts were awash in water pollution cases, the riparian doctrine had emerged as a powerful weapon against the era's severe environmental challenges.[8]

Waterfront property owners, businesses, and others dependent on lakes and rivers fought industrial and municipal water pollution with riparian law throughout much of the English-speaking world during the following century, and in some places continue to do so. In Great Britain, for example, the Anglers' Co-operative Association fights pollution by defending riparian rights in county courts. The Association has won all but two of the hundreds of cases it has argued since its founding in 1948.[9]

In Canada, riparian law originally applied everywhere except Quebec, where similar civil law rules held.[10] But like other common law doctrines, riparian law survives only where politicians or bureaucrats haven't extinguished it through statutes and regulations. Riparian rights remain strongest in Atlantic Canada and Ontario.[11] In the Western provinces, where riparian law would have impeded mining and irrigation, statutes have governed water allocation since the late nineteenth century; even there, however, riparians may retain rights to clean water.[12] For various reasons, including the financial risks entailed in court cases and the courts' frequent reluctance to frustrate industry, Canadians now rarely enforce their riparian rights.[13] But when they do, as evidenced by Hazen Gauthier's challenge to the Sudbury Rotary Club, riparian rights remain powerful tools for environmental protection.[14]

The common law allows riparians to use an unlimited amount of water for "ordinary" purposes, which traditionally included only domestic and subsistence agricultural activities.[15] In most jurisdictions, they may use additional water for certain reasonable "extraordinary" purposes, such as irrigation or manufacturing, connected with their property.[16]

Riparians do *not* have a right to divert water for use off their property. In 1875, the House of Lords (Britain's ultimate judicial appeal court) forbade a waterworks company from diverting a stream in order to supply the English town of Swindon.[17] A diversion of such magnitude would not qualify as an ordinary, reasonable use, the law lords explained; and extraordinary uses were allowed only if connected with riparian land. Almost 40 years later an Ontario court, preventing an entrepreneur from providing the village of Thornhill with water from the Don River, echoed the law lords' decision: to divert water from riparian land, and to consume it for purposes unconnected with that land "would be, not only an unreasonable use of the water, but would be a use altogether outside and beyond the right of the riparian proprietor to use the water."[18]

A riparian's right to use water confers no right to abuse it. Extraordinary water users may not interfere with other riparians' property rights: they must return the water to the watercourse substantially undiminished in volume and unaltered in quality. As early as 1858 the courts determined that a tanner in Lower Canada must not block the River Yamaska's flow to a downstream mill;

they found that the tanner had the right to hold back water to propel his tannery's wheels and machinery—an extraordinary use—only if "he does not thereby interfere with the rights of other proprietors."[19] Similarly, in deciding an 1893 case against a Scottish mining company, one British law lord noted, "I am not satisfied that a riparian owner is entitled to use water for secondary [i.e., extraordinary] purposes, except upon the condition that he shall return it to the stream practically undiminished in volume and with its natural qualities unimpaired."[20] His colleague added, "it is not permissible in such a case for a man to use his own property so as to injure the property of his neighbour."[21]

Riparian law is extraordinarily potent, prohibiting *any* sensible change in the water's quality. In the Scottish case noted above, a distiller obtained an injunction preventing an upstream coal mine from discharging hard water into a stream; while still pure and drinkable, the stream was no longer fit for the manufacture of whiskey. Twenty years later, a New Brunswick court ruled against an iron company whose operations discoloured the Nepisiquit River.[22] More recently, in the 1950s, at the behest of a fishing club and a local landowner, a British court restrained upstream industries whose thermal pollution killed fish.[23]

Riparians can sue polluters to protect their rights even if they have suffered no evident harm; once interference with a riparian right is established, damage is presumed.[24] In fact, as Hazen Gauthier so aptly demonstrated, riparians who can demonstrate that a proposed activity will likely violate their rights may act even *before* a stream has been polluted or diverted. Riparians' rights to unaltered water exist whether or not they use the water, and whether or not its alteration interferes with any of their activities. That a Trinidadian land owner in one 1918 case put to no use whatsoever either the river flowing through his property or the property itself didn't prevent the court from recognizing his right to the natural flow of the river.[25] The law thus enables riparians to prevent polluters from establishing the right to carry on longstanding activities (called a "prescriptive right") that might interfere with future water uses.

As with nuisance law, existing water pollution does not justify further pollution. Courts have not cared that, because a dozen other industries polluted a river, restraining one would not restore the water's purity. If every polluter could defend himself on the ground of existing pollution, the reasoning goes, riparians could never repair the environment.

The issue arose in an early twentieth-century case against a New York salt manufacturer accused of depleting a creek's flow and contaminating it with salt. The company tried to defend itself on the grounds that a dozen other salt works also diminished and polluted the creek. The judge, however, found that others' contribution to the problem in no way lessened the defendant's obligation; if anything, it *increased* it. "The fact that other salt manufacturers are doing the same thing as the defendant, instead of preventing relief, may require it," the judge explained. He then cited an earlier decision on the matter:

> Where there is a large number of persons mining on a small stream, if each should deteriorate the water a little, although the injury from the act of one might be small, the combined result of the acts of all might render the water utterly unfit for further use; and, if each could successfully defend an action on the ground that his act alone did not materially affect the water, the prior appropriator might be deprived of its use, and at the same time be without a remedy.[26]

Nor, under traditional riparian law, may polluters violate an individual's rights in order to promote a greater good, be it private or public. Although no longer always the case, courts long refused to consider the economic or social costs of prohibiting pollution; they ruled against companies that had invested considerable capital in their works, those that employed hundreds of people, and those representing a region's leading—sometimes only—industries. Municipalities frequently failed to convince the courts to allow polluting sewage disposal systems in the name of the greater good. The courts, however, generally made one concession to the public interest: they delayed injunctions in order to give industrial and municipal polluters time to clean up.

A case in 1900 against a paper mill whose wastes polluted a creek illustrates the courts' traditional refusal to balance private economic factors when choosing a remedy. In issuing an injunction against further pollution, the Indiana court refused to weigh the paper mill's $90,000 construction costs against the plaintiffs' material damages, which amounted to just $250. The court noted that the creek's condition constituted a nuisance which caused damages "immeasurable by a pecuniary standard." In this context, the size of the company's investment was irrelevant:

> The fact that [the] appellant has expended a large sum of money in the construction of its plant, and that it conducts its business in a careful manner and without malice, can make no difference in its rights to the stream. Before locating the plant the owners were bound to know that every riparian proprietor is entitled to have the waters of the stream that washes his land come to it without obstruction, diversion, or corruption, subject only to the reasonable use of the water, by those similarly entitled, for such domestic purposes as are inseparable from and necessary for the free use of their land; and they were bound, also, to know the character of their proposed business, and to take notice of the size, course, and capacity of the stream, and to determine for themselves, and at their own peril, whether they should be able to conduct their business upon a stream of the size and character of Brandywine creek without injury to their neighbors; and the magnitude of their investment and their freedom from malice furnish no reason why they should escape the consequences of their own folly.[27]

A dozen years later, in a similar New York case, a judge who refused to consider the financial burdens an injunction would place upon a pulp mill explained, "It has always been the boast of equity that any substantial injustice might be corrected by it to even the humblest suitor, and that the financial size of such a suitor's antagonist was not important."[28] The Court of Appeals later confirmed that balancing an injunction's great cost to the pulp mill against the plaintiff's relatively small injury would be unjustified: "Although the damage to the plaintiff may be slight as compared with the defendant's expense of abating the condition, that is not a good reason for refusing an injunction. Neither courts of equity nor law can be guided by such a rule, for if followed to its logical conclusion it would deprive the poor litigant of his little property by giving it to those already rich."[29]

In fact, the courts' refusal to consider an injunction's economic impact on a defendant remained so common that, according to the judge in Hazen Gauthier's case against the Rotary Club, "It is trite law that economic necessities of the defendants are irrelevant in a case of this character."[30]

So, too, have courts refused to consider the *public* costs of their injunctions. In rejecting the public good as a justification for pollution, judges have frequently soared to inspiring rhetorical heights. Behind the rhetoric have been some of the most powerful environmental protection decisions in common law history.

In the New York salt case previously discussed, the manufacturer tried to defend its polluting ways in the name of the public good. Salt manufacturing, it averred, was the region's leading industry. The defendant alone employed more than 100 men and women. To shut it down—to say nothing of the dozen other salt mines that might be subject to similar actions—would harm the public interest. But the Court of Appeal judge objected. Requiring the interest and convenience of the individual to give way to the general good, he warned, "would amount to a virtual confiscation of the property of small owners in the interest of a strong combination of capital."[31]

In defending individual rights against the interests of industry the judge cited an early coal mining decision:

> It was urged that the law should be adjusted to the exigencies of the great industrial interests of the commonwealth, and that the production of an indispensable mineral . . . should not be crippled and endangered by adopting a rule that would make colliers answerable in damages for corrupting a stream into which mine water would naturally run. . . . The consequences that would flow from the adoption of the doctrine contended for could be readily foretold. Relaxation of legal liabilities and remission of legal duties to meet the current needs of great business organizations, in one direction, would logically be followed by the same relaxation and remission, on the same grounds, in all other directions. One invasion of individual right would follow another, and it might be only a question of time when, under the operations of even a single colliery, a whole countryside would be depopulated.[32]

The judge then launched into his own passionate defence of individual rights:

> The lower riparian owners are entitled to a fair participation in the use of the water, and their rights cannot be cut down by the convenience or necessity of the defendant's business. . . . While the courts will not overlook the needs of important manufacturing interests, nor hamper them for trifling causes, they will not permit substantial injury to neighboring property, with a small but long-established business, for the purpose of enabling a new and great industry to flourish. They will not change the law relating to the ownership and use of property in order to accommodate a great business enterprise. According to the old and familiar rule, every man must so use his own property as not to injure that of his neighbor; and the fact that he has invested much money and employs many men in

carrying on a lawful and useful business upon his own land does not change the rule. . . .[33]

Some contemporary courts continue to uphold the tradition of placing individual rights before the public good. When considering Hazen Gauthier's bid to save Lake Ramsay, Judge Dunlap refused to allow his respect for the Rotary Club's mission—to raise money for its work with crippled children—to influence his decision.[34] "It is unfortunate," he said, "that in the circumstances of this case the rights of a riparian land proprietor come into conflict with the laudable objects of a charitable pursuit formulated and prosecuted with sincerity and dedication. . . . None the less, the most honourable of intentions alone at no time can justify the expropriation of common law rights of riparian owners."[35]

In the absence of a specific law to the contrary, even government itself cannot justify violating people's property rights to clean water in the name of the public good. As one judge explained at the end of the nineteenth century:

> I know of no duty of the Court which it is more important to observe and no power of the Court which it is more important to enforce than its power of keeping public bodies within their rights. The moment public bodies exceed their rights, they do so to the injury and oppression of private individuals, and those persons are entitled to be protected from injury arising from the operations of public bodies.[36]

Similarly, in his decision on a 1928 challenge to the storm sewage disposal practices of Edmonton, Alberta, a Supreme Court judge acknowledged that the city represented the collective rights of its ratepayers, who required sewers. "But these rights," he explained, "are necessarily restricted by correlative obligations. Although held by the municipalities for the benefit of all the inhabitants, they must not—except upon the basis of due compensation—be exercised by them to the prejudice of an individual ratepayer."[37] The judge echoed the decision from an early sewage disposal case: "[W]hatever the consequences, and much as the result may cause inconvenience, the principle must be upheld that, unless Parliament otherwise decrees, 'public works must be so executed as not to interfere with private rights of individuals.'"[38]

Riparian rights, protecting lakes and rivers from obstruction, diversion, and corruption, complete the trio of property rights most commonly used in the defence of nature. Together, trespass, nuisance and riparian rights have effectively empowered people to preserve or restore clean land, air and water—*too* effectively, apparently, for governments, which have worked assiduously to undermine property rights and the environmental protection they have fostered.

Notes

1.   Blackstone, *Commentaries on the Laws of England*, Volume 3, 191-2.

2.   *Gauthier et al.* v. *Naneff et al.* (1970), [1971] 1 O.R. 97 at 99 (H.C.J.).

3.   Legal scholars disagree about who has riparian rights. According to Rueggeberg and Thompson, riparian rights "belong only to those who own the banks of rivers, lakes or other bodies of water" (*Water Law and Policy Issues in Canada*, 4). Similarly, Percy explains that "the riparian doctrine restricts water rights to those who own property that adjoins a body of water" (*The Framework of Water Rights Legislation in Canada*, 73).

Others define riparians more broadly. According to McNeil and Macklem, "Every person who is in lawful possession of land adjacent to water, whether as a freeholder, leaseholder or in some other capacity, has riparian rights" (*Aboriginal, Treaty and Riparian Rights in the Moose River Basin*, 1).

Campbell *et al.* straddle the issue, suggesting first that the riparian "doctrine provides occupiers of land bordering a natural stream (riparian land) with certain rights to the use and flow of water" but later mentioning "rights which are incidental to the ownership of land" ("Water Management in Ontario," 479, 480).

4.   *Gauthier* v. *Naneff, op. cit.* at 101.

5.   See Appendix C for riparian rights case summaries.

6.   The roots of riparian law can be traced back even further. According to Chief Justice McRuer, "The origin of the common law applicable to this subject goes back to and beyond Roman law" (*McKie et al.* v. *The K.V.P. Co. Ltd.*, [1948] 3 D.L.R. 201 at 209).

The discussion in this paragraph is based in part on Harvey, "Riparian Water Rights."

7.   McLaren, "Nuisance Law and the Industrial Revolution," 323-4.

8.   By the 1850s, while some justices still referred to nuisance law in their decisions in water pollution cases, the riparian doctrine as we know it was "clear and settled" (*Embrey and Another* v. *Owen* (1851), 6 Exch. 353, 155 E.R. 586). Also see *Wood and Another* v. *Waud and Others* (1849), 3 Exch. 748, 154 E.R. 1047, an early case in which the court distinguished between ordinary and extraordinary water uses.

9.   Anglers' Co-operative Association, *ACA Review*; and personal communication with Anglers' Co-operative Association staffer, June 16, 1994.

For a description of the Association and its goals, membership, and strategies, see *Martell and Others* v. *Consett Iron Co. Ld.* (1954), [1955] 1 Ch. 363.

The Association is discussed at greater length in Chapter 13.

10. In *Miner* v. *Gilmour* (1858), 12 Moo. P.C. 131, 14 E.R. 861 at 870, the Privy Council's Lord Kingsdown noted, "it did not appear that, for the purposes of this [riparian] case, any material distinction exists between the French and the English law." Also see Percy, *op. cit.*, 72; Rueggeberg and Thompson, *op. cit.*, 5; and Canadian Environmental Law Research Foundation, "An Overview of Canadian Law and Policy Governing Great Lakes Water Quantity Management," 199-20.

11. According to Percy, "Riparian rights remain the basis of water allocation in Ontario and the Atlantic provinces" (*op. cit.*, 72). Similarly, Lucas explains that in Ontario, riparian laws "continue to govern the legal character of water rights" (*Security of Title in Canadian Water Rights*, 20). And McNeil and Macklem note that the doctrine remains valid on Indian reserves, where provincial legislation cannot override it (*op. cit.*, 7).

12. According to Harvey, "the riparian right to unpolluted water is alive and well" (*op. cit.*, 523). Also see Percy, *op. cit.*, 19.

13. Percy notes that "despite their undoubted existence, [riparian rights] are rarely enforced" (*op. cit.*, 75). According to Sharpe, there have been few reported Ontario riparian cases in the last three decades (*Injunctions and Specific Performance*, 197-8). And the Canadian Environmental Law Research Foundation suggests that the doctrine will now be used only in the most extraordinary cases (*op. cit.*, 112).

14. According to Rueggeberg and Thompson, "Many lawyers believe . . . that in the interests of water quality, the riparian owner's right to sue for injury where an upstream user might be discharging harmful contaminants is still a powerful means of preserving high quality conditions" (*op. cit.*, 6).

15. More recently, courts have stretched the meaning of ordinary to encompass waterpower, provided that the power is used on the riparian land, or even, in some industrial areas, manufacturing. See McNeil and Macklem, *op. cit.*, 2, and Campbell *et al.*, *op. cit.*, 481.

16. In the 1891 case, *Ellis* v. *Clemens*, Mr. Justice Street suggested that "the general rule which I gather from the cases is that any user which inflicts positive, repeated, and sensible injury upon a proprietor above or below is not to be considered a reasonable user" (21 O.R. 227 at 230).

17. *The Directors, etc. of the Swindon Waterworks Company Limited* v. *The Proprietors of the Wilts and Berks Canal Navigation Company* (1875), L.R. 7 H.L. 697.

18. *Watson* v. *Jackson* (1914), 19 D.L.R. 733 at 745 (Ont. S.C.).

19. *Miner* v. *Gilmour, op. cit.* at 870.

20. *John Young and Company* v. *The Bankier Distillery Company and Others*, [1893] A.C. 691 at 696 (P.C).

21. *Ibid.* at 699.

22. *Nepisiquit Real Estate and Fishing Company, Limited* v. *Canadian Iron Corporation, Limited* (1913), 42 N.B.R. 387 (Ch.).

23. *Pride of Derby and Derbyshire Angling Association Ld. and Another* v. *British Celanese Ld. and Another* (1952), [1953] 1 Ch. 149 (C.A.). This case is discussed at length in Chapter 13.

24. See, for example, *McKie et al.* v. *The K.V.P. Co. Ltd., op. cit.* at 216. Also see Canadian Environmental Law Research Foundation, *op. cit.*, 113; Estrin and Swaigen, *Environment on Trial*, 115; and Campbell *et al., op. cit.*, 503.

25. *Stollmeyer and Others* v. *Trinidad Lake Petroleum Company Limited, and Others*, [1918] A.C. 485 (P.C.).

26. *Strobel et al.* v. *Kerr Salt Co.*, 164 N.Y. 303, 320, 58 N.E. 142 at 148, 51 L.R.A. 687, 79 Am. St. Rep. 643 (N.Y. Ct. App. 1900) citing *Hill* v. *Smith*, 32 Cal. 166.

27. *Weston Paper Co.* v. *Pope et al.*, 155 Ind. 394, 57 N.E. 719 at 721, 56 L.R.A. 899 (1900).

28. *Whalen* v. *Union Bag & Paper Co.* First appeal: 145 App. Div. 1, 129 N.Y. Supp. 391 at 393 (1911).

29. *Whalen* v. *Union Bag & Paper Co.* Second appeal: 208 N.Y. 1, 5, 101 N.E. 805 at 806 (1913).

30. *Gauthier* v. *Naneff, op. cit.* at 103.

31. *Strobel et al.* v. *Kerr Salt Co.*, *op. cit.* at 145.

32. *Ibid.* at 146, citing *Coal Co.* v. *Sanderson*, 1878 trial decision, subsequently considered in 113 Pa. St. 126, 6 Atl. 453 (1886). Judge Vann acknowledged that a higher court had, in the name of the community interest in natural resource development, overturned this decision, but noted that "Courts of the highest standing have refused to follow the Sanderson Case" and that "its doctrine was finally limited by the court which announced it" (at 147).

33. *Ibid.* at 147-8.

34. During the hearing the judge noted, "My sympathy is with what the Sudbury Rotary Club is doing, but I must confine my interpretation to legal grounds." *Sudbury Star*, September 10, 1970.

35. *Gauthier* v. *Naneff, op. cit.* at 103.

36. *Roberts* v. *Gwyrfai District Council*, [1899] 2 Ch. D. 608.

37. *Malcolm Forbes Groat and Walter S. Groat* v. *The Mayor, Aldermen and Burgesses, being the Corporation of the City of Edmonton*, [1928] S.C.R. 522 at 533.

38. *Ibid.* at 534, citing *Attorney General* v. *Birmingham.*

Part II

The Erosion of Common Law Property Rights

4

In the Name of the Public Good

When there is a dispute between certain persons, the duty of the government is to see that everything is done in the public interest. . . .
Ontario Premier Frost, 1950[1]

On April 31, 1950, *An Act respecting The KVP Company Limited* received royal assent. With one stroke of the pen, the Ontario government wiped out an entire community's property rights, and with them, citizens' power to protect their river from an upstream polluter. The story of the KVP Act dramatically illustrates the significance of common law rights to clean water and governments' willingness to override these rights in the name of the "public good." It is a story about a community's struggle for a clean river—a struggle against the pulp mill that dumped its wastes into it. The courts tried to protect the river; the government, concerned as always about jobs, protected the pollution.

The battle over the Spanish River began in 1946, when the Kalamazoo Vegetable Parchment Company (KVP) revived a long-dormant kraft pulp and paper mill in Espanola, Ontario. Other companies had operated earlier mills on the site, but impending bankruptcy had shut down the last—run by the Abitibi Power and Paper Company—in 1930. The site stayed inactive for the next 16 years, except for three, when it served as a prisoner-of-war camp.

During those 16 years, the Spanish River, assisted by nature, had thrived. A 1934 flood had flushed contaminants from the river, restoring prime habitat. By the 1940s, the abundance of game fish had made the river and its surroundings a popular tourist resort area.

The opening of the KVP plant in 1946 changed all that. The river began to smell. Repulsive odours, often likened to the stench of rotten cabbage, permeated the river's 35-mile course to Lake Huron's north channel; they were even detectable ten miles out into the channel. And in the winter, according to the provincial fish and wildlife overseer, a hole cut in the ice would release a smell that would "nearly knock you down."[2]

KVP's operations ruined the taste of this northerly river's water. Farm animals found it repelling. People living beside the river could no longer draw their drinking water from it. Even boiled water tasted and smelled so bad that it couldn't be used for cooking or washing.

Each day, the mill released between three-and-a-half and five tons of chemically contaminated wood fibres which lodged in the river bed, accumulated in large foul-smelling masses, and eventually rose to the surface and drifted downstream. These stinking masses robbed the water of oxygen. Some blamed the river's huge numbers of dead and dying fish on oxygen starvation. Whatever the reason, fishing declined substantially.

Sadly, much of KVP's pollution was unnecessary. Kraft mills elsewhere used alternative methods—settling basins, for example —for effluent disposal. Before the mill had started up, a downstream landowner had urged its manager to pipe the effluent to sand flats nearby. But the manager had refused. "It is," he had said, "a matter of economics."[3]

Not surprisingly, those living downstream from the mill started complaining shortly after operations resumed. Supported by the downstream community and by local wildlife organizations, six men, all of whom owned land along the Spanish River, launched five lawsuits against KVP. One had a summer house on his property; several operated tourist camps; some farmed their land; and one, who owned a water lot on the river, was a commercial fisherman. All requested damages and an injunction. Their cases were tried together.

High Court Chief Justice McRuer found that the KVP Company had both violated the plaintiffs' riparian rights and committed a nuisance. He awarded damages totalling $5,600 and issued an injunction prohibiting KVP from altering the character or quality of the water; he then suspended the injunction for six months to allow KVP time to find other means of disposing of its effluent. Seven months later, the Ontario Court of Appeal affirmed his decision.[4]

In his judgment, Chief Justice McRuer noted that KVP's pollution had changed the river's character. Riparian law, he explained, prohibits any such alteration; under the law, a person living beside a river has a right to the flow of water in its natural state. Whether or not the change causes damage, or interferes with someone's water use, is irrelevant.

The Chief Justice rejected the all too common argument that

the social benefits of an activity can justify pollution. KVP had long advanced this argument; as its manager had once asked a downstream landowner, "What are a few fish compared with what we are doing for the country?"[5] But the Chief Justice refused to take into consideration KVP's economic importance. "In my view," he explained, "if I were to consider and give effect to an argument based on the defendant's economic position in the community, or its financial interests, I would in effect be giving to it a veritable power of expropriation of the common law rights of the riparian owners, without compensation."[6]

Chief Justice McRuer also rejected KVP's suggestion that an agreement with the government allowed it to pollute. A clause in the agreement stated, "No refuse, sawdust, chemicals or matter of any other kind, *beyond that reasonably necessary for the operation of the Company herein*, which shall be or may be injurious to game and fish life shall be placed or deposited in any river, stream or other waters."[7] The Chief Justice denied that this agreement amounted to a permit to pollute, explaining that legislation —not merely an agreement between the Crown and the polluter— would be required to deprive the plaintiffs of their rights.

The provincial government rose to the challenge, introducing legislation to crush the property rights of those living downstream from pulp and paper mills. Its amendments to the ludicrously named Lakes and Rivers Improvement Act empowered courts to consider the public interest before restraining a polluting mill: judges could refuse to grant an injunction if "the importance of the operation of the mill to the locality in which it operates and the benefit and advantage, direct and consequential, which the operation of the mill confers on that locality and on the inhabitants of that locality" outweighed the private injury inflicted by the mill.[8]

The debate on the new legislation reeked of hypocrisy. The Attorney General defended the blatantly anti-environmental law with pro-environmental rhetoric. His government had done all in its power to cut down pollution, he claimed. "Our attitude towards pollution," he said, "would be the same as our attitude towards sin. We are all against it."[9]

Only one MPP argued that the legislature should preserve both property rights and the Spanish River. William Dennison, of the Co-operative Commonwealth Federation (CCF, the New Democratic Party's predecessor), urged the government not to interfere in the KVP case: "I plead with the honourable Minister to do nothing in connection with this case which will affect the rights of these people who will take this company to the highest tribunal in the land, to get that pollution stopped."[10] His plea fell on deaf ears.

The politicians trampled once-sacred property rights—and the environment these rights so effectively protected—because they feared that jobs were at stake. Believing KVP's threats to close the mill—a position branded by some as "company bluff"[11]—they wanted to prevent the loss of 1500 jobs.

The politicians may have also feared that property rights threatened the entire pulp and paper industry. In its response to the court decision against it, KVP had promoted such a fear. "This is vital to us," one company official had explained. "You just can't run a sulphate plant without a very large amount of effluent, in the form of a liquor. To handle this effluent like you would an ordinary disposal plant where the stuff is filtered, is a far bigger problem than most people realize. It is very important to the whole industry, not only our plant, but all other sulphate plants."[12] At a time when troubles in the wood industry had left two to three thousand northern Ontarians out of work, the government felt a "public responsibility" to keep pulp and paper mills operating.[13]

Armed with the recent amendments to the Lakes and Rivers Improvement Act, KVP went to the Supreme Court of Canada, where it asked for a new trial on the issue of whether or not an injunction should be granted. On October 4, 1949, the court handed down its ruling: the injunction against the KVP pulp mill would stand. The court denied that the new legislation empowered it to overturn the injunction in this case. It could not, it explained, "give a judgment that was impossible in law at the time of the decision of the Court of Appeal."[14]

Mr. Justice Kerwin noted that while the Ontario Judicature Act allowed courts to substitute damages for an injunction, courts had always zealously guarded riparian rights, including the right to an injunction. He cited an earlier judgment from the British Privy Council on the issue: "The grant of an injunction is the proper remedy for a violation of right according to a current of authority, which is of many years' standing and is practically unbroken."[15]

The judge reviewed the courts' historical commitment to awarding injunctions; he attributed the tradition to a determination to avoid legalizing the violation of others' property rights by anyone willing to pay damages. An injunction should be waived, he said, only if damages provided "a complete and adequate remedy."[16] In the KVP case, damages could clearly not meet such a test. And so the injunction would stand, although it would be stayed for an additional six months. Six weeks later, the court refused KVP's request for permission to apply for future extensions.

Undeterred, mill management, labour unions, and several municipal associations organized a major lobbying effort. Delegations from Espanola, carrying a petition from 2000 residents, visited political leaders, requesting that they dissolve the injunction against KVP. On February 6, 1950, Premier Frost assured one delegation, "Leave it to me!"[17]

True to his word, 18 days later the Premier informed the legislature of his intention to "take whatever steps may be necessary to bring about the continued operations of this company so that the employment conditions in Espanola shall not be disturbed and that the development of the community will not be retarded."[18] Within a month the government introduced *An Act respecting The KVP Company Limited* to the sound of applause from the gallery. The act, as promised, would dissolve the injunction.[19]

Once again, legislators debated the act with considerable hypocrisy. Premier Frost prefaced his policy statement on the act with a paean to both environmental quality and individual rights: "[W]e do not regard lightly the matter of pollution of our streams. Indeed, we think it is a very serious matter. . . . We do not hold lightly the rights of individuals to protect their interests in the courts of this land. That is, in itself, a very important matter."[20] The Premier later insisted, "The government is most desirous of doing everything possible to prevent the pollution of our lakes and streams."[21] Everything, that is, but allow people to exercise their rights to clean water.

In defence of KVP, the Premier suggested that pollution is inevitable in modern society. "[W]e do recognize," he said, "that in these days of industrialization and . . . increase of population in areas of the province that we are bound to get a certain amount of pollution in our lakes and streams." Nevertheless, he assured his colleagues, "it is the policy of the government to keep any pollution at the lowest possible level."[22]

As is still so often the case, jobs preceded environmental protection on the government's agenda. The Attorney General frankly stated his position: "We are just not interested in preserving the quality of the water in the river as far as it is possible, as we are in preserving the means of employment for these people."[23] He later elaborated on his government's priorities: "[W]e sometimes have to balance the difficulties arising out of the interests of an industry, and all that that means, in providing employment and good living conditions for several thousands of people, and the ill effects which almost always follow when you have a civilized community living in a town or city. . . . [T]he development of the north country depends upon industry, and we cannot allow industry to close down."[24]

Few MPPs raised objections to the proposed act. Several expressed revulsion over pollution from pulp mills around the province. The Leader of the Opposition warned of a time when companies, demanding special consideration, would hold the threat of job losses over the government and the local populace. But none advocated allowing KVP's injunction to stand. Even William Dennison, earlier defender of individual rights, denied that the mill should be closed down; he instead proposed giving it five or ten years to clean up. And so *An Act respecting The KVP Company Limited* passed third reading on March 30, 1950, five days before the injunction was to have taken effect. It received royal assent a month later.

Unfortunately, the government's protection could not assure KVP's stability.[25] Since the Spanish River Pulp and Paper Company's establishment in 1899, the mill at Espanola had lurched from one financial crisis to the next. Payroll problems beset the mill as early as 1914. Temporary shutdowns, layoffs, changes in ownership, and ultimately bankruptcy plagued operations in the following decades. Nor did things look up after the government rescued KVP in 1950. The mill was shuffled from one owner to the next. Brown Company, which purchased KVP in 1966, blamed the sharp drop in its earnings on the money-losing Espanola mill. In the late 1970s, E. B. Eddy (the mill's current owner) required $25 million of government assistance. But even large federal and provincial grants could not ensure the profitability of the mill, which continued to run operating losses.[26]

Nor did government intervention improve the state of the

environment. Although the KVP Act had required the Research Council of Ontario to develop methods to clean up the Spanish River, the pollution continued for many years, driving tourist operators out of business and taking its toll on commercial fishermen, farmers, and the general public.[27]

The mill's successive owners promised to clean up the river, but reneged because of the financial costs of doing so. For example, in 1969, senior management told local citizens that E. B. Eddy "was not a Company with a magic wand or the millions needed to reduce the pollution of the Spanish River to zero."[28] The company did begin to implement pollution reduction measures in the 1970s.[29] But not until the next decade (when the International Joint Commission declared the Lower Spanish River an Area of Concern) did cleanup begin in earnest.[30] Tragically, new abatement measures did not prevent 1983's large chemical spill, in which 18,000 gallons of highly toxic 'soap' flowed from a holding tank into a sewer, and from there into the Spanish River. The spill killed over 120,000 fish.[31]

The KVP story justifies a postscript. After the passage of the KVP Act, Leslie Frost enjoyed another eleven years as Premier. Upon retiring from politics, he became a member of KVP's board of directors.[32]

Notes

1. Ontario Premier Leslie Frost, *Ontario Legislative Assembly Debates*, February 24, 1950, A-9.

2. *McKie et al.* v. *The K.V.P. Co. Ltd.*, [1948] 3 D.L.R. 201 at 206 (Ont. H.C.).

3. *Ibid.* at 219.

Several MPPs also insisted that KVP's pollution was preventable. According to William Dennison, "there is a scientific method available whereby these companies can remove from the water they are dumping into the streams in that country, the chemicals and the sewage and the solids which pollute the streams, and they can recover a good deal of those chemicals, and use them over again, providing they are prepared to pay the price required for the equipment which does the job" (*Debates, op. cit.*, March 29, 1949, 1457).

Another MPP, C. W. Cox, explained, "There is a remedy for pollution, and they are using it, in other places. . . . I have with me a rather comprehensive report issued by the Manager of one of the paper mills [in Wisconsin], in which he points out it is entirely feasible to solve the pollution problem, with respect to pulp and paper mills" (*Ibid.*, March 23, 1950, B-3 - B-4).

4. *McKie* v. *K.V.P. Co. Ltd.* (1948), [1949] 1 D.L.R. 39 (Ont. C.A.).

The Court of Appeal reworded the injunction to read as follows: "This Court Doth Order and Adjudge that the Defendant be, and it is hereby, restrained from discharging or permitting to be discharged from the Defendant's works mentioned in the pleadings, into the waters of the Spanish River, any substance or matter that, to the injury of the Plaintiff, affects the quality or character of the waters of the said River where the Plaintiff's lands border upon it, or that causes the said waters to become less pure than otherwise they would be" (at 41-2).

5. *Sudbury Daily Star*, November 23, 1948.

6. *McKie et al.* v. *The K.V.P. Co. Ltd.*, [1948] *op. cit.* at 214.

7. *Ibid.* at 218, emphasis added.

8. *An Act to amend the Lakes and Rivers Improvement Act*, section 39 (1) (a). The government introduced the act in February, 1949; it received royal assent on April 1, 1949.

9. *Debates, op. cit.*, March 29, 1949, 1461, 2.

10. *Ibid.*, 1459.

11. Morrison, *Espanola on the Spanish*, 171.

12. *Sudbury Daily Star*, April 16, 1948.

13. Attorney General Leslie Blackwell, *Debates, op. cit.*, March 29, 1949, 1462.

14. *The K.V.P. Co. Ltd.* v. *Earl McKie et al.*, [1949] S.C.R. 698 at 701.

15. *Ibid.* at 701-2, citing *Stollmeyer* v. *Petroleum Development Company Limited, and Others*, [1918] A.C. 485 (P.C.).

16. *Ibid.* at 703.

17. Morrison, *op. cit.*, 171.

18. *Debates, op. cit.*, February 24, 1950, A-10.

19. The act maintained people's rights to bring legal actions against KVP, but limited possible remedies to damages. It also set up an arbitration mechanism to resolve disputes and assigned to the Research Council of Ontario responsibility for developing pollution abatement methods for KVP.

20. *Debates, op. cit.*, February 24, 1950, A-5.

21. *Ibid.*, A-8.

22. *Ibid.*, A-6, A-8.

23. Dana Porter, *Debates, op. cit.*, March 21, 1950, B-6.

24. *Debates, op. cit.*, March 23, 1950, B-13 - B-14.

25. For the information in this paragraph I have relied on Morrison, *op. cit.*, 10-11, 85-86, 182-5, 192-3.

26. Phil Hearn, E. B. Eddy, personal communication, May 10, 1993. Mr. Hearn said he thought that the mill had lost money in two of the last three years. George Weston Limited's 1992 Annual Report confirms that E. B. Eddy Paper and Forest Products ran operating losses in 1991 and 1992. It does not, however, provide specific figures for the Espanola mill.

27. Morrison, *op. cit.*, 171-2, 183.

28. *Ibid.*, 192.

29. The measures were not entirely effective, however. In a 1988 decision regarding E. B. Eddy, a provincial court justice noted that the mill continued to pollute the Spanish River. Under both start-up and operating conditions, he said, the mill "usually and normally" discharged deleterious substances (*R.* v. *E. B. Eddy Forest Products Limited* (1992), 5 F.P.R. 63 at 87).

30. For information on improvements made in the 1980s, see Ontario Ministries of the Environment and Natural Resources and Environment Canada, *Status Report, Spanish River—Harbour Area, Remedial Action Plan (RAP)*, 1-12.

31. Michael John Powell, regional fisheries biologist for the Ministry of Natural Resources, provided this estimate at the trial of *R.* v. *E. B. Eddy Forest Products Limited, op. cit.* at 74.

32. Morrison, *op. cit.*, 171.

5

Growth at All Costs

With any province, such as this, growing as it is, it is impossible not to affect the conditions of people and of streams and watersheds, as compared to the way they were before. They must be affected.

                                              Ontario Premier Frost, 1956[1]

Nineteen fifty-five was a bad year for Ontario's municipal polluters. In separate cases, courts ruled that two municipalities—Woodstock and Richmond Hill—must stop dumping raw sewage into local rivers. But the municipalities needn't have worried: the provincial government came to their rescue before the injunctions took effect.

Woodstock had constructed its sewage disposal plant in 1922

for a population of 9,000. In the following decades, the plant failed to keep up with the city's growth. Improperly maintained and operated, it could not handle the waste from 16,000 residents; the sewage simply overflowed into the Thames River, or received inadequate treatment before being discharged there.

Mr. Burgess, who operated a dairy farm just downstream from the sewage outlet, found one of his cows mired in the Thames in 1947. He inspected the river, which he found "slimy and stinking, with solid matter flowing downstream." The condition worsened over the next several years. The cows developed dysentery, decreased their milk production, and aborted their calves. Mr. Burgess sold them at a loss. He stopped renting out pasture land, and he stopped selling sod to landscape gardeners, since he had no cattle to keep it short.

In 1955, Mr. Burgess went to court, where he sought and obtained an injunction and damages. The judge who heard the case found that Woodstock's pollution of the river constituted a nuisance which should be restrained. Citing the KVP case, he simply explained, "where there is pollution of a watercourse, then an injunction ought to be granted."[2] The judge did, however, make one concession: he stayed the injunction for 18 months, giving Woodstock a chance to upgrade its plant.

Meanwhile, the Village of Richmond Hill was undergoing a similar trial, with a similar result. In 1952 the village had constructed a sewage disposal plant that discharged its effluent, along with storm-sewer water, into a branch of the Don River. Because the sewage plant was too small for Richmond Hill's population and because chlorination was improperly controlled, the formerly clear stream became dark and dirty, its fish and watercress disappeared, its banks became littered with toilet paper and condoms, and the surrounding area began to smell of sewage.

Fed up with the mess being created by the sewage plant, Annie Stephens, who owned land along the Don, filed a lawsuit claiming that Richmond Hill had violated her riparian rights. The judge who heard the case in 1955 agreed that a riparian has the right to the natural flow of a stream, "without sensible alteration in its character or quality," and need not suffer damages in order to obtain an injunction.[3]

Richmond Hill argued that an injunction against it would harm the public welfare: not only would it deprive its own citizens of the only affordable method of sewage disposal, but it could also adversely affect 95 per cent of the province's other municipalities with similar systems. The judge responded with a passionate defence of the court's role in preserving individual rights:

> [I]t is not for the judiciary to permit the doctrine of utilitarianism to be used as a make-weight in the scales of justice. . . .
>
> It is the duty of the State (and of statesmen) to seek the greatest good for the greatest number. To this end, all civilized nations have entrusted much individual independence to their Governments. But be it ever remembered that no one is above the law. Neither those who govern our affairs, their appointed advisers, nor those retained to build great works for society's benefit, may act so as to abrogate the slightest right of the individual, save within the law. It is for Government to protect the general by wise and benevolent enactment. It is for me, or so I think, to interpret the law, determine the rights of the individual and to invoke the remedy required for their enforcement.[4]

The judge therefore concluded that Mrs. Stephens was entitled to a broad injunction; he perpetually restrained Richmond Hill from discharging effluent or storm overflow into the Don and from polluting it in any manner. He then suspended the injunction for one year. Five months later the Court of Appeal affirmed the injunction.

At issue in both the Woodstock and Richmond Hill trials was

the question of statutory authority. Normally, polluters can protect themselves with "the defence of statutory authority" if their pollution results inevitably from a government-authorized activity. In licensing an activity, the thinking goes, the government licenses its inevitable results; otherwise, of what use would a licence be?

Both Woodstock and Richmond Hill argued that their permission, under the Public Health Act, to operate sewage treatment plants gave them statutory authority to pollute. The courts rejected these arguments, explaining that regardless of whether the Department of Health had lawfully approved the municipalities' sewage treatment plans, water pollution was neither an anticipated nor an inevitable result. The municipalities, albeit at great expense, could have installed larger plants or considered land-based alternatives, such as sewage-farms.[5]

It took the provincial government only six months to respond to the court's conclusion that "the Public Health Act does not authorize a municipality to interfere with riparian rights."[6] On March 20, 1956, the government introduced An Act to amend The Public Health Act. The act dissolved the injunctions against Woodstock and Richmond Hill. It went even further, deeming any sewage project approved by the Department of Health to be operated by statutory authority. In the words of the Attorney General, "This means that the courts would not have power to grant an injunction to stop the operation of a sewage disposal plant to the inconvenience and detriment of all the inhabitants of the municipality."[7] The Leader of the Opposition described the bill more bluntly, explaining that it empowered the Department of Health to allow municipalities to pollute Ontario's rivers: "[O]nce The Department of Health gives approval, each one of these streams—in effect—can have sewage dumped into it."[8]

A month earlier, the government had introduced An Act to establish the Ontario Water Resources Commission, purportedly to end "the pollution problem" in the province. The act empowered the OWRC to build and operate water supply and sewage disposal systems. The following year, the government authorized the commission to establish operating standards for sewage works and set water quality regulations.[9] As the OWRC assumed responsibility for water quality from the Department of Health, it also acquired the department's power to authorize water pollution. It correspondingly gained that department's power to deprive citizens of their riparian rights—which traditionally permitted *no* sensible alteration in water quality. The OWRC Act so completely superseded riparian rights that there have been few riparian cases reported in the province since.[10]

The debates surrounding both the Public Health Act amendments and the OWRC Act illuminate the government's approach to pollution. In the mid-1950s, most legislators assumed that population growth and industrial development inevitably led to pollution. As one MPP suggested, "wherever we have progress in industry, we have to contend with polluted water."[11]

The politicians' insistence on pollution's inevitability verged on dishonesty. The Minister of Health admitted that treating most waste was not a technical problem. Others, most obviously the courts, also believed that pollution could—and must—be stopped. The real issue in dispute was not whether pollution could be stopped, but who should pay to stop it. The government argued that taxpayers—rather than polluters—should bear responsibility for clean-up costs. Premier Frost explained his commitment to shouldering the tremendous costs of cleaning up industrial pollution as follows:

> I think it is reasonable and common sense to regard the fact that concentrations of industry create obligations. To regard them merely as possibilities for additional revenue is completely the wrong conception. . . . It will take everything Ontario receives from corporation and personal income taxes

to pay for the incidence of industry only, and then it will not be sufficient.[12]

As for polluting municipalities, many of them lacked the capital—or the credit to borrow money—to pay for repairing or expanding their sewage systems. And so the provincial government would have to come to their rescue, despite its own tight financial situation. This was not just the governing party's position; the Leader of the Opposition agreed wholeheartedly:

> [T]he municipalities in this province are not in a financial position to carry the full burden that will be imposed upon them by the type of corrective measures which will be proposed to them in the next few years. I believe quite sincerely that the Province of Ontario will have to come to the aid of these municipalities, and they will have to be given grants in order to lessen the financial impact upon the municipal taxpayers for these services.[13]

Ultimately, of course, the two new acts shifted the burden not only to the provincial government but also to the victims of pollution. As is so often the case, the government pursued the public good by depriving victims of their rights. The public interest, the Attorney General explained, "must be paramount in the matter of injunction proceedings." The people of Woodstock and Richmond Hill "must live and have health and sanitation, no matter what happens. That is the first consideration."[14] But the courts had not suggested otherwise; they had simply insisted that sanitation not occur at the expense of some citizens.

The politicians worried about a snowball effect if people were to retain—and use—their property rights. Pollution victims had increasingly begun to exercise their common law rights to clean water. One MPP described the situation as follows:

> In too many cases, a municipality takes its water from a relatively pure stream, and discharges its sewage below its own

water intake but above its neighbour's intake. Interest in this problem, I find, is much greater than ever before. There is a growing realization on the part of the public that it is a trespass on the rights of their neighbours and of themselves for un-treated effluent to be discharged from municipal or industrial sewers into a stream or lake which serves others.[15]

The legislators well knew that many municipalities used their rivers as sewers and could therefore be subject to lawsuits. One MPP remarked on the pollution plaguing the Humber and Don Rivers. Another described the Grand River as "nothing more or less than an open sewer," thanks in part to the city of Brantford's spewing into it raw sewage from 50,000 people. Another noted that even Ottawa had no sewage disposal plant. And Toronto's pollution had become the subject of international protest. The Attorney General suggested that, in all, 65 Ontario municipalities could be affected if people started exercising their common law rights to clean water.

When the Premier suggested that the new Public Health Act "modernizes and straightens out a situation which undoubtedly has been at loose ends for a number of years"[16] he was saying that the legislation transferred responsibility for making decisions about water quality from individuals to government. But he could not say that the government could be trusted with the responsi-bility. Government had in the past proven reluctant to enforce its own laws. For example, the Public Health Act had long prohib-ited pollution. One section stipulated that "no garbage, excreta, manure, vegetable or animal matter or filth shall be discharged in any of the lakes, rivers, streams or other waters in Ontario." Another section empowered the Department of Health to issue mandatory orders to establish or improve sewage treatment plants.

Yet the Department of Health had refused to exercise its power to prevent pollution. When it did issue clean-up orders, municipalities simply ignored them, confident that the government would not enforce them. Even the Premier admitted that his government's orders had been "more disregarded than they have been observed."[17] He blamed their ineffectiveness on municipalities' financial problems.

New legislation failed to correct the situation. Almost a year later, during the debates regarding further amendments to the Public Health and OWRC Acts, the Opposition accused the government of failing to enforce its environmental laws. The Minister of Health could recall only one time that the government had pursued a mandatory clean-up order under the former version of the Public Health Act; even that had ended in failure. "As far as I know," the Minister admitted, "in the annals of our history, there was one order where the court order was carried out and they were fined $100 a day, some 20 or 30 years ago; that is the top fine. It mounted up to $75,000 or so, and the government of the day forgave them or whatever one likes to call it."[18]

Sadly, the OWRC showed no signs of using its new powers more forcefully than had the Department of Health. Although by 1957 the commission had issued two mandatory clean-up orders—one for Sarnia and one for Trenton—it seemed likely to be as understanding as its predecessors: in neither case had it set a deadline for compliance.[19]

In allowing sewage treatment plants to violate people's riparian rights, Ontario's legislators provided a brazen example of government's desire to promote growth at all costs. But they were by no means the first or last to do so. The Ontario Water Resources Commission Act and the amendments to the Public Health Act joined a growing list of laws designed to encourage industrial development at the expense of the environment and those who depend upon it. Nor have riparians been the only victims of such laws. Those living downstream from sewage treatment plants share a fate with countless others living besides railroads, nuclear power plants and other nuisances. Their rights sacrificed for "the public good," they find themselves increasingly unable to control the environmental degradation whose costs they must bear.

Notes

1. Ontario Premier Leslie Frost, *Legislature of Ontario Debates, Official Report—Daily Edition*, March 26, 1956, 1536.

2. *Burgess* v. *The City of Woodstock*, [1955] O.R. 814 at 823.

3. *Stephens* v. *The Village of Richmond Hill*, [1955] O.R. 806, aff'd [1956] O.R. 88.

4. *Ibid.* [1955] at 812-3.

5. These comments appeared in the Richmond Hill decision, which the justice in the Woodstock case referred to as a conclusion "by which I am bound and with which I agree" (at 818).

6. *Burgess* v. *Woodstock*, *op. cit* at 818, citing *Stephens* v. *Richmond Hill*, *op. cit.* The Woodstock decision was issued on September 12, 1955.

7. A. K. Roberts, *Debates*, *op. cit.*, March 27, 1956, 1575.
   The act also substituted compensation (set by the Ontario Municipal Board) for injunctions. See sections 6 (1) (22) and 6 (2) through 6 (4).

8. F. R. Oliver, *Debates*, *op. cit*, March 26, 1956, 1537.

9. For a summary of the OWRC's powers see Anisman, *Water Pollution Control in Ontario*, 378 ff.

10. Sharpe, *Injunctions and Specific Performance*, 198.

11. A. Cowling, *Debates*, *op. cit.*, February 28, 1956, 574.

12. *Ibid.*, 563.

13. *Ibid.*, 565.

14. *Debates*, *op. cit.*, March 27, 1956, 1578.

15. W. Murdoch, *Debates*, *op. cit.*, February 12, 1957, 286.

16. L. Frost, *Debates*, *op. cit.*, March 26, 1956, 1536.

17. *Debates*, *op. cit.*, February 28, 1956, 562.

18. M. Phillips, *Debates*, *op. cit.*, February 11, 1957, 263.

19. L. Frost, *Debates, op. cit.*, March 28, 1957, 1778.

6

The Defence of Statutory Authority

The Legislature is supreme, and if it has enacted that a thing is lawful, such a thing cannot be a fault or an actionable wrong.

Lord Halsbury, 1901[1]

On June 26, 1970, Canada's deputy Governor General gave royal assent to *An Act respecting civil liability for nuclear damage.* In so doing, he perpetrated one of Canada's greatest insults to both property rights and the environment.[2]

The Nuclear Liability Act completely exempts nuclear designers, manufacturers and suppliers, such as Westinghouse and General Electric, from any financial liability resulting from a nuclear accident—even if the accident is caused by their negligence or wilful wrongdoing. Under the act, a manufacturer who falsifies safety documents or a supplier who knowingly sells defective equipment remains immune from civil lawsuits brought by accident victims.

The act also protects the operators of nuclear generating stations. It limits their liability to $75 million per station, which, as Chernobyl's billions of dollars of damages so dramatically illustrate, falls far below the potential costs of a major accident. In fact, a severe accident at a Canadian reactor could be expected to cost between $375 million and $75 billion.[3]

The act limits the period in which the victims of smaller accidents may file claims to within ten years of the accident—even though cancers and genetic abnormalities would often take decades longer than that to show up.

Furthermore, the act restricts victims' access to the courts. If, after an accident, claims are expected to exceed $75 million, victims must take their claims not to court but to a special commission that would decide how to divide the available compensation. Parliament could—but would not be required to—step in and allocate tax dollars to pay some of the claims. If no additional funds were allocated, victims who could have collectively lost a billion dollars could recover just $75 million, or seven cents on their dollar.[4]

In short, the Nuclear Liability Act deprives people harmed by a nuclear accident of their common law rights. In the absence of the act, nuclear operators would be fully liable under a branch of nuisance law named after the famous nineteenth-century case of *Rylands* v. *Fletcher*.[5] In that case the court ruled that "the person who for his own purposes brings on his lands and collects and keeps there anything likely to do mischief if it escapes, must keep it in at his peril, and, if he does not do so, is *prima facie* answerable for all the damage which is the natural consequence of its escape."[6] The rule under *Rylands* v. *Fletcher* would internalize the costs and risks of nuclear power; it would ensure that utilities assumed financial responsibility for the consequences of their chosen method of electricity generation. In contrast, under the Nuclear Liability Act, the victims and the taxpayers will end up sharing the vast bulk of the costs of any severe accident.

Tragically, in shifting financial responsibility for a nuclear accident, the act increases the likelihood of one occurring. Protection from liability reduces incentives to prevent accidents. Safety measures cost money, and electric utilities, under pressure to minimize costs, must find it hard to justify large safety expenditures if their liability is limited. Furthermore, protection from liability lowers the costs of nuclear power, thereby encouraging utilities to build more reactors (instead of safer alternatives) and increasing the level of this dangerous activity.[7]

Why would Parliament pass such an outrageous law? Although the federal Liberal government couched the bill's introduction in rhetoric about "protection for the people of this country,"[8] it failed to obscure its real goal: protection of the nuclear industry. It admitted, "the fear of being held liable for radiation injury could cause anxiety, for example, to manufacturers of equipment used in nuclear installations about the possibility of being exposed to exceptionally large damage claims."[9]

The opposition parties seemed to agree that such anxiety would not serve the public interest. Clean, cheap nuclear power, described by one Progressive Conservative MP as "a double boon for mankind," offered "an opportunity we cannot afford to miss."[10] An MP from the New Democratic Party added that Canada was becoming increasingly dependent on nuclear energy—an energy which could soon drive planes and even cars.[11] Someone had to accept responsibility for the risks associated with this growing industry. Insurance companies, well aware of potentially gargantuan costs, refused to bear unlimited risk.

And so, the MP concluded, the risks and costs of an accident would fall on the public's shoulders: "Whenever disasters of this kind take place the public, through taxes and other disaster measures, are required to pick up the tab."[12]

Governments have long asked taxpayers and the affected public to pick up the tab for the environmental harm wrought by industry. In order to do so, they have had to override or modify the common law with statutes and regulations enabling polluters to violate others' property rights with impunity.

Thus governments have given polluters who are challenged in court a prized defence: "the defence of statutory authority." The courts' long-standing familiarity with those five words illustrates the consistency with which governments have legalized nuisances over the last two centuries, indemnifying polluters from liability for what would otherwise be actionable wrongs.

Courts, in determining whether governments have indeed indemnified particular activities, generally distinguish between permissive and mandatory statutes. Under the former, which maintain industries' discretion over operating methods and locations, industries are expected to act in conformity with private property rights and cannot claim the defence of statutory authority. For example, a company's obligation to maintain a highway cannot justify its use of damaging road salt when instead it could have used a harmless de-icing agent. Similarly, the right to generate electricity does not authorize a company to create a nuisance; it must choose a generating method and location that will not interfere with others' property rights.

It is when the harm is an *inevitable* consequence of a legislatively authorized activity that a polluter can claim the defence of statutory authority. In mandating an activity or authorizing something to be done in a specific manner or location, the reasoning goes, the legislature sanctions all of its unavoidable consequences, including those that would have previously been forbidden. This is based on the principle of law that "he who grants something is deemed to also grant that without which the grant would be worthless" (in Latin, *cuicunque aliquis quid concedit concedere videtur et id sine quo res ipsa esse non potuit*).[13] Without legislative protection from liability, people would retain their right to challenge in court the inevitable results of statutorily authorized activities; legal actions could lead to injunctions against offending activities, thus thwarting the will of the legislature. Not surprisingly, legislators have written the laws—have set the rules governing the courts, in other words—so as to avoid that outcome.

Two judges of the Supreme Court of Canada have recently questioned the wisdom of the inevitability test, and with it the value of the defence of statutory authority. Chief Justice Dickson concurred with Mr. Justice La Forest that inevitability itself should not excuse exemption from tort liability. The fact that an operation will inevitably damage some individuals does not explain why those individuals should be responsible for paying for that damage. "Arguments about inevitability," the judges agreed, "are essentially arguments about money. . . . '[I]nevitable' damage is often nothing but a hidden cost of running a given system." Their conclusion? "The costs of damage that is an inevitable consequence of the provision of services that benefit the public at large should be borne equally by all those who profit from the service." The judges added that requiring the body that provides a service to bear the costs of its operations could serve as a valuable deterrent: "[I]f the authority is to bear the costs of accidents . . . it may realize that it is more cost-effective to forestal [*sic*] their occurrence."[14] Unfortunately, the judges do not seem to have succeeded in weakening the almost universal respect that the defence of statutory authority has enjoyed for over 200 years.

Although government-authorized nuisances are as old as the rights they violate, they long remained exceptions to the rule. Medieval mining regulations provide some of the earliest examples of governments overriding common law property rights. In the thirteenth century, several revenue-hungry European governments vigorously promoted mining. They gave miners free land and exempted them from military service. Many of the miners' perks came at the expense of local landowners: the governments encouraged miners to prospect on private property, allowed them to cut privately owned trees, and authorized them to divert streams. To ensure that the miners' victims couldn't fight back, the governments freed the miners from the jurisdiction of local magistrates.[15]

Government-sanctioned property rights violations became more common in the late eighteenth century when American governments passed a series of Mill Acts in order to promote their favoured form of economic development. Designed to encourage the construction of mills and to protect mill owners from expensive lawsuits, they permitted the owners to flood neighbouring lands. Although they provided for monetary compensation, they deprived victims of the rights to injunctions, punitive damages, or self-help actions that they would have otherwise enjoyed under the common law of trespass or nuisance.[16]

British acts of that era likewise protected certain ventures from common law liability. As early as 1792, the courts determined that the public interest warranted indemnifying public works authorized by Parliament. As the Chief Justice explained in that year, without liability exemptions "every Turnpike Act, Paving Act, and Navigation Act would give rise to an infinity of actions. . . . Some individuals suffer an inconvenience under all these Acts of Parliament; but the interests of individuals must give way to the accommodation of the public."[17]

Some of the most dramatic early illustrations of statutory

authority can be found in the British, American, and Canadian laws protecting railway companies from common law liability. Railways, the first of which were chartered in Britain in the late 1820s, mushroomed in the following decades; the British Parliament authorized the construction of over 400 between 1844 and 1846.[18] As steam locomotives became commonplace, their noise, vibration, and smoke, along with the danger of fires set by escaping sparks, became frequent problems.

Lawsuits involving nuisances caused by trains were common. A British innkeeper complained that the vibrations from trains passing through a nearby tunnel ruined the beer stored in his cellar.[19] A New York riparian sought damages when a railroad bridge caused his land to flood.[20] The owner of an English cotton mill complained that the danger of sparks flying from engines travelling the adjacent railway required him to purchase costly insurance and reduced the value of his property.[21] A New Brunswick farmer sought compensation for a barn lost to a fire started by the local train.[22]

It rapidly became apparent, however, that the legislation authorizing the railways had overridden people's common law rights to stop such nuisances. Those harmed could not expect the courts to issue injunctions against the railway companies; in fact, unless the legislation so provided, they couldn't even count on being financially compensated for their losses.

Rex v. *Pease*, an 1832 English case in which users of a highway complained that the noisy, smoky locomotives on an adjacent railway line alarmed their horses and caused accidents, established the extent to which governments had immunized railway companies from liability for the damages they caused. The railway company defended itself on the grounds that Parliament, in authorizing its operations, undoubtedly took into consideration—and therefore tacitly authorized—the nuisances caused by steam locomotives. It likely did so, the company added, because locomotives served a public interest by facilitating the cheap transport of coal; the benefits of highway use, in short, should "be sacrificed to the greater public benefit derived from the undertaking."[23] The court agreed that Parliament had, without qualification, authorized both the construction of the railroad parallel to the highway and the use of locomotives upon it. Although Parliament must have known that the railroad would inconvenience highway travellers, it had failed to impose any duty to screen the railway or to otherwise lessen its impacts. One could reasonably presume, therefore, that "the Legislature intended that the part of the public which should use the highway should sustain some inconvenience for the sake of the greater good to be obtained by other parts of the public in the more speedy travelling and conveyance of merchandise along the new railroad."[24]

The courts confirmed the validity of the railroads' defence of statutory authority in *Vaughan* v. *The Taff Vale Railway*, an 1860 case against a company whose sparking locomotive had set fire to a woods. The judges who heard that case agreed that they could not hold the company responsible for the fire. As one explained, "although the use of a locomotive engine must have been accounted a nuisance unless authorized by the legislature, yet, being so authorized, the use of it is lawful, and the defendants are not liable for an accident caused by such use without any negligence on their part."[25]

Four years later Horatio and Mary Brand filed a now famous claim against the Hammersmith and City Railway Company, whose vibrating, noisy, smoky trains travelled the rails beside their property. The railroad's vibrations reduced the value of their house and gardens and ensured that they would command a reduced rent in the future. When the Brands requested compensation for their losses, the lower court ruled against them, explaining that Parliament, in expressly authorizing the use of locomotives, had overridden the common law and its protection of individuals' property rights. The statutes that replaced the common law—the Lands and Railway Clauses Consolidation Acts of 1845—did not stipulate that the companies must compensate for the effects of their operations. Requiring the railway company to compensate the Brands would therefore interfere with the power conferred upon it by the legislature.

One of the judges who heard the case explained that Parliament had acted in the public interest:

> It would be almost impossible to construct a railway in the metropolitan district, or in any large town, without creating more or less inconvenience to a great number of persons; and it may be that the legislature may have thought that as to injuries resulting from the ordinary use and exercise of the powers conferred on railway companies to run locomotive engines, it was expedient to exempt railway companies from the multitudinous claims which might be made in respect of such injuries; and therefore the legislature may be supposed to have determined that private rights should yield to the public convenience.[26]

The judge then suggested that it was not merely expedient to protect the railway companies; it was also *necessary*, since inflicting upon them large penalties "might possibly prevent the increase of railways altogether."[27]

The House of Lords upheld this decision after an unusually controversial hearing at which some law lords argued that the Brands deserved compensation and others insisted that compensation was inappropriate since the legislature had not provided for it.[28] Most agreed that in the absence of statutory authorization, the railway's vibrations would have constituted a nuisance which neighbours could have enjoined. No longer could the Brands sue for nuisance, however.[29] As Mr. Justice Blackburn explained, "[I]f the Legislature authorizes the doing of an act (which if unauthorized would be a wrong and a cause of action) no action can be maintained for that act, on the plain ground that *no Court can treat that as a wrong which the Legislature has authorized*, and consequently the person who has sustained a loss by the doing of that act is without remedy, unless in so far as the Legislature has thought it proper to provide for compensation to him."[30] *Rex* v. *Pease*, he said, had decided the matter back in 1832; *Vaughan* v. *Taff Vale* had followed. Huge sums had been invested in railways on the strength of those decisions. And so, regardless of those original decisions' soundness, they ought now to be considered the law.

One law lord did point out the inequity of this reasoning. Mr. Baron Bramwell could not imagine that a company would be allowed to increase its profits by refusing to compensate the victims of its nuisances. Arguments about the necessity of creating nuisances, he protested, were really arguments about costs. For example, a railway company intent on preventing fires might station employees along its tracks to prevent sparks from igniting nearby grass. Since doing so would cost a considerable sum, the company would find it cheaper to simply risk starting fires. But there was no reason that the company—and ultimately the fare-paying passengers who benefited from the system—should not bear those risks and costs:

> Admitting that the damage must be done for the public benefit, that is no reason why it should be uncompensated. It is to be remembered that that compensation comes from the public which gets the benefit. It comes directly from those who do the damage, but ultimately from the public in the fares they pay. If the fares will not pay for this damage, and a fair profit on the company's capital, the speculation is a losing one, as all the gain does not pay all the loss and leave a fair profit. Either, therefore, the railway ought not to be made, or the damage may well be paid for.[31]

The law lord failed to persuade his colleagues or to modify the well established thinking on the issue of statutory authority.

Brand v. *Hammersmith* was to be extensively cited over the years, including in a 1901 case brought against the Canadian Pacific Railway Company for a fire set by sparks from one of its locomotives. In that case, CPR acknowledged that under common law it would have been liable for damages caused by fires that its trains started. It argued, however, that in authorizing the use of locomotives, Parliament had also authorized the use of fire and the occasional accidental escape of sparks. It claimed that Parliament had, in other words, indemnified railroad companies against the anticipated and inevitable results of using locomotives. The Privy Council agreed. "[I]t would be a repugnant and absurd piece of legislation," the Lord Chancellor suggested, echoing *Brand* v. *Hammersmith*, "to authorize by statute a thing to be done, and at the same time leave it to be restrained by injunction from doing the very thing which the Legislature has expressly permitted to be done."[32]

Statutes authorizing nuisances now abound. Their forms are legion. Sometimes they are quite frank. Like the KVP Act discussed earlier, laws may shield a single polluter. Or, like the Public Health Act, they may expressly confer statutory authority on a whole class of polluters—in that case, those who operate sewage treatment plants. Entire industries may also be protected by liability limitations, such as those conferred by the Nuclear Liability Act or the Canadian Shipping Act, which limits risk through the Maritime Pollution Claims Fund.[33]

Some statutes substitute damage awards for injunctions against polluters. The KVP Act, it will be recalled, overruled the Supreme Court's injunction against a polluting pulp mill; the law decreed that downstream victims would have to be content with damage awards. Almost three decades earlier, the Ontario government had passed The Damage by Fumes Arbitration Act forbidding courts to hear cases about sulphur fumes. Instead, a government-appointed arbitrator would award damages; in no circumstances would the arbitrator issue injunctions.[34]

Ontario's Mining Act similarly deprived victims of their common law rights to enjoin polluters. The court noted the loss in a 1962 case in which northern Ontario cottage owners protested a uranium mine's contamination of their lake.[35] The judge who heard the case acknowledged that under the common law, the cottagers would have been entitled to water unaltered in character or quality, and furthermore, that a violation of their property rights would, traditionally, have entitled them to an injunction. The situation at hand, however, was governed not by common law but by the Mining Act, which conferred the right to discharge tailings and other waste and denied pollution victims an injunction; it merely provided for compensation for damages. As the judge noted, "[T]he effect of the statute is to terminate the common law right whereby the owner can secure protection of his property."[36] New Brunswick's Judicature Act achieves the same end by different means: it prohibits anyone harmed by the discharge from a manufacturing or industrial plant from seeking an injunction against it without permission from the Minister of Justice.

Then there are the myriad regulations and standards that sanction industrial discharges that would under common law be considered nuisances. The Ontario Water Resources Act grants statutory authority to those discharging effluent sanctioned by a Ministry of Environment certificate of approval.[37] One would be hard pressed to find in such certificates water quality standards that are as stringent as those imposed under riparian law, which traditionally allowed *no* alteration of water quality.

Regulatory protection is, of course, not limited to polluters of water. Regulations govern air emissions, odours, and noise levels. Control orders issued under Ontario's Environmental Protection

Act regulations are known in the field as "pollution mandates." Ontario's Farm Practices Protection Act exempts farmers from liability for odour, noise, and dust, provided they do not violate specified laws. Thanks to the act, an Ontarian can no longer go to court to request an injunction against a neighbouring farmer whose operations would, in the absence of the act, constitute a nuisance.[38]

In case after case, government regulations have made it easier—and cheaper—for industries to pollute. Polluters have long understood that they benefit from regulation. As one industry advisor noted, "No industry offered the opportunity to be regulated should decline it. Few industries have done so."[39] The legislative erosion of traditional common law property rights has provided enormous subsidies to polluting industries. Manufacturers have been allowed to use others' property for free, or at greatly reduced costs. The costs, of course, have not disappeared simply because polluters have not had to bear them. Instead, they have been externalized: the victims of pollution have been forced to underwrite the activities that harm them. This redistribution of costs is in effect a redistribution of wealth, typically from individuals to industry.[40]

While the erosion of property rights may have helped some industries to thrive, those industries have often been unviable, harming the economy as a whole as well as the environment. And they have often survived at the expense of more promising industries which have failed to secure special regulatory treatment. Furthermore, in relieving polluters from responsibility for the consequences of their actions, governments have removed a strong incentive for environmentally responsible behaviour. Under a common law liability regime, it is in an industry's own financial interest to avoid harming others. Otherwise, it may face injunctions or large damage awards. Experience in diverse fields confirms that strict liability increases incentives for responsible behaviour. Stricter product liability laws in the United States have led to the improved safety of many products. Similarly, increased medical malpractice premiums have prompted doctors to change their procedures.[41]

Conversely, immunizing people or industries from risk and responsibility decreases their level of care. After Quebec adopted a no-fault automobile insurance system in 1978, automobile fatalities rose; Australia's no-fault scheme similarly increased fatalities. Likewise, industries that, thanks to government regulation, do not bear the costs of environmental destruction are unlikely to invest adequately in systems that preserve clean air, land, and water.[42]

The public seems blissfully unaware of the perverse results of much environmental regulation. Environmentalists habitually call for further government intervention to stop pollution. Nobel Prize-winning economist Ronald Coase explained that economists share that approach:

> When they are prevented from sleeping at night by the roar of jet planes overhead (publicly authorized and perhaps publicly operated), are unable to think (or rest) in the day because of the noise and vibration from passing trains (publicly authorized and perhaps publicly operated), find it difficult to breathe because of the odour from a local sewage farm (publicly authorized and perhaps publicly operated) and are unable to escape because their driveways are blocked by a road obstruction (without any doubt, publicly devised), their nerves frayed and mental balance disturbed, they proceed to declaim about the disadvantages of private enterprise and the need for Government regulation.[43]

More than three decades later, those concerned about the environment continue to cling to the illusion that our land, air and water can only be saved by further government action. Far too few yet realize the extent to which regulations, designed to protect particular industries and promulgated in the name of the public good, are environmental culprits.

Notes

1.   Lord Halsbury, the Lord Chancellor, in *Canadian Pacific Ry. Co.* v. *Roy* (1901), C.R. [12] A.C. 374 at 389 (P.C.).

2.   In 1987 Energy Probe, the City of Toronto, and 11 prominent Canadians launched a constitutional challenge to the Nuclear Liability Act on the grounds that it both violated the Canadian Charter of Rights and Freedoms and exceeded the federal government's jurisdiction. After a series of appeals by nuclear utilities failed to prevent the case from being tried, the trial began in October 1993; the following spring, the judge decided in favour of the government and the electric utilities. Appeals may leave the constitutionality of the act unresolved for several years. For more information see *Energy Probe et al.* v. *The Attorney General of Canada et al.* (1994), 17 O.R. (3d) 717 (Ont. Ct. Gen. Div).

3.   Theresa McClenaghan, plaintiffs' opening statement in *Energy Probe et al.* v. *Attorney General of Canada.*

4.   Michael Trebilcock, testifying as an expert at *Energy Probe et al.* v. *The Attorney General of Canada*, October 14, 1993, Transcript Volume 3, 288.

5.   *Ibid.*, 286.

6.   *Rylands* v. *Fletcher* (1865), L.R. 1 Ex. 265, aff'd (1868), L.R. 3 H.L. 330.

7.   For a lengthy discussion of this issue see Trebilcock and Winter, *The Impact of the Nuclear Liability Act on Safety Incentives in the Nuclear Power Industry.*

8. Mr. R. J. Orange, Parliamentary Secretary to the Minister of Energy, Mines and Resources, *Commons Debates*, February 6, 1970, 3316.

9. *Ibid.*, 3315.

10. Mr. Louis-Roland Comeau, *ibid.*, 3316.

11. Mr. Mark Rose, *ibid.*, 3318.

12. *Ibid.*, 3319.

13. For an extensive discussion of this issue, see the Supreme Court decision in *Tock et al.* v. *St. John's Metropolitan Area Board* (1989), 64 D.L.R. (4th) 620.

In her decision for the majority Madame Justice Bertha Wilson reviewed in great detail the case history of the defence of statutory authority (starting with the early railway cases) and stated the principles to be derived from them. She distinguished between the inevitable results of legislation that imposes a duty or confers a specific authority and the results of legislation that confers a discretionary authority. Only the former, she concluded, have been statutorily authorized.

Madame Justice Wilson noted disapprovingly that some recent cases have not followed these principles. "[T]he inevitable consequences doctrine is now being applied without regard to the type of statutory authority conferred on the public body," she warned. "In my view," she concluded, "to the extent that some of the more recent cases are inconsistent with the early principles, they should not be followed."

The *Tock* decision has been followed in at least seven cases since, and has been considered in several others. For commentary on the extent to which the decision has narrowed the defence of statutory authority, see Harvey, "Riparian Rights," 522, and Rankin, *An Environmental Bill of Rights for Ontario*, 30-1.

14. *Tock et al.* v. *St. John's Metropolitan Area Board, ibid.* at 645-8.

15. Gimpel, *The Medieval Machine*, 93-9.

16. Horwitz, *The Transformation of American Law 1780-1860*, 47-51.

17. *The Governor and Company of the British Cast Plate Manufacturers* v. *Meredith and Others* (1792), 4 T.R. 794, 100 E.R. 1306 at 1307.

18. Britain and several of the United States chartered railroads in the late 1820s. Canada began construction of its first line in 1835 ("Railway," *Encyclopaedia Britannica*).

19. *The London and North-Western Railway Company* v. *Bradley* (1851), 3 Mac. & G. 336, 42 E.R. 290.

20. *Bellinger* v. *New York Central Railroad*, 23 N.Y. 42 (1861).

21. *Stockport, Timperley and Altringham Railway Company* (1864), 33 L.J. 251 (Q.B.).

22. *Robinson* v. *New Brunswick Railway Company* (1884), 11 S.C.R. 688.

23. *The King* v. *Edward Pease and Others* (1832), 4 B. &. Ad. 30, 110 E.R. 366 at 370.

24. *Ibid.* at 371.

25. *Vaughan* v. *The Taff Vale Railway Company* (1860), 5 H. & N. 679, 157 E.R. 1351 at 1355 (Ex.).

26. *Brand and Wife* v. *Hammersmith and City Railway Company* (1865), 1 L.R. 130 at 143-4 (Q.B.).

27. *Ibid.* at 146.

Traditional wisdom has it that railroads were responsible for the development of entire nineteenth-century economies. Ironically, as the work of 1993 Nobel economist Robert Fogel demonstrates, American railroads were far more dispensable than previously thought. Had railroads failed because they were unable to assume their full costs, the country, developing alternative methods of transportation, would likely have experienced comparable economic growth. (See the *New York Times*, "A Talent for Rewriting History" and "Economic Scene"; and the *Wall Street Journal*, "Chicago Rules.")

28. *The Directors, &c., of the Hammersmith and City Railway Company* v. *G. H. Brand and Mary C. Louisa, his Wife* (1869), L. R. 4 H.L. 171.

29. Mr. Baron Bramwell took exception to this argument. He insisted that the decisions in *Rex* v. *Pease* and *Vaughan* v. *The Taff Vale Railway Company* were wrong. If the legislature had intended to grant the power to create nuisances, he said, it would have explicitly said so. He concluded that the plaintiff's right of action had not been taken away.

30. *Ibid.* at 196, italics added.

31. *Ibid.* at 191.

32. *Canadian Pacific Ry. Co.* v. *Roy, op. cit.* at 388.

33. Block, "Environmental Problems, Private Property Rights Solutions," 291.

In a debate over the Nuclear Liability Act, MP Mark Rose noted the parallels between that act and the Canada Shipping Act. "When we were considering the Canada Shipping Act," he explained, "a subclause covering unlimited liability for [oil] spills was taken out of the act on the grounds that no insurance company would cover all the damage caused by such a disaster" (*Commons Debates, op. cit.*, 3319).

34. For information on the circumstances surrounding The Damage by

Fumes Arbitration Act see Dewees and Halewood, "The Efficiency of the Common Law."

A riparian's legal challenge to sawmills that deposited their wastes in the Ottawa River prompted one of the earliest Canadian laws substituting damages for injunctions. In 1885, fearful that the lawsuit could shut down the polluting mills, the Ontario legislature passed *An Act respecting Saw Mills on the Ottawa River*. The act ordered judges to weigh the lumber trade's economic importance against the plaintiff's injury before granting an injunction. For more information see McLaren, "The Tribulations of Antoine Ratté."

35. *Re Faraday Uranium Mines Ltd. and Arrowsmith et al.* (1962), 32 D.L.R. (2d) 704.

36. *Ibid.* at 718.

37. Campbell *et al.*, "Water Management in Ontario," 506, and Estrin and Swaigen, *Environment on Trial*, 406.

Legal commentators debate the degree to which the Ontario Water Resources Act replaces the common law. According to the Canadian Environmental Law Research Foundation, the common law has been "relegated to a very modest role in resolving disputes over competing water uses" ("An Overview of Canadian Law and Policy Governing Great Lakes Water Quantity Management," 111).

In contrast, Lucas, Percy, McNeil and Macklem, and Campbell *et al.* assert that the act does not abolish riparian rights. The latter explain: "The grant of a permit does not remove any of the common law obligations of the permittee, but requires him in addition to conform to the stipulations of the permit. Thus, an 'extraordinary' user who obtains a permit is still subject to the riparian rights doctrine. . . . In effect, the permit represents an upper limit upon the rate of extraordinary water use so long as the withdrawal it authorizes is equal to or less than that which a court would consider 'reasonable'" (*op. cit.*, 483-4. Also see Lucas, *Security of Title in Canadian Water Rights*, 20; Percy, *The Framework of Water Rights Legislation in Canada*, 76-7; and McNeil and Macklem, *Aboriginal, Treaty and Riparian Rights in the Moose River Basin*, 3).

Percy notes, however, that in a riparian challenge, "a court might consider the terms of the permit in assessing the reasonableness of the holder's use" (*The Framework of Water Rights Legislation in Canada*, 87).

38. Estrin and Swaigen, *op. cit.*, 13.

39. Owen and Braeutigam, *The Regulation Game*, 2.

40. Horwitz, *op. cit.*, 70, 100-1; Ellickson, "Alternatives to Zoning," 694-9; and Block, "Economists and Environmentalists," 17.

41. Trebilcock and Winter, *op. cit.*, 11.

For more on the deterrent value of liability, see Wright and Linden, *Canadian Tort Law*, Chapter 1; and Bardach and Kagan, *Going By the Book*, 271-83.

The experience of Florida's fertilizer industry illustrates how differently polluters will behave when the costs of their pollution are "internalized." In the 1950s, a number of phosphate fertilizer companies polluted the air with fluorides, which settled onto neighbouring grasslands, where cattle grazed. Many cattle developed fluorosis; their joints stiffened, rendering them so completely immobilized that they starved to death. Faced with the options of reducing fluoride emissions or purchasing polluted lands (so their emissions would hurt only themselves), the companies chose the latter. In order to avoid spending $16 million installing pollution-control equipment, they spent $25 million buying 200,000 polluted acres. Only then did they realize that to protect revenues from their new grazing lands, it made financial sense to install the pollution-control equipment (Crocker and Rogers, *Environmental Economics*, 93-112).

42. Trebilcock and Winter, *op. cit.*, 10, 22.

43. Coase, "The Problem of Social Cost," 26.

7

Blinded Justice

Harold Perry is a shaken man.

And unless he moves his business, he will be for the rest of his working days.

With a ruling from Ontario's highest court yesterday, his legal battle to stop the rumblings of Toronto subway cars beneath his Bedford Rd. offices came to an abrupt stop.

Three Ontario Court of Appeal judges unanimously overturned a lower-court ruling that the Toronto Transit Commission must pay Perry damages for being a nuisance and remove a 'frog' that forms the crossover of two rail lines at the busy St. George station, right outside his door.

The judges also blasted the trial judge for suggesting the 'frog' be removed, saying it was a cavalier idea that could have compromised the safety of TTC passengers and besmirched the transit authority's reputation.

People working in a commercial area can't expect the same degree of tranquility they would find in a residential neighbourhood, the court said.

While they may cause disruption, transportation networks provide a public service so essential that it outweighs noise complaints or other difficulties for people who work nearby, the judges said.

The Toronto Star, 1993[1]

Governments aren't the only ones who have eroded common law property rights in the name of the public good. The courts themselves have modified both the rules governing liability and the remedies available to those whose rights have been violated, all too often leaving people powerless to oppose environmental degradation.

As demonstrated throughout Part One, ancient common law

property rights shielded the environmental interests of property owners from those who would attack them. Rights brought with them strict environmental responsibilities: the use of one's own property could not interfere with another's use and enjoyment of his property. However, as industry developed, those who feared the costs and constraints of property and property rights tried to redefine them. Property, they contended, was to be *used* and not merely enjoyed. Property rights should therefore safeguard the right to *develop* property as well as the right to be protected from others' uses. They argued, in other words, that a person's property rights should serve as both a sword to slash others' rights and a shield to defend his own, with the courts as arbiters.

While courts in the United States often sympathized with such arguments, British and Canadian courts maintained more conservative views.[2] Even they, however, sporadically made concessions to industrialization.

An English court first legalized a previously unacceptable nuisance in 1858. In *Hole* v. *Barlow*, a man objected to his neighbour's brick-making. The baking process, he complained, created noxious vapours that rendered his home "uncomfortable, unhealthy, unwholesome, and unfit for habitation."[3] The trial judge's instructions to the jury betrayed his greater concern for polluting industries than for their victims:

> [I]t is not every body [*sic*] whose enjoyment of life and property is rendered uncomfortable by the carrying on of an offensive or noxious trade in the neighbourhood, that can bring an action. If that were so . . . the neighbourhood of Birmingham and Wolverhampton and the other great manufacturing towns of England would be full of persons bringing actions for nuisances arising from the carrying on of noxious or offensive trades in their vicinity, to the great injury of the manufacturing and social interests of the community. I apprehend the law to be this, that no action lies for the use, the reasonable use, of a

lawful trade in a convenient and proper place, even though some one may suffer annoyance from its being so carried on.[4]

When the jury determined that the brick burning was indeed "reasonable," Mr. Hole appealed on the grounds that the judge had misdirected the jury. But the Court of the Common Pleas found no fault in the judge's instructions. One judge defended them as follows: "The common-law right which every proprietor of a dwelling-house has to have the air uncontaminated and unpolluted, is subject to this qualification, that necessities may arise for an interference with that right *pro bono publico* [for the public good], to this extent, that such interference be in respect of a matter essential to the business of life, and be conducted in a reasonable and proper manner, and in a reasonable and proper place." "[P]rivate convenience," he concluded, "must yield to public necessity."[5]

This radical departure from precedent delighted polluters, who frequently cited it in trying to defend their nuisances. The character of a neighbourhood, they argued, should determine whether an activity was permissible; manufacturing districts were convenient, reasonable, and proper places in which to create noise or emit fumes.

Such reasoning did not sit well with a higher British court, however: the Exchequer Chamber overruled it four years later. In that case, which similarly involved the "noxious and unwholesome vapours, fumes, stinks and stenches" resulting from brick-making, the court found that *Hole* v. *Barlow* had not been well decided.[6] What would constitute a "reasonable" use or a "convenient" place, the majority of the judges wondered? As far as they were concerned, a place where an activity would incommode someone else would be inconvenient. Changing the law to allow one to cause nuisance to another, they warned, would "lead to great inconvenience and hardship."[7]

Regardless of the court's rejection of *Hole* v. *Barlow*, polluters continued to cite it in defence of their nuisances. In 1865, a copper smelter tried to use it as a defence against the claims of a local manor owner, saying that the industrial character of the neighbourhood made it a reasonable and proper place to carry on its business. The House of Lords rejected the company's argument but did concede that courts should consider the character of the neighbourhood in some cases. In a decision that courts would refer to frequently in future years, one law lord distinguished between nuisances resulting in personal discomfort and those resulting in material injury or financial harm. Courts, he said, should consider the character of the neighbourhood only in the former cases:

> If a man lives in a town, it is necessary that he should subject himself to the consequences of those operations of trade which may be carried on in his immediate locality, which are actually necessary for trade and commerce, and also for the enjoyment of property, and for the benefit of the inhabitants of the town and of the public at large. If a man lives in a street where there are numerous shops, and a shop is opened next door to him, which is carried on in a fair and reasonable way, he has no ground for complaint, because to himself individually there may arise much discomfort from the trade carried on in that shop. But when an occupation is carried on by one person in the neighbourhood of another, and the result of that trade, or occupation, or business, is a material injury to property, then there unquestionably arises a very different consideration. . . . [T]he submission which is required from persons living in society to that amount of discomfort which may be necessary for the legitimate and free exercise of the trade of their neighbours, would not apply to circumstances the immediate result of which is sensible injury to the value of the property.[8]

The compromise as laid down in that case was accepted in both England and Canada; it still applies today. Courts continue to distinguish between nuisances resulting in "mere" personal inconvenience, discomfort or annoyance and those causing actual damage to health or property. The former, unless substantial, may be justified by the character of the neighbourhood in which they occur. The latter, in contrast, readily entitle a complainant to his remedy.[9] In 1989, two Canadian Supreme Court judges summarized the law as follows:

> The courts attempt to circumscribe the ambit of nuisance by looking to the nature of the locality in question and asking whether the ordinary and reasonable resident of that locality would view the disturbance as a substantial interference with the enjoyment of land. . . . [T]hese criteria find their greatest application in cases where the interference complained of does not consist of material damage to property but rather interference with tranquility and amenity. . . . In the presence of actual physical damage to property, the courts have been quick to conclude that the interference does indeed constitute a substantial and unreasonable interference with the enjoyment of property.[10]

This approach shows common sense. One living in the country expects purer air than one living in a city. Likewise, one living in a residential neighbourhood expects greater quiet than one living in a manufacturing district.

Canadian courts have also accommodated industrialization by robbing victims of their most powerful remedies. At one time, those whose property rights had been violated could count on obtaining injunctions against those responsible. In fact, at one time certain courts had no choice but to issue injunctions. Not until 1858 did the British Parliament empower Chancery courts to award damages in lieu of injunctions. Ontario's 1877 Judicature Act gave Ontario courts the same authority.

Courts have often cited the public interest when exercising their new power. Early this century, one Ontario judge—Mr.

Justice Middleton—became notorious for placing his concern for the public good before the rights of individuals.[11] He did so in 1914, when Vaux and Jessie Chadwick went to court to stop Toronto from using its new electric pumps at a nearby water pumping station. While he acknowledged that the pumps' vibration, humming, and buzzing constituted a nuisance, he refused to issue an injunction. The pumping of water, he explained, "is necessary for municipal purposes."[12] And so he would choose the option, granted by the Judicature Act, of substituting damages for an injunction.

Mr. Justice Middleton did not limit this special treatment to municipalities; private polluters soon discovered that they, too, could benefit from his concerns for the general welfare. Between 1916 and 1920, a number of farmers sued copper and nickel smelters near Sudbury, Ontario, complaining that sulphur dioxide in the smelters' smoke damaged their crops and soil, contaminated their water, and injured their animals. Mr. Justice Middleton tried six of the cases together. In a decision that broke new ground in Canadian law, he allowed the pollution to continue in the name of the common good. Since mines inevitably produced smoke, he reasoned, forbidding smoke could ruin the industry. That must not happen: "The Court ought not to destroy the mining industry—nickel is of great value to the world—even if a few farms are damaged or destroyed." The judge even suggested that the farmers benefited from the mines: closing the mines would destroy the community, and thus the market for the farmers' goods, forcing the farmers to move. Such remarks must have sounded offensively patronizing to the farmers, who would not have sought injunctions had they determined the mines to be in their best interest. Nor, likely, would the farmers have taken much comfort from the judge's conclusion, which sounded more like that of a government than a court of law: "There are circumstances in which it is impossible for the individual so to assert his individual rights as to inflict a substantial injury upon the whole community."[13]

Concern for the public good similarly influenced the court in a mid-1930s case in which a man from Kingsville, Ontario, sued a tobacco processing plant whose fumes sickened his family. Although the Court of Appeal found that the tobacco company had indeed created a nuisance, it refused to grant an injunction against it. The court worried that an injunction would disadvantage the defendant and the community far more than it would benefit the plaintiff: the factory employed 200 people, who would lose their jobs as a result. "[T]his," said one judge, "is to be avoided if at all possible. The public good can never be absent from the mind of the Court when dealing with a matter of discretion."[14]

Fortunately, the above decisions are exceptions to the rule. Textbooks continue to hold that "It is no defence that the nuisance, although injurious to the individual plaintiff, is beneficial to the public at large."[15] Injunctions remain the favoured remedy in both English and Canadian property rights cases, especially where trespass or a violation of riparian rights has occurred, and generally, but somewhat less categorically, in nuisance cases.[16] The Ontario High Court noted in 1984 that "the defence of 'general benefit of the community' . . . is not available in answer to a claim for nuisance. There has been consistent rejection of that notion by the highest Canadian courts."[17] Five years later a Canadian Supreme Court judge confirmed the courts' reluctance to override common law property rights. "The courts," he said, "strain against a conclusion that private rights are intended to be sacrificed for the common good."[18]

A number of factors have contributed to the courts' reluctance to substitute damages for injunctions. Judges have long understood that many injuries cannot be monetized. How, one law lord wondered as early as 1859, can someone prove the exact quantity of pecuniary loss he has sustained? What, for example, is the value of a business's lost customers?[19]

Only victims themselves can know what value they place on a good night's sleep, or how much money they would be willing to accept for breathing foul air. When a judge or jury awards damages, however, the victims do not determine the amount. Substituting damages for an injunction therefore amounts to forcing the victim to sell his property rights at a price set by the court. It amounts, in short, to giving a defendant the power of expropriation.

In contrast, injunctions allow the victim to negotiate his own price. If his environment is priceless, he may simply tell the polluter to go away. Alternatively, he may bargain away his rights or reach a compromise that benefits both him and the polluter.[20]

Furthermore, only injunctions can prevent the recurrence of property rights violations. In allowing damages to replace injunctions, courts in effect license continuing wrongs—a role which they generally reject. A British judge warned in 1894 that the court must not become "a tribunal for legalizing wrongful acts. . . . [T]he Court has always protested against the notion that it ought to allow a wrong to continue simply because the wrongdoer is able and willing to pay for the injury he may inflict."[21] With some important exceptions, his successors have paid him heed.

Notes

1. *Toronto Star*, "Court derails man's bid to stop subway noise."

2. For information on the American experience of courts transforming the common law to benefit industry, see Horwitz, *The Transformation of American Law 1780-1860*, especially 2, 3, 17, 19, 31, 37, 40, 70, 99. Epstein challenges Horwitz's view in "The Social Consequences of

Common Law Rules," 1729.

For information on the Canadian experience, see Risk, "The Law and the Economy in Mid-Nineteenth-Century Ontario," 122; and Nedelsky, "Judicial Conservatism in an Age of Innovation," 281-310.

3.   *Hole* v. *Barlow* (1858), 4 C.B. (N.S.) 334, 140 E.R. 1113 at 1114 (C.P.).

For a discussion of this case in the context of the weakening of nuisance law in the nineteenth century, see Brenner, "Nuisance Law and the Industrial Revolution," 408-32.

4.   *Hole* v. *Barlow, ibid.* at 1114.

5.   *Ibid.* at 1118.

6.   *Bamford* v. *Turnley* (1860), 3 B. & S. 62, 122 E.R. 25, aff'd (1862), 3 B. & S. 66, 122 E.R. 27 (Ex.).

7.   *Ibid.* at 30.

8.   *The Directors, etc. of the St. Helen's Smelting Co.* v. *William Tipping* (1865), 11 H.L.C. 642, 11 E.R. 1483 at 1486.

According to both Brenner and Nedelsky, *St. Helen's Smelting Co.* v. *Tipping* was "arguably the most important nuisance case of the era" (*op. cit.*, 413 and 316 respectively).

9.   For further information, see Estrin and Swaigen, *Environment on Trial,* 110; Canadian Environmental Law Research Foundation, "An Overview of Canadian Law and Policy Governing Great Lakes Water Quantity Management," 115; Campbell *et al.*, "Water Management in Ontario," 503-4; and Nedelsky, *op. cit.*, 287-8, 317.

10.   *Tock et al.* v. *St. John's Metropolitan Area Board* (1989), 64 D.L.R. (4th) 620 at 639-40.

11. McLaren calls the notion that a judge may consider the social utility of a nuisance before issuing an injunction against it "the brain child" of Mr. Justice Middleton; he later refers to the notion as "the Middleton thesis" ("The Common Law Nuisance Actions and the Environmental Battle," 554-5).

12. *Chadwick* v. *City of Toronto* (1914), 32 O.L.R. 111 at 113.

13. *Black* v. *Canadian Copper Co.*, etc. (1917), 12 O.W.N. 243 at 244, aff'd (1920), 17 O.W.N. 399 (C.A.).

Dewees and Halewood point out that a court injunction would not have shut down the nickel industry. Seasonal, locational and technological alternatives in use elsewhere would have enabled Canadian Copper (INCO's predecessor) to reduce not only local agricultural damage but also the acid damage wreaked on Canadian lakes and forests ("The Efficiency of the Common Law," 3, 14, 16-9).

No one today accepts acid damage as necessary. The great economic and environmental costs of acid rain—not generally recognized until the 1970s and 1980s—might have been avoided had property rights been enforced early this century.

14. *Bottom* v. *Ontario Leaf Tobacco Co. Ltd.*, [1935] O.R. 205 at 206 (C.A.).

15. Heuston and Buckley, *Salmond & Heuston on the Law of Torts*, 79.

16. In *Shelfer* v. *City of London Electric Lighting Co.*, [1895] 1 Ch. 287 at 322-3, one justice explained that a court should substitute damages for an injunction only if the injunction would be oppressive and the injury was small and could be easily estimated and compensated by money. That 1894 decision has since been frequently followed.

For more information on when courts grant injunctions, see Sharpe, *Injunctions and Specific Performance*, 6, 180-201; Nedelsky, *op. cit.*, 301-3; and Estrin and Swaigen, *op. cit.*, 108-10. For information on the extent to which British courts favoured early industrial development see McLaren, "Nuisance Law and the Industrial Revolution," 341-65.

17. *Buysse et al.* v. *Town of Shelburne* (1984), 6 D.L.R. (4th) 734 at 740.

18. *Tock* v. *St. John's Metropolitan Area Board, op. cit* at 651.

19. *The Directors, &c., of the Imperial Gas Light and Coke Company* v. *Samuel Broadbent* (1859), 7 H.L.C. 600, 11 E.R. 239 at 243.

20. Property rights case law illustrates both that people with clearly defined rights have long negotiated with would-be polluters and that they frequently place limits on how much they are willing to bargain away.

Wood v. *Sutcliffe* tells of a dispute between the users of a Yorkshire stream. In the first decades of the nineteenth century, worsted wool spinners had used the pure stream to wash wool and generate and condense steam. When an upstream factory began to pollute the stream, the spinners threatened to sue. To avoid litigation, the factory owners offered to annually pay the spinners £2 per horse-power for the right to pollute the water. The spinners agreed, and sunk a well from which they could draw the pure water they needed. But the spinners were not content to let the stream deteriorate further, and launched lawsuits against other polluters in both 1849 and 1851. (1851), 2 Sim. (N.S.) 163, 61 E.R. 303. Also see *Wood and Another* v. *Waud and Others* (1849), 3 Ex. 748, 154 E.R. 1047.

Walker v. *McKinnon Industries Ltd.* chronicles the dispute in St. Catharines, Ontario, between a florist and a neighbouring foundry. Although fumes and soot from the foundry blocked the sunlight from the florist's greenhouses and injured his plants, the florist at first chose to negotiate rather than sue. World War II raged, and the courts seemed unlikely to restrain a company that manufactured urgently needed munitions. The florist and the foundry owners reached agreements regarding damages and temporary easements for the pollution. When the pollution continued after the war ended, however, the florist launched a court action for both damages and an injunction. [1949] 4 D.L.R. 739 (Ont. H.C.), aff'd [1950] 3 D.L.R. 159 (Ont. C.A.), aff'd [1951] 3 D.L.R. 577 (P.C.).

The possibility of a polluter obtaining the consent of his victims has been raised in other cases, including *Embrey* v. *Owen* (1851), 6 Exch. 353 at 370 and *Roberts* v. *Gwyrfai District Council*, [1899] 2 Ch. D. 608 at 608, 610. Also see Campbell *et al.*, "Water Management in Ontario," 504.

21. *Shelfer* v. *City of London Electric Lighting Company, op. cit.* at 311, 315-6.

Part III

Common Law Failings

8

The Courts v. The Common Man

All the filth of the town—dead horses, dogs, cats, manure, etc. heaped up together on the ice, to drop down, in a few days, into the water which is used by almost all the inhabitants on the Bay shore . . .

The Canadian Freeman, circa 1832[1]

In the nineteenth century Toronto's waterfront was a cesspool. The municipal government located its first landfill dumps on the water's edge in 1835. That same year it started emptying its sewers into the harbour . . . and didn't stop for three-quarters of a century. Rotting garbage and raw sewage soon filled the shoreline slips, necessitating frequent dredging. In response, the city simply extended its sewers further into the harbour. By mid-century, a two-foot-thick carpet of sewage stretched more than 300 feet from the shore.[2]

The government wasn't the only polluter. Companies drained manure from their cowsheds into nearby Ashbridges Bay. People dumped trash into the water. In the winter, they tossed it onto the frozen lake, knowing that it would sink in the spring melt.

Incredibly, the city drew its drinking water from the fetid harbour. The contaminated water (described by the *Globe* as "drinkable sewage"[3]) sickened Torontonians. Cholera broke out in 1832, and again and again during the following decades. Typhoid fever followed.[4]

Toronto was by no means unique. In fact, it was one of the age's cleaner cities, described in 1884 as "the healthiest on the American continent."[5] Britain's industrial towns may have been the most polluted. There the Industrial Revolution transformed pastoral landscapes into wastelands of appalling filth and ugliness. One district's saturation with smoke and coal dust earned it the name "the Black Country." Chemical vapours destroyed virtually all of another district's trees, gardens and crops. Once-clear rivers ran like ink. They stank and, in one case, burned. Friedrich Engels described the view from a Manchester bridge in 1844:

> At the bottom flows, or rather stagnates, the Irk, a narrow, coal black, foul smelling stream full of debris and refuse, which it deposits on the shallower right bank. In dry weather, a long string of the most disgusting, blackish green, slime pools are left standing on this bank, from the depths of which bubbles of miasmatic gas constantly arise and give forth a stench unendurable even on the bridge forty or fifty feet above the surface of the stream. But besides this, the stream itself is checked every few paces by high weirs, behind which the slime and refuse accumulate and rot in thick masses. Above the bridge are tanneries, bone mills and gas works, from which all drains and

refuse find their way into the Irk, which receives further the contents of all the neighbouring sewers and privies.[6]

Why did desecration such as Toronto's and Manchester's occur? Blame falls in part on the governments that utterly failed to enforce their own laws, such as the 1834 act requiring Toronto to provide "good and wholesome water" to its residents. While that city's bylaws regarding nuisances, sanitation, and public health multiplied throughout the nineteenth century, and government increased its powers to regulate pollution, water quality deteriorated.[7] Laws and regulations aimed at cleaning up air and improving public sanitation proved similarly ineffective in Britain.[8]

While the histories of Toronto's filthy harbour and Britain's squalid rivers illustrate governments' failure to protect the environment, they also raise questions about the effectiveness of common law property rights—then and now—in preventing pollution. Since riparian law forbade water pollution, why didn't Torontonians and their British counterparts use their riparian rights to prevent the contamination of their lakes and rivers? Why, for that matter, didn't *all* pollution victims—at least those in common law jurisdictions—use their property rights to fight the environmental destruction wrought by industrialization? While some of the answers to these questions are certainly found in both the governments' and the courts' higher regard for the abstraction they called the public good, other factors—including an absence of concern, the difficulties of court challenges, and people's ignorance of their rights—further explain the common law's failure to protect the environment.

Many nineteenth-century townspeople were indifferent to water pollution. Children swam in Toronto's foul harbour. Almost no one understood the health effects of pollution. Torontonians blamed cholera, for example, on virtually everything other than contaminated water. Some thought it originated from putrid or humid air. Others linked the disease to filthy houses and habits. Still others blamed intemperance, jailing drunkards or putting them in stocks in order to stem the spread of the disease.[9]

Even those knowingly suffering from pollution often saw it as an inevitable and acceptable price of progress. Such was frequently the case in England during the Industrial Revolution, when many who favoured industrialization were willing to exchange clean air and water for jobs, consumer goods, and public services. Smoke and noise meant work for those living near the belching factories. Industrial workers, under the strict control of their polluting employers, didn't dare complain. Other incentives encouraged those who weren't employed by polluters to trade away their common law rights. In some cases, property values rose in industrial areas. In other cases, manufacturers paid neighbours not to complain. And where victims were also polluters, refraining from enforcing their common law rights could be reciprocated to their benefit.[10]

The high cost of litigation deterred many from enforcing their common law property rights. Suing polluters was expensive—so expensive that legal action was out of the question for almost all but the wealthy. A select committee examining air pollution in one region of England in 1862 reported that average workingmen could simply not afford to bring nuisance actions against polluters.[11] Even those who could afford litigation often found it cheaper to simply move away from the squalor.[12]

Further complicating legal action was the victim's obligation to prove not just that he was injured, but that he was injured by one particular polluter. With only the unaided human eye to trace the paths of poisons, British landowners hired runners to follow the plumes emanating from factories. Manufacturers responded by raising smokestacks and dispersing fumes.[13] Tracing the source of a pollutant in a heavily industrialized area presented further challenges. The 1862 select committee noted, "[W]here several works are in immediate juxtaposition, the difficulty of tracing the damage to any one, or of apportioning it among several, is too great as to be all but insuperable."[14] It was also difficult to establish a causal connection between a poison and an injury: how could one *prove* that emissions from a neighbouring factory caused one's illness?

Torontonians no longer throw animal carcasses into their harbour. British factories don't blot out the sun with soot. Rivers rarely catch fire. Yet pollution is likely of greater concern today than in the nineteenth century. Ironically, despite more affluence and better education about pollution's consequences, people are now less able to fight pollution: they have lost many of the rights that they so often failed to exercise in the past. Yet, where common law property rights remain, those using them to protect the environment face fewer impediments. Social and technological advances have overcome many of the factors preventing industrialization's early victims from asserting their rights.

Several factors, while less severe than a century ago, continue to impede the enforcement of common law property rights. Although legal aid has increased the poor's access to the courts, litigation remains prohibitively expensive for many. Lawyers' bills, court costs, witness fees, and the threat of having to pay the other party's legal costs in the event of an unsuccessful suit (the rule in Canada) often deter court actions.[15] The exercise of property rights, as with other rights, continues to be a rich man's prerogative, and will remain so until the court system is reformed to provide equal justice for all.[16]

Even the best court reforms would leave some litigation prohibitively expensive. As a general rule, high transaction costs resulting from unavailable information, costly negotiations or other factors reduce the courts' effectiveness in fighting pollution. When many people suffer minor, cumulative damages from many small polluters, no individual has an incentive to sue; each costly suit would bring inconsequential relief. No one, for example, could sue every smog-producing driver that passes his home, and suing one or two would not measurably clear the air. Such cases call for government regulations that, in reducing emissions from numerous minor sources, make a major difference in air quality.

Tracing an environmental poison to its source can be difficult, especially if there is a time lag between the release of the poison and the appearance of its effects, or if there are numerous potential sources.[17] But technological advances are rapidly overcoming many barriers to enforcing property rights. Chemical "fingerprinting" (using methods such as gas chromatography and mass spectrometry) enables victims to match a pollutant to a polluter. As the technology becomes both cheaper and more powerful, law firms, banks and insurance companies are increasingly adopting it to prove environmental liability.[18]

Chemical fingerprinting also allows companies to shield themselves from liability for pollution not of their making—often a strong incentive for adopting the technique. In 1993 a geochemist used gas chromatography and mass spectrometry to trace oil in Price William Sound to a 1964 spill, bolstering Exxon's contention that the 1989 Exxon Valdez disaster was not responsible for all of the oil fouling the sound.[19]

Various tagging methods could also enable people to trace water or air pollutants to their sources. Odorants (such as the mercaptan now added to natural gas), dyes, or isotopes could "brand" chemicals. Government agencies and utilities have demonstrated one such pollution-tracing technique in the American Southwest, where, after injecting deuterated methane into smokestacks, they traced sulphur dioxide from an Arizona power plant to haze in a national park in Utah.[20]

Even if pollutants can be traced, it is often difficult—or impossible—to prove that they caused particular damages complained of. But here, too, barriers are beginning to fall. Molecular fingerprinting, while not as developed as chemical fingerprinting, shows extraordinary potential for establishing polluters' liability for the health effects of their emissions. Different carcinogens produce unique mutations in one gene: radon, ultraviolet light, and tobacco tar, for example, leave recognizable fingerprints. Genetic analysis may therefore soon make it possible to identify the carcinogen responsible for a tumour.[21]

In those instances where proof remains impossible, victims using the common law may still be able to stop pollution. A civil case asserting one's common law rights demands a less rigourous standard of proof—a 51 per cent likelihood—than does a statutory prosecution, which requires proof beyond a reasonable doubt.[22]

Both court reforms and scientific advances may well, at least indirectly, help overcome the widespread ignorance of the law that remains one last impediment to people enforcing their now limited rights.[23] In the 1940s and 1950s, a handful of well-publicized law suits alerted Ontarians to the nature and extent of their common law property rights, and to their usefulness in protecting the environment.

Even lawmakers had been unaware of the power of riparian rights before people living along the Spanish River won their 1948 lawsuit against the KVP pulp mill. The Ontario CCF's conservation-minded William Dennison complained that, when trying to put a stop to de Havilland's pollution of Black Creek in 1944, "I did not know about the English law at that time, or I would have suggested he take the thing to court." The common law's potential was also news to his Liberal colleague, who noted, "I am interested to know that the only way we can get rid of the pollution is through the court."[24]

In the 1950s, court challenges to polluting sewage systems further increased interest in using property rights to clean up lakes and rivers. An Ontario Progressive Conservative MPP described the growing awareness in 1956: "Interest in this problem, I find, is much greater than ever before. There is a growing realization on the part of the public that it is a trespass on the rights of their neighbours and of themselves for untreated effluent to be discharged from municipal or industrial sewers into a stream or lake which serves others."[25]

New tools will inevitably prompt successful cases against polluters—cases that will alert others to the attainability of clean air, land, and water. Inspired by the possible, they too may well turn to the courts.

Notes

1. Francis Collins, editor of the *Canadian Freeman*, *circa* 1832, cited by Glazebrook, *The Story of Toronto*, 68.

2. For more information on the nineteenth-century pollution of Toronto's harbour, see Armstrong, *Toronto*, 70, and *City in the Making*, 32, 210-11; Kerr and Spelt, *The Changing Face of Toronto*, 69, 72-3; Kluckner, *Toronto: The Way It Was*, 110, 166-8; Middleton, *Municipality of Toronto Canada*, Volume 1, 198, 331-2, 344, 368; Reindeau, "Servicing the Modern City," 161-2; Rust-D'Eye, *Cabbagetown Remembered*, 48; and Toronto Harbour Commission, *Toronto Harbour*, 14.

3. *Globe*, March 18, 1882, cited by Careless, *Toronto to 1918*, 144.

4. For information on the health effects of Toronto's contaminated water see Armstrong, *Toronto*, 65, 123; Careless, *op. cit.*, 51, 71, 73; Glazebrook, *op. cit.*, 29, 67, 79-80, 175; Kluckner, *op. cit.*, 168;

Middleton, *op. cit.*, 167-8, 235, 331, 344; and West, *Toronto*, 101-3.

5.   Mulvany, *Toronto*, 246.

6.   Engels, *The Condition of the Working Class in England*, cited by McLaren, "Nuisance Law and the Industrial Revolution," 323-4. For more information on nineteenth-century Britain's environmental blight, also see Hoskins, *The Making of the English Landscape*, 167-172; and Brenner, "Nuisance Law and the Industrial Revolution," 416-9, 429.

7.   Nor did the 1911 Toronto Harbour Commission Act alleviate the problem. Under the THC's jurisdiction, the harbour became infamous for its toxic water and sediments, and was designated an "Area of Concern," first by the Great Lakes Water Quality Board and later by the International Joint Commission.
     For information on early environmental regulation in Toronto, see Armstrong, *Toronto*, 68, 109, 123; Careless, *op. cit.*, 59, 145; Glazebrook, *op. cit.*, 77; Middleton, *op. cit.*, 198; and Mulvany, *op. cit.*, 59, 247.

8.   Brenner, *op. cit.*, 425-8.

9.   See references in notes 2 and 4.

10.   Brenner, *op. cit.*, 408, 420, 430, 432; and McLaren, *op. cit.*, 353, 357, 360.

11.   The House of Lords Select Committee on Noxious Vapours, discussed by Brenner, *op. cit.*, 416-25. Also see McLaren, *op. cit.*, 346-9, 360.

12.   Hoskins, *op. cit.*, 167.

13.   McLaren, *op. cit.*, 349-50.

14.   Cited by Brenner, *op. cit.*, 425.

15.   Even a simple civil claim may be prohibitively expensive. With

lawyers' fees starting at about $1,000 a day (and most lawyers needing one day to prepare for each day in court) and witness fees in the $2,000 range, a four-day hearing may cost $10,000. A defendant with deep pockets may call numerous witnesses, prolonging the hearing and increasing its costs. More complicated legal challenges may be still more expensive: it may cost a plaintiff over $500,000 to take a constitutional challenge to the Supreme Court of Canada.

A successful plaintiff will likely recover some of his costs. An unsuccessful plaintiff, however, will likely have to bear not only his own costs but also those of his opponent.

For more information on the prohibitive cost of civil suits see Estrin and Swaigen, *Environment on Trial*, xix, 7, 51, 67, 120.

McLaren suggests that the increased availability of information and the emergence of environmental groups (who may provide inexpensive assistance) should offset some of the costs of making and proving one's case in court ("The Common Law Nuisance Actions and the Environmental Battle," 509).

16. Allowing lawyers to charge contingency fees would be one way of increasing the courts' accessibility.

17. For information about the extent to which barriers to enforcing one's property rights in the courts remain, see Dewees, "The Comparative Efficacy of Tort Law and Regulation for Environmental Protection," 11-16. Also see Bardach and Kagan, *Going By the Book*, 272, 275, 281.

18. "Fingering pollution," *The Economist*, 91-2; *Wall Street Journal*, "CAT Scan May Soon 'Map' Air Pollution."

19. *New York Times*, "A New Slant on Exxon Valdez Spill."

20. Anderson and Leal, *Free Market Environmentalism*, 166. Also see Smith, "Controlling the Environmental Threat to the Global Liberal Order," 11, 21; and Stroup and Shaw, "The Free Market and the Environment," 39.

21. *New York Times*, "Cells May Bear Mark Of Each Cancer Agent."

22. Estrin and Swaigen, *op. cit.*, 52-4.

23. Bardach and Kagan, *op. cit.*, 273.

24. William Dennison and J. D. Baxter, *Ontario Legislative Assembly Debates*, March 29, 1949, 1459, 62. Ironically, the debate occasioning these remarks resulted in amendments to the Lakes and Rivers Improvement Act—the first step in the extermination of property rights along the Spanish River described in Chapter 4.

25. William Murdoch, *Legislature of Ontario Debates, Official Report—Daily Edition*, February 12, 1957, 286. These remarks, too, occurred in a debate resulting in the further erosion of Ontarians' property rights.

9

Governments Gutting Their Holdings

The forest trees that in the olden time—
The people's glory and the poet's pride—
Tempered the air and guarded well the earth
And, under spreading boughs, for ages kept
Great reservoirs to hold the snow and rain,
From which the moisture through the teeming year
Flowed equably but freely—all were gone . . .
Their precious bales exchanged for petty cash,
The cash that melted and had left no sign;
The logger and the lumbermen were dead;
The axe had rusted out for lack of use;
But all the endless evil they had done
Was manifested in the desert waste. . . .

Great cities that had thriven marv'lously
Before their source of thrift was swept away
Faded and perished, as a plant will die
With water banished from its roots and leaves;
And men sat starving in their treeless waste
Beside their treeless farms and empty marts,
And wondered at the ways of Providence.

> *Report of Ontario's Royal Commission on*
> *Forest Reservation and National Park, 1893*[1]

Nineteenth-century conservationists who were concerned about the loss of Ontario's trees should have wondered not at the ways of Providence but at the ways of their governments, who had done everything in their power to raze the primeval forests. When the above poem was penned, government policies had propelled more than a century of forest destruction.[2]

France's military needs first governed forestry policy in what is now Canada. After the French withdrawal in 1763, Britain's Royal Navy—having denuded Great Britain—looked to Canada for oak and pine for its ships' hulls and masts. In the nineteenth century, revenue generation replaced fleet building as the force driving deforestation. Earnings from the early civilian timber trade were to support the British Crown. Later, the government of the United Canadas, followed by provincial governments, planned on constructing roads and public buildings with timber revenues.

Maximizing revenues demanded maximizing cuts, or so went government logic. From the 1820s onward, the government required loggers to fell a minimum amount of timber within a specified period; non-compliers would lose their licences. It was a policy of economic folly. The "minimum cut" provisions, applied regardless of demand, periodically saturated the market with worthless wood and depressed the timber industry. An 1842 regulation specifying that an annual licence could be renewed only if the licensee had cut down 5,000 feet per square mile brought about the first depression in the timber market. In response, the government was forced in 1846 to reduce the minimum cut to 1,000 feet; further reductions occurred two years later.

The government experimented with other ways of ensuring that its trees would not remain standing, including directing loggers to fell all trees, regardless of their value. In another variation, in 1851 the government levied a charge on timber holdings that would double each year that the forest remained uncut. Like the minimum cut, the charge encouraged over-production, forcing loggers to cut unneeded lumber to avoid losing their rights to the trees. Not surprisingly, another severe depression in the timber market soon occurred.

Loggers vigorously protested the minimum cut requirements and other disincentives to conservation. But it was beyond their power to act: the government owned the resource and the government set the rules. Had the government not refused to sell timber lands, or had it at least sold secure property rights to the timber itself, financial self-interest would have driven loggers to conserve. Holding timber lands in their natural state, waiting for time and renewed demand to increase their value, would have enabled loggers to avoid—or at least ride out—the frequent depressions. They did just that whenever they could get away with it. The government termed this holding practice "specula-tion," and renewed its efforts to fell the trees.[3]

Ironically, during the industry's early years, regulations forcing the cutting of trees failed to produce the anticipated revenues. Monitoring and collection proved difficult and costly. "I have found it impracticable," the Commissioner of Crown Lands reported in 1839, "to collect any important amount of duties on timber cut upon Government lands in other parts of the Province and the expenses attending the attempts to do so have borne much too large a proportion of the sums collected."[4]

Governments soon discovered a new reason to raze their forests: job creation. In 1872, the Ontario government justified a controversial sale of logging rights north of Lake Huron by arguing that new sawmills would employ settlers in the area. The same motives later prompted government support for the pulp and paper industry; an 1892 agreement, establishing the pattern for future pulp contracts, offered favourable rates for the right to cut timber if the company hired three hundred hands for ten months of the year.

Meanwhile, agricultural settlement paralleled timber develop-ment in destroying Ontario's forests. During and after the American War of Independence, the British government provided retreating troops and United Empire Loyalists with free grants of land along the lakes and rivers of what is now Southern Ontario. Throughout the following century, the government continued to lure settlers with the promise of free land, first in Southern

Ontario and later between the upper Ottawa River and Georgian Bay.

But these land grants had strings attached: the government insisted that the land be developed. "Settlement duties" varied from time to time but generally included residing on the land, clearing and cultivating a certain number of acres within a specified period, and constructing a house. Settlers who failed to perform their duties could not acquire title—could not establish property rights—to their land. The threat of losing uncleared land prompted many settlers to cut their trees wastefully, or even to burn them.

Other incentives also encouraged needless deforestation. The Free Grant and Homesteads Act of 1868 created a "use-it-or-lose-it" regime in pine trees. The government allowed settlers to cut pine while clearing and fencing their land and building homes and barns, but reserved for itself the pine remaining once the settlers had acquired their titles. What settler in his right mind would conserve his pine trees?

Ironically, much of the land cleared by settlers proved unsuitable for farming. Surveyors, it turned out, had incorrectly assumed that all soil supporting trees could also support crops. Moreover, land grants proved too small to farm successfully, and were often too far from agricultural markets. As a select committee admitted in 1863, "[S]ettlement has been unreasonably pushed in some localities quite unfit to become the permanent residence of an agricultural population."[5] By the end of that year, most of the settlers in the Ottawa-Huron country had left the land. And twenty years later, farmers were being urged to plant trees on their non-arable lands.

The economic folly of the governments' forestry and agricultural policies was clear from the beginning. The environmental consequences were less obvious. Although at least one scientist warned of the dangers of deforestation as early as 1847, not until the 1860s and 1870s did the public begin to appreciate the extent of the damage. Agricultural land clearing and forestry had dried up streams, increased fire-hazards, spread tree diseases, and threatened fish and wildlife. And forests were continuing to fall at an alarming rate. In 1871, Sir John A. Macdonald warned, "We are recklessly destroying the timber of Canada and there is scarcely the possibility of replacing it."[6] The following year an article in the *Canadian Monthly* echoed the alarm: "We are wasting our forests, habitually, wickedly, insanely, and at a rate which must soon bankrupt us in all that element of wealth."[7] Eight years later, a speaker warned the United Fruit Growers Association of Ontario, "If something is not speedily and effectually done . . . we shall, before many years have swept their onward course, find ourselves compelled to forever inhabit a dismal treeless waste and an unfruitful region."[8] Speakers at the 1882 American Forestry Congress worried that marketable Canadian and American timber supplies were nearing their end, and bemoaned the effects of deforestation, including climate change, soil erosion, and flooding.

The government was slow to respond. Finally, after the 1893 Royal Commission on Forest Reservation and National Park reported that "the wholesale and indiscriminate slaughter of forests brings a host of evils in its train,"[9] the province took a preliminary step: it established Algonquin Park in order, among other things, to preserve the primeval forest.

Park designation did not, however, protect Algonquin's forest from logging. From the park's earliest days, lumbermen already licensed to cut pine in the region were allowed to continue. And as other species, such as birch, became needed, the government amended the law to allow their harvest. Other reserved lands fared similarly; when the government reserved the Temagami forests in 1901, it refused to exclude lumbering.

Despite increasing public concern about the dwindling

forests, government-sponsored deforestation persisted in the new century. Jobs continued to eclipse profitable logging, conservation, and equity on political agendas. In 1935, hoping to create 10,000 jobs, the Ontario government reduced mills' dues and licence fees on the condition that the operators hire a certain number of people. "The putting of men back to work," it explained, was more important "than the real or apparent losses in certain lines of revenue."[10] The following year, putting men to work similarly inspired the Forest Resources Regulation Act, which empowered the Minister of Lands and Forests to seize timber limits from companies slow to cut timber. Under the act the Minister redistributed several thousand square miles of timber lands that had until then been held out of production.

Creating forestry industry jobs remains a cornerstone of provincial forest management policies, with governments' short-term perspectives blinding them to the counterproductive nature of programs that create jobs by destroying wealth. In 1989, the Ontario government sold trees to logging companies at an average of just 85 cents apiece to prop up the industry.[11] Minimum cut requirements remain in effect, requiring loggers to harvest trees regardless of demand, market price, or profitability. And forestry agreements continue to allow for the reallocation of uncut wood to those who promise to harvest it.

The government also continued in this century to push agricultural development on unsuitable land. Soon after a "Clay Belt" running through Cochrane, Kapuskasing and Hearst, Ontario, was discovered in 1900, the government opened up the area to free land grants. By 1920, the government had spent $800,000 settling 101 veterans near Kapuskasing. But it became increasingly clear that arable farming in the Clay Belt, with its harsh climate and distance from markets, would be unprofitable. By 1957, only two of the original grant recipients remained in the Kapuskasing area.[12]

Ontario is by no means alone in destroying its forests. In fact, it is the destructive behaviour of other provinces that has earned Canada its reputation as "Brazil of the North." Virtually all provinces promote deforestation in the name of job creation. They do so not only at the environment's peril but also at considerable—even absurd—economic cost. Alberta has given massive subsidies to foreign pulp and paper corporations in order to put people to work; the jobs have cost the government hundreds of thousands of dollars each. Saskatchewan is reported to have spent almost a million dollars per job in one pulp and paper job creation endeavour. Ironically, despite the governments' efforts, Canadian forests produce fewer jobs per volume of wood cut than do those of any other industrialized country.[13]

In British Columbia, where 96 per cent of productive forest land is publicly owned, the government has done much to encourage unsustainable forestry practices. Throughout much of this century, its policies were driven by the significant revenues generated by timber operations. Logging filled not only the provincial coffers but also politicians' pockets; in the 1940s and 1950s, the Minister of Forests awarded tree farm licences (a euphemism for tree *harvest* licences) to large corporations that made political contributions to his party.[14]

As in other provinces, in British Columbia job creation has replaced revenue generation as the primary motivating force behind forestry policy. The province subsidizes logging by collecting only a fraction of its lumber's value from those who cut it; one estimate of its forgone revenue exceeds $2 billion a year.[15]

An obsession with jobs produces not only bad economic policy (at the expense of even more jobs) but also bad environmental policy. British Columbia has gained international notoriety for endorsing clear-cutting of its ancient rainforests. In one infamous 1993 announcement, the government, driven by its concern for forest industry jobs, allowed logging in 67 per cent of the old-growth forests of Clayoquot Sound. The decision to permit clear-cutting in one of the world's few remaining large temperate rainforests outraged environmentalists around the globe.[16]

The government of British Columbia, like its counterpart in Ontario, prompts loggers to cut trees they view as valueless. Described by the Minister of Forests as "use it or lose it," the province's policy controlling cuts penalizes holders of tree farm licences who fail to harvest the minimum required.[17] Not wanting to lose their timber allocations, operators create logs for which there is no demand—often from trees which, when standing, had considerable recreational or ecological value.

Nor is the problem confined to Canada. The U.S. Forest Service is notorious for promoting uneconomic logging in national forests.[18] American government agencies even try to circumvent federal laws in aid of the forest industry. Although logging in the federally owned old-growth forests of the Pacific Northwest threatens the spotted owl and violates the Endangered Species Act, a cabinet committee tried in 1992 to exempt certain timber operations from the act. The administration renewed its efforts in 1994. Its goal? Preserving forest industry jobs.[19]

Forestry policy illustrates the extent to which governments have depleted public resources. Other resources—from minerals to fisheries to rivers with power-generating potential—have received similar treatment in the name of revenue generation, growth, industrialization, job creation, or other perversions of "the common good."[20]

Tragically, the public has been powerless to prevent the devastation. Property rights, which can so effectively protect private resources, have been of no use. One can only protect that which one owns, and all too often it is the government—not the public—that owns Canada's natural resources.[21] As long as they continue to own public lands and resources, governments will be free to destroy them to achieve their ends.

Property rights have similarly failed to prevent the *pollution* of public resources. The common law saviours—trespass laws, nuisance laws, and riparian rights—have traditionally been linked to property ownership or occupancy; they have arisen from harm to individuals' private interests. Common law property rights have not empowered people to protect public resources. As the jurist Sir William Blackstone explained more than two centuries ago, "[T]he law gives no *private* remedy for anything but a *private* wrong."[22] Since individuals lack proprietary interest in public resources, they often have no cause of action for damages done to those resources.

Public nuisances, or pervasive nuisances, affect many people rather than select individuals. Normally, in the case of public nuisances, individuals lack the "standing" to sue: they lack the right to stand before a court. Only the attorney general, intended to be the guardian of the public interest, may take action on behalf of the public at large. Blackstone defended this practice on practical grounds: "[T]he damage being common to *all* the queen's subjects, no *one* can assign his particular proportion of it; or, if he could, it would be extremely hard if every subject in the kingdom were allowed to harass the offender with separate actions."[23]

Hickey v. *Electric Reductions Co. of Canada* illustrates the common law's failure to safeguard public property. In that famous 1970 Newfoundland case, commercial fishermen sought an injunction against poisonous discharges from a phosphorous plant into Placentia Bay. Although the court acknowledged that the pollution, by harming the fish, may have jeopardized the fishermen's livelihoods, it decided that they lacked the standing to sue: first, they had no property interest in the fish, and second, their damages did not differ in both kind and degree from those of the general public, all of whom had the right to fish in public waters and all of whose rights had been violated to the same degree.[24]

Had the fishermen's damages differed in kind and degree, they could have challenged the public nuisance. As Blackstone explained, "[W]here a private person suffers some extraordinary damage, beyond the rest of the queen's subjects, by a public nuisance . . . he shall have a private satisfaction by action."[25] This remains the case: an individual has a right of action to abate a public nuisance if his property has been damaged or if he can show "special damage"; he must have experienced a harm both greater than and qualitatively different from that of other members of the public.[26]

Ontario's Environmental Bill of Rights, proclaimed in 1994, relaxed public nuisance standing restrictions in the province and introduced harm to a public resource as a new cause of action.[27] However, the bill included the government's favourite escape clause: it empowered the court, after considering economic and social concerns, to dismiss an action if doing so would be in the public interest. The government thus ensured that short-term job creation would remain a valid excuse for destroying the province's resources.

Notes

1. Ontario's Royal Commission on Forest Reservation and National Park, *Report*, 1893, cited by Lambert, *Renewing Nature's Wealth*, 10. (Line 18 of Lambert's version reads "sate" rather than "sat.")

2. Unsustainable forest management dates back even farther. Economic and environmental folly characterized the forestry practices of generations of English kings, who, between the sixteenth and

eighteenth centuries, stripped vast royal woods to meet their revenue requirements. Adam Smith described the equally wasteful practices of many eighteenth-century European governments:

> Though there is not at present, in Europe, any civilized state of any kind which derives the greater part of its public revenue from the rent of lands which are the property of the State; yet, in all the great monarchies of Europe, there are still many large tracts of land which belong to the crown. They are generally forest; and sometimes forest where, after travelling several miles, you will scarce find a single tree; a mere waste and loss of country in respect both of produce and population (*An Inquiry into the Nature and Causes of the Wealth of Nations*, Book 4, 233).

For the following discussion on the history of Ontario's forestry and agricultural policies I have relied on Albion, *Forests and Sea Power*; Lambert, *op. cit.*; Mussell, "Property Rights in the Development of Ontario Forest Tenures"; Nautiyal, "Forest Tenure Structure in Ontario"; and Nelles, *The Politics of Development*.

3. Anderson and Leal discuss the extent to which economic considerations led late nineteenth-century lumbermen in the American Great Lakes states to log or, alternatively, to conserve their privately held forests. In what the authors describe as both economically efficient and environmentally beneficial speculation, owners often delayed harvesting stands that would, uncut, increase in value faster than would alternative investments (*Free Market Environmentalism*, 37-50).

4. Commissioner Sullivan, *Report on the Public Departments*, 1839, 158, cited by Lambert, *op. cit.*, 45.

Revenues generated by timber development gained importance during the second half of the nineteenth century. Between 1867 and 1899, Ontario's timber industry supplied approximately 28 per cent of provincial revenues. Warnings from opposition MPPs and academics that timber represented capital rather than a source of current revenues fell on deaf ears.

Ontario's forests were also an important source of political capital, especially in the first decades of the twentieth century. Donations to the party in power helped lumbermen obtain timber limits. Before provincial elections, it was not unusual for the government to "auction off" timber with neither advertisement nor competition.

5.   The Select Committee on the State of the Lumber Trade, cited by Ontario Royal Commission on Forestry, *Report*, 1947, 8-9, cited by Lambert, *ibid.*, 91.

6.   Ontario Ministry of Natural Resources, *White Pine*, 41.

7.   Captain N. W. Beckwith, *Canadian Monthly*, June, 1872, 527, cited by Lambert, *op. cit.*, 158.

8.   Commissioner of Agriculture and Arts, *Report*, 1880, 146, cited by Lambert, *ibid.*, 177.

9.   Royal Commission on Forest Reservation and National Park, *op. cit.*, 9, cited by Lambert, *ibid.*, 169.

10.   The Department of Lands and Forests, *Annual Report*, 1935, 10, cited by Lambert, *ibid.*, 339.

11.   For more information on governments' incentives to destroy forests, see Solomon, "Save the Forests—Sell the Trees," excerpted in Dolan and Lindsey, *Economics*, 887-8. I am also grateful to Al Mussell for information on this issue.

12.   Denise Call, the Ministry of Agriculture and Food's agricultural representative for Cochrane North, notes that the Clay Belt now hosts a number of productive farms; thanks to the adoption of new techniques (funded by more government grants), farmers now see the northern climate as a "particularity" rather than a disadvantage (personal communication, November 21, 1994).

13.   Cooperman provides a province-by-province description of expensive and destructive forest practices in "Cutting Down Canada," 55-63.

14.   Drushka, *Stumped*, 15, 31, 72, 176, 265.

15. Personal communication with Ben Parfitt (co-author, with M'Gonigle, of *Forestopia*), July 26, 1994.

The Western Canada Wilderness Committee points out the extent to which political rather than financial gain motivates forestry policies: in past years the government has earned less in stumpage fees than it has spent running the forest service. (Personal communication with Paul George, executive director, February 23, 1994.)

16. For more information on the Clayoquot decision, see articles in the *Globe and Mail* dated April 14, May 1, May 3, and May 12, 1993.

In another infamous decision, in 1990 the Social Credit government gave MacMillan Bloedel permission to log the temperate rainforest of the upper Carmanah Valley, despite the low economic return expected for both the government and the forestry giant. (See the *Globe and Mail*, "Carmanah logging called poor investment," and the *Financial Post*, "Carmanah no winner for MB?") As of 1994, however, no logging had occurred.

17. Drushka, *op. cit.*, 52. Drushka discusses another disincentive to conservation on 79.

18. Anderson and Leal explain that timber programs in U.S. national forests not only destroy the environment but also regularly lose money (*op. cit.*, 52-4). Also see Dolan and Lindsey, *op. cit.*, 885; Grumbine, "Policy in the Woods," 253; *Wall Street Journal*, "Hayek's Heirs Contemplate Greener Pastures"; *New York Times*, "Choice of Chief Upsets Ranks of Forest Service"; and Miller, "Land of the Free," 68.

19. *Financial Post*, "Logging gets OK in spotted owl area"; and *New York Times*, "White House Seeking to Ease Ban on Logging in Owl Areas."

20. Nelles, *op. cit.*, discusses the extent to which Ontario governments have confused the public interest with the interests of selected industries. A century of governments intent on promoting rather than regulating mineral extraction, logging, and waterpower development left the people of the province no better off—indeed, likely worse off—than they would have been had the resources been in private hands.

21. Provincial governments own 80 per cent of Canada's productive forest land; the federal government owns 11 per cent; 430,000 private woodlot owners own the remaining 9 per cent.

Forest ownership in the three provinces with the greatest amount of productive forest land is as follows:

Quebec:

87.6% provincial; 0.4% federal; 12% 120,000 private owners

British Columbia:

95% provincial; 1% federal; 4% 21,000 private owners

Ontario:

84% provincial; 1% federal; 15% 169,000 private owners

(1986 figures from Forestry Canada's *Forestry Facts*, 10, 60, 63, 75.)

22. Blackstone, *Commentaries on the Laws of England*, Volume 3, 193.

23. *Ibid.*

For more information on public nuisance see Horwitz, *The Transformation of American Law 1780-1860*, 76-7; Ontario, *Report of the Task Force on the Ontario Environmental Bill of Rights*, 11-3, 91-2; and Estrin and Swaigen, *Environment on Trial*, 112-3, 812.

24. *Hickey* v. *Electric Reductions Co. of Canada* (1972), 21 D.L.R. (3d) 368, cited in Canadian Environmental Law Research Foundation, "An Overview of Canadian Law and Policy Governing Great Lakes Water Quantity Management," 118-9. Also discussed as *Hickey* v. *Electric Reduction Co.* (1970), 2 Nfld. & P.E.I.R. 246, 21 D.L.R. (3d) 368 (Nfld.S.C.) in *Report of the Task Force on the Ontario Environmental Bill of Rights*, 12; in the *Financial Post*, "Bracing for environmental rights bill"; and by Wright and Linden, *Canadian Tort Law*, 17-2 - 17-5.

25. Blackstone, *op. cit.*, 193.

26. Canadian Environmental Law Research Foundation, *op. cit.*, 118-9, Ontario, *Report of the Task Force on the Ontario Environmental Bill of Rights*, 91-2, and Epstein, "The Social Consequences of Common Law Rules," 1731.

27. Bill 26, *An Act respecting Environmental Rights in Ontario*, received royal assent December 14, 1993, and was proclaimed on February 15, 1994.

Section 103 (1) of the act states: "No person who has suffered or may suffer a direct economic loss or direct personal injury as a result of a public nuisance that caused harm to the environment shall be barred from bringing an action without the consent of the Attorney General in respect of the loss or injury only because the person has suffered or may suffer direct economic loss or direct personal injury of the same kind or to the same degree as other persons." Section 84 (1) states: "Where a person has contravened or will imminently contravene an Act, regulation or instrument prescribed for the purposes of Part V and the actual or imminent contravention has caused or will imminently cause significant harm to a public resource of Ontario, any resident in Ontario may bring an action against the person in the court in respect of the harm and is entitled to judgment if successful."

10

The Taxman's Axe

The growth-rate of a tree slows as it reaches maturity until it no longer uses the full growth potential of the land it stands on. When this occurs the tree should be cut, since it is preventing the realization of the full growth potential of the site.

Ontario Department of Lands and Forests, 1967[1]

We agree with the [Ontario government's] Green Paper that land should not be allowed to lie idle.

The Prospectors and Developers Association of Canada, 1989[2]

In 1993, Ontario's woodlots began to fall beneath the taxman's axe.[3] That year the government, infamous for clearing public lands, turned its attention to the private sector. By dramatically increasing realty tax costs on privately owned forest lands, it forced their exploitation and development.

Provincial tax assessors had long discriminated against forest land, valuing it not at its current use but at some higher potential use, or theoretical "market value," that a better financial steward than the forest owner could marshal.[4] The best potential use of most forest land, the entrepreneurial tax assessors decided, was not forestry, recreation, or wildlife protection but residential development. Thus all woodlands in Ontario, except Christmas tree plantations, sugar bush and others qualifying as farms, were assessed on their theoretical development potential, limited only by what local zoning bylaws allowed.

For two decades, a tax rebate shielded forest owners from market value assessment: the Managed Forest Tax Rebate, ranging from 50 to 100 per cent, was available to all who promised to maintain their forest cover for ten years. Citing budgetary constraints, the government cancelled the rebate in 1993. Forest owners would now pay full taxes based on their land's development potential.

Market value assessment forced landowners who couldn't afford to pay high taxes on low yields to destroy their forests. Property tax increases, in some cases measuring 500 per cent over three years, prompted thousands to reduce or abandon their management plans, terminate planting, or accelerate the cutting of their woodlands; others subdivided their property into estate or cottage lots.[5]

Forest owners vividly described the environmental effects of market value assessment in five submissions to Ontario's Fair Tax Commission. Assessments based on theoretical rather than actual uses force owners to liquidate their forests, complained one tree farmer to the commission. Another woodlot owner elaborated that the tax burden imposed by the assessment of his forest's theoretical highest end-use value left him with just three options: parcelling his land, selling it as one piece for development, or logging it unsustainably. He confessed to imprudently harvesting timber in order to meet his increased costs. "Wildlife will suffer first," he mused. "We will all lose in the end."[6]

Particularly hard hit by the tax changes was Peter Schleifenbaum, manager of the Haliburton Forest and Wild Life Reserve Limited, central Ontario's largest privately owned forest.[7] Mr. Schleifenbaum's parents had purchased the property in 1961, after a logging company had stripped it of its best timber and most of its market value. Using natural regeneration and selective cutting, they nursed the land back to a rich, productive, and profitable venture. The Schleifenbaums' forestry program paid off: within three decades the forest boasted the highest volume of timber per acre of any comparable hardwood area in central Ontario.

The Haliburton Forest and Wild Life Reserve wasn't just a working forest. It was also a recreational haven for thousands of visitors each year. Bordering Algonquin Provincial Park, its 50,000 acres encompassed 50 lakes, huge hardwood and ever-green expanses, and the homes of countless fish, fowl, and wildlife. Its 340 semi-wilderness campsites made it the largest private campground in North America. In the summer it offered birding, fishing, hiking, canoeing, 270 kilometers of mountain bike trails . . . and an "environmental music" course taught by the renowned Canadian composer R. Murray Schafer. Hunting dominated the three-week season each fall. Snowmobilers and cross-country skiers used the forest in the winter. Throughout the year, an old logging camp on the property served as a base camp for an extensive outdoor education program.

A government assessment based on the property's value if subdivided into cottage lots pushed the annual realty tax bill to $200,000, and left Mr. Schleifenbaum wondering how he could resist destroying at least part of his wilderness. The Haliburton Forest's revenues could not support such a tax bill.[8] Developers had offered considerable sums for lakefront land. Intensive logging would also pay handsomely; Mr. Schleifenbaum could strip his land in four years, invest the $20 million the timber would bring in, and live very comfortably on the interest.

That prospect held little appeal for one steeped in a European tradition emphasizing long-term stewardship over short-term gain and valuing the security that comes from knowing that the land and resources will be there for the next generation.[9] "We really are stewards," Mr. Schleifenbaum lamented. "We believe in it. But we're being penalized if we leave our land forested. This is not a climate in which private forestry can survive."[10]

Other tax policies similarly penalized Ontarians who didn't deforest their land. In 1994, the Erin Mills Development Corporation, faced with an annual $11,000 realty tax bill on ten forested acres that had survived urbanization in Mississauga, chopped down the trees and planted wheat. Lower assessments on agricultural land, along with a 73 per cent rebate on farm realty taxes, motivated the devastation.[11] From the company's perspective it was an economically responsible action. As general manager Randy Griffin explained, "We don't like to cut it all down. But when you're trying to reduce your taxes, these are the things you've got to do."[12]

Ontario's non-profit Conservation Authorities had to sell off lands in order to pay their 1994 property taxes.[13] Like forests, conservation lands had long been subject to unrealistically high taxes as a result of market value assessment and the absence of a separate assessment category for conservation lands. The Ministry of Revenue relied primarily on nearby residential land values (rather than on current land use) to establish the value of conservation lands, as if flooding the residential market with the conservation lands would not have depressed land values. It even assessed flood plains and protected areas—lands that potential purchasers would be unable to develop—as residential lands, giving them a tax value *higher* than their market value. As municipalities implemented market value assessment in the 1970s, assessments on conservation lands skyrocketed. By 1980, assessments had increased between 139 and 428 per cent, depending on the category of land, and taxes had increased between 44 and 222 per cent.

Like forest owners, conservation authorities had been shielded from the increasing taxes by a rebate: the Conservation Land Tax Rebate. And like forest owners, when they lost the rebate in 1993 they faced huge tax bills. Property taxes on conservation lands increased by $3.6 million as a result of the tax change, with one authority's bill alone nearing $1.2 million.[14]

Several conservation authorities had to sell lands as a consequence of the tax change.[15] The Ganaraska Forest, suddenly saddled with a $150,000 tax bill on its 11,000 acres of newly-minted "residential" land, had no choice but to shed some of its property. The prospect of losing forest to developers outraged Ganaraska's chief administrator. "Somewhere in the tax shuffle," she complained, "the environment got lost."[16]

While discriminatory realty taxes have compelled the owners of forests and conservation lands to exploit or sell their land, discriminatory mining land taxes have forced owners of mining lands to *give* their property to the government. In 1991 the Ontario government proclaimed a new Mining Act. The act and its regulations introduced huge increases in the mining land tax: from $1.24 per hectare in 1991 to $8.00 per hectare in 1996, or more than a 500 per cent increase over five years.[17]

By changing the definition of mining rights, the act also extended the number of taxable properties. Its predecessor had applied to properties in which sub-surface rights had been sold separately from surface rights—the norm after 1913. In contrast, the new act encompassed mining rights on *any* land, including that for which the purchasers of the surface had been granted sub-surface rights.[18] The tax even applied to lands granted under the 1869 Mining Act, which had stated that the properties would not be taxed; "such lands, ores and minerals," the government had then promised, "shall henceforth be free and exempt from every such royalty, tax or duty."[19]

The tax hike made selling taxable properties increasingly difficult. No market existed for properties encumbered by taxes four times higher than their neighbours'. Even mining companies wouldn't buy taxable land; they could lease land from the government for a fraction of what, as owners, they would pay in mining land taxes.

Unable to either pay the mining tax or sell their land, owners were forced to surrender their property—without compensation—to the government. Depending on their location, some lost their sub-surface rights; others forfeited the land itself. According to Minister of Mines Gilles Pouliot, that was the whole idea: the tax, he explained, "has always been intended as a means of returning land to the Crown."[20]

Those who lost "only" their mining rights had to put up with the disruption and loss associated with allowing others to mine their lands. Under the Mining Act, a mining company could enter private land with only a day's notice in order to assess its mineral potential. If, after prospecting, exploring and excavating, it chose to develop a mine on the property, it had to compensate the landowner for damages. But the rules contained no provisions for compensation for intangible losses, such as disruption of a wilderness. Worse, it was the mining commissioner, rather than the landowner, who had the power to decide if the compensation were adequate.

The province's rationale for taking mining rights and land? The government, valuing the wealth, jobs, and export earnings generated by mineral development, believed that too many private landowners allowed their property to lie idle.[21] In 1961, the Public Lands Investigation Committee had discovered the conservationist tendencies of those owning mining lands: only a small fraction of them actually mined their property. In an effort to encourage landowners to mine, or to free up their lands for others to mine, the government quintupled the mining lands tax in 1969. The increase had its desired effect: landowners returned 400,000 acres—more than a quarter of all lands under mining patents—to the Crown in the next 20 years.

But the taxes weren't sufficiently high to force everyone's hand. Some landowners continued to discourage mining by requiring companies working on their property to share their profits. Others refused outright to develop their mines. "Let me tell you," Mines Minister Pouliot explained, "there are widows in Arizona who own property in Ontario, and because they own it mines are not being developed. The only way that mines will develop and Ontario will prosper is if we take their properties away from them."[22]

Tax policies that drive environmental destruction are by no means strictly an Ontario phenomenon. Governments the world over, seeking the revenues and jobs generated by forestry, try to discourage private woodlot owners' tendencies to conserve.[23] The latter generally place a higher value on their trees than do the former. They don't cut at a loss, and they don't cut to create jobs. When they do cut their trees, they generally command prices two or three times higher than those earned by their governments. They tend toward selective cutting, natural regeneration and other sustainable forestry practices. And they often simply refuse to cut their forests, instead preserving them for their recreational or spiritual value.

Sweden responded to such recalcitrance by forbidding wild, unmanaged stands of trees, and requiring its reluctant citizens to harvest at least half of their trees within a decade after they mature. Finland took the tax route, taxing the owners of standing woodlots on the amount they would have earned if they had harvested rather than preserved their trees.

Some American states, too, tax woodlot owners on their potential rather than actual revenues. A commission established by the U.S. Congress called property taxes one of the most significant problems facing privately held forest lands in the northeastern United States. It warned that by basing taxes not on current use but on what the land could theoretically be worth if developed, governments encourage owners to sell their forests. Many private landowners, it explained, simply can't afford to hold on to undeveloped land.[24]

Governments use carrots as well as sticks to pressure private owners to deforest their land. In the 1980s the government of Prince Edward Island was concerned about the preservation of the private woodlots comprising 92 per cent of the island's productive forest land:[25] landowners weren't cutting their trees fast enough to supply the province's mills. Although some made small clearcuts for firewood and lumber, few could afford (or wanted) to access remote parts of their property or to purchase heavy equipment or chemicals, and their woods didn't provide sufficient returns to warrant large investments. And so the province, aided by the federal government, introduced subsidies to encourage woodlot owners and forest contractors to build roads into their woods, to rip trees out by their roots, to clear-cut, to burn, to create plantations of single species, and to spray herbicides and pesticides.[26]

Federal-provincial forest resource development agreements have done similar harm to the forests in other Maritime provinces. First signed in the 1970s in response to the threat of wood scarcities, the agreements have subsidized intensive forest management practices such as clear-cutting, single-species planting, and the use of herbicides and pesticides in New Brunswick and Nova Scotia.

Provincial governments, dependent on the revenues, jobs, and electoral support provided by large pulp and paper companies, have also acted on their own to encourage private woodlot owners to cut their trees and sell them cheap. In Nova Scotia, where 31,000 small woodlot owners hold 70 per cent of the province's productive forest land, the Forest Improvement Act aimed at boosting pulpwood production on small woodlots. The 1965 act, passed in response to projected pulpwood shortages, directed forest operators to "use every effort to harvest all possible saleable wood of commercial value." Not surprisingly, forest owners widely opposed the act on the grounds that it overrode private property rights. But the Premier defended the act in the name of the public good. "We are either serious about making the most of our forests or we're not," he explained. "I think if we are serious we have to carry through, and encourage our people to follow certain practices that will mean a great deal to our province in the future."[27]

Governments have shown that they are not up to the task of preventing resource degradation or pollution; indeed, they have often actively encouraged it. In order to generate revenue and create jobs, they have gutted their holdings. Citizens have been powerless to prevent environmental degradation because they have had no formal claim to the threatened resources; they have lacked property rights to them.

Governments have also destroyed resources they don't own, pressuring private owners to raze their forests and to mine their soils. When the owners have resisted, governments have overridden their property rights, forcing them through unreasonable taxes or outright expropriation to comply.

It is long past time for responsibility for natural resources to be shifted away from governments and back to the individuals and communities that have strong interests in their preservation. Such a shift can best be accomplished by strengthening property rights and by assigning property rights to resources now being squandered by governments.

Notes

1.   Lambert, *Renewing Nature's Wealth*, 413.

2.   The Prospectors and Developers Association of Canada's comments on *Ontario's Mines and Minerals, Policy and Legislation: A Green Paper*, released by the Ministry of Northern Development and Mines in December 1988; cited in Ontario Ministry of Northern Development and Mines, *Mining Act Backgrounder*.

3.   The phrase "falling under the taxman's axe" comes from the *Mississauga News*, "Stop the Axes."

4.   The following discussion of provincial tax assessment policies and the Managed Forest Tax Rebate is based on personal communication with a number of bureaucrats, including Betty Vankerkhof, private woodlands policy officer with the Ministry of Natural Resources, and David Buttle, valuation analyst with the Ministry of Finance's Assessment Division, March 14, 1994.
     For more information on the impacts of federal and provincial tax policies on conservation, see Denhez, *You Can't Give It Away*.

5.   Personal communication with Lynn McIntyre, secretary/treasurer of the Ontario Woodlot and Sawmill Operators Association, March 16, 1994, regarding an informal membership poll conducted by the association in 1993; personal communication with Arthur Mathewson, chair of the Ontario Forestry Association's Private Woodlands Committee, May 2, 1994; and the Ontario Forestry Association's *Taxed to Death*. A poll of the 8,000 landowners who had lost the Managed Forest Tax Rebate revealed that 78 per cent of the more than 3000 respondents were reducing or abandoning their management efforts. Forty per cent planned to reduce or terminate planting and 31 per cent had stopped improving stands. Twenty per cent had sold or planned to sell their property.

6. Eyvind Fogh's brief to the Fair Tax Commission's Mississauga hearing and Arthur Mathewson's brief to the Fair Tax Commission's Kingston hearing. Both submissions appeared in Ontario Forestry Association, *Forest People*, 6-8.

These warnings did not fall on deaf ears: the commission recommended that managed forests' assessments should be based on the forests' current uses, rather than on their potential residential uses. (Ontario Fair Tax Commission, *Fair Taxation in a Changing World: Highlights*, 97, 126.)

7. For the following discussion of the Haliburton Forest and Wild Life Reserve I have relied on personal communication with Peter Schleifenbaum and dozens of brochures and (often undated) newspaper and magazine clippings provided by him. Also see the *Globe and Mail*, "Private Ontario woodlots under a tax."

8. In 1993, the Haliburton Forest's gross revenues from logging and recreation approached $1 million a year, with expenses eating up about half that amount.

9. In fact, Mr. Schleifenbaum's forest would become far more valuable in a generation. Three decades of growth would allow the high-quality hardwoods to reach maturity, after which time they could be sold for lumber, bringing in higher revenues than the poorer quality trees cut in previous years for pulpwood or firewood.

In addition to providing current and future revenues, the uncut forest had considerable non-monetary value for one who loved nature. Clearly, for Mr. Schleifenbaum these values combined exceeded the $20 million he could have earned from stripping the forest.

10. At the time of writing, Mr. Schleifenbaum had not yet chosen a course of action. Pressing for changes in provincial tax policies, he hoped to avoid having to choose between selling off land for development and increasing his logging operations.

11. Unlike forest land, agricultural land is not assessed at its market value. Farmland's value is based on the price that a farmer would pay for land that he intended to farm. In addition, farmers with a gross farm production value of over $7,000 benefit from the Farm Rebate Program.

Since its introduction in 1970, the program has enabled farmers to get back between 25 per cent and 100 per cent of their land taxes. Not surprisingly, the elimination of the forest rebate has sent many scrambling for the farm rebate.

12. *Mississauga News*, "Developer denuding land for tax break"; and personal communication with Randy Griffin, March 14, 1994.

13. The following discussion is based on: *Financial Post*, "Conservationists blast 'nature tax'"; *Toronto Sun*, "This land is your land?"; personal communication with Rebecca Goodwin, coordinator of Natural Heritage League, March 23, 1994; personal communication with Russ Powell, natural heritage coordinator, Ministry of Natural Resources, March 28, 1994; personal communication with Murray Stephen, general manager, Halton Region Conservation Authority, March 25, 1994; and the Halton Region Conservation Authority, "Submission to Fair Tax Commission," May 31, 1993.

14. The Metro Toronto Conservation Authority's extensive holdings pushed its bill to almost $1.2 million. The Hamilton Region Authority, with holdings just one-quarter the size of Metro's, faced a bill of almost $600,000—a whopping $78.55 per acre per year.

According to Jan Street, manager of communications for the Association of Conservation Authorities of Ontario, the Ministry of Natural Resources later provided some funding to ease the Conservation Authorities into their new tax situation (personal communication, November 29, 1994).

15. Jill McColl, at the Association of Conservation Authorities of Ontario, surveyed the province's 39 authorities. Seven had sold lands in 1993/94 (three of the sales, however, were not prompted by tax increases). Nine others had initiated sales in that period. Seven or eight had decided not to sell lands (personal communication, May 2, 1994).

16. Personal communication with Gayle Wood, staff chairman of the Association of Conservation Authorities of Ontario and chief administrative officer of the Ganaraska Conservation Authority, March 23, 1994.

17. Mining Act, *Revised Statutes of Ontario 1990*, Chapter M.14. Bill 71 was introduced as *An Act to Amend the Mining Act of Ontario* by the Liberal government in October, 1989, and received royal assent six weeks later. The NDP government proclaimed the act in June, 1991.

The following discussion is based on personal communication with Michelle Watkins, land tax administrator for the Ministry of Northern Development and Mines, March 8, 1994, and November 29, 1994; Ontario Ministry of Northern Development and Mines, *Mining Act Backgrounder*; personal communication with Charles Ficner, an owner of mining land and mining rights who has strenuously objected to the new act, March 9, 1994; and numerous documents provided by Charles Ficner, including communication with several MPPs.

18. Michelle Watkins, land tax administrator for the Ministry of Northern Development and Mines, denies that redefining mining rights affected the number of properties eligible for the tax (personal communication, March 22, 1994). The act, however, seems to contradict her position. Section 189 (1) (c) indicates that "all mining rights in, upon or under lands in a municipality patented under or pursuant to any statute, regulation or law at any time in force authorizing the granting of Crown lands for mining purposes" are liable for the tax. The definition of mining rights therefore appears to be essential in determining which rights are liable to the tax. If, as Ms. Watkins asserts, no new properties were put on the tax roles when the definition was changed, it is possible that the province was taxing properties that it should not have been taxing.

At least one MPP believes that the definition of mining rights is critical. On June 7, 1993, MPP Bob Chiarelli introduced Private Member's Bill 43, *An Act to amend the Mining Act*, in the Ontario Legislature. The bill would restore the previous definition of mining rights in order to "prevent landowners whose surface rights and mineral rights have not been dealt with separately from being taxed under Part XIII of the *Mining Act*." As of March 1994, the bill had not received second reading.

19. *An Act Respecting Mining, Revised Statutes of Ontario*, Chapter 29, Volume 1, 1877.

When the government contemplated changing the Mining Land Tax, it was aware of this early provision. See Ontario Ministry of

Northern Development and Mines, *Ontario's Mines and Minerals*, 36.

20. *Financial Post*, "Confiscating Ontario private property."
In its *Mining Act Backgrounder*, the Ministry of Northern Development and Mines confirmed the Minister's statement: "An 'acreage tax' was never intended for the sole purpose of generating revenue. Since its inception, the tax was applied to encourage the holders of mining rights to return those rights to the Crown if there was no intention to explore, develop and produce the mineral resources on their lands."
The rules governing the forfeiture of sub-surface and surface rights are somewhat ambiguous. The act empowers the government to "declare *the lands or mining rights . . .* forfeited to and vested in the Crown" if a landowner is three years in arrears on his mining land tax payments. According to ministry staff, those paying municipal or provincial land taxes forfeit "only" their mining rights, while those not on realty tax rolls forfeit both their mining and surface rights.

21. The Ministry of Northern Development and Mines proclaimed mining's virtues in *Ontario's Mines and Minerals*, 1. In a section entitled "Retaining Title," after noting that many mining lands lie dormant and unexplored, the ministry explained, "[A] basic principle is to ensure that the limited amount of mining lands within the province is actively explored and developed in an orderly and expedient manner to the benefit of Ontario"; it then recommended establishing "a mechanism that would encourage continued exploration of mining lands conveyed in the past" (15).
The mining land tax's main target is clearly undeveloped land; the act permits the minister to exempt from taxation lands that have been subdivided, farmed, or used for a variety of other purposes, such as natural gas production.

22. *Financial Post*, "Confiscating Ontario private property."
The government defends itself on the grounds that it is only trying to encourage people to use land for the purpose for which it was originally granted. The General Mining Act, however, under which some of the taxed lands were sold, permitted "mining lands" to be used for many other purposes, including some, such as cultivation, that would prevent mining.
Furthermore, the original-grant justification is not in keeping with

other government policies. For example, the government doesn't object to lands originally granted as agricultural lands now being used for other purposes.

23. For more information on governments' incentives to destroy forests, and private woodlot owners' tendency to conserve, see Solomon, "Save the Forests—Sell the Trees," excerpted in Dolan and Lindsey, *Economics*, 887-8; and Sandberg, *Trouble in the Woods*, 18, 169.

24. *New York Times*, "Property Tax Changes Are Urged to Help Preserve Northeast Forest," reporting on recommendations of the Northern Forest Lands Council.

25. The ownership estimates for PEI and Nova Scotia (following) appear in Forestry Canada's *Forestry Facts*, 53, 55.

26. Cooperman, "Cutting Down Canada," 61; personal communication with Gary Schneider, Environmental Coalition of PEI, March 15, 1994; and Bruno Peripoli, "Forest policy misguided," 7-8.

27. *Nova Scotia Debates*, February 22, 1965, 536-7; and Sandberg, *op. cit.*, 1-3, 13-4, 18-9, 142-3, 170, 178-80.

Part IV

Nature's Case for Restoring Strong Property Rights

11

Alienable Rights

I think the problem is that by enshrining private property rights in the Constitution at this point, we would be signalling that we want things done differently from the way they've been done in the past.

William Andrews
West Coast Environmental Law Association, 1991[1]

When in 1991 the Canadian government proposed entrenching property rights in the Constitution, many environmentalists balked. Career environmentalists almost unanimously warned that including property rights in the *Canadian Charter of Rights and Freedoms* would weaken government's power to plan and legislate. Landowners and businesses, they cautioned, would fight unconstitutional pollution regulations in the courts. Even unsuccessful court challenges could tie up legislation, create uncertainty, and cost considerable sums, chilling government actions.[2]

Others objected that stronger property rights would give the judiciary too much power. "The courts," the Canadian Environment Network warned, "will be second-guessing the legislatures." Pollution Probe went further, saying that the courts would become the primary decision makers in environmental disputes, gaining an essentially legislative role.[3]

Several organizations feared that charter-based property rights could confer the right to pollute. According to Pollution Probe, "When we talk about property rights, what we're really saying is that everybody can do what they want with their property." Although the organization admitted that such a right would be subject to the rights of other property holders, it warned that victims would bear the onus of showing that they had been harmed by the pollution. And no protection would be accorded to the environment for its own sake.[4]

Lay environmentalists soon joined the chorus of those opposed to entrenching property rights in the Constitution. Those persuaded that property rights would harm the environment included organizations as diverse as the Ontario Coalition Against Poverty, the Coalition of Provincial Organizations of the Handicapped, the Congress of Black Women of Canada, and the Ontario Coalition for Better Childcare.[5] MPs from the New Democratic Party called property rights "an incredible red flag" for environmentalists.[6] Apocalyptic rhetoric reached new heights in the *Globe and Mail*'s letters column, where a geography professor warned that the property rights proposition "is a legal licence for corporations to exploit land, water and air resources to the fullest extent possible, over as much area as possible, in the shortest time possible, regardless of consequences."[7]

Virtually all of the environmentalists' concerns were

unfounded. Some reflected an ignorance of the law and of legal history; others, a blinding bias towards centralist regulatory approaches to the environment.[8]

Experience in the United States demonstrates that property rights need not impede government's ability to legislate environmental protection. That country, whose constitution protects property rights, generally enjoys higher environmental standards than Canada.[9] There, property rights have not interfered with the federal government's ability to make and enforce strong environmental protection laws—even those that infringe property rights. The U.S. Supreme Court has never used property rights to strike down federal environmental protection statutes and regulations.[10]

Property rights are even less likely to strait-jacket Canadian governments. While rights entrenched in the Canadian Charter can't be overridden as easily as their unentrenched counterparts, the Charter itself limits the extent to which individual rights can inhibit government action. No Charter right is absolute. Section 1 of the Charter allows governments to balance individual rights against the public interest; it empowers them to violate rights to the extent justified in a free and democratic society. Importantly, the courts, rather than the governments themselves, determine whether the violation is justified.[11] But the Charter also allows governments to act without court sanction: Section 33 permits federal and provincial legislators who are determined to override rights to do so notwithstanding their Charter protection. In short, while the Charter both raises the legal hurdle and increases the political costs of overriding individual rights, it does not disempower governments.[12]

Stronger property rights, as their opponents fear, could indeed lead to frequent court challenges. But there is nothing wrong with people pursuing justice. Frivolous cases should be—and are—avoided: courts simply refuse to hear them. Serious cases should be encouraged. Citizens' challenges to laws violating their property rights—laws sanctioning pollution at their expense—should be *celebrated* by environmentalists. Court challenges would likely abate over the years following the entrenchment of property rights; as courts struck down laws offending people's rights to clean land, air and water, governments would be increasingly reluctant to pass new laws allowing pollution, giving victims fewer reasons to go to court.

To the extent that property rights would shift responsibility from governments to individuals working through the courts, the environment would benefit. All too often governments have used their sweeping powers to legislate environmental destruction rather than protection. Even outspoken opponents of property rights acknowledged during the constitutional debate that governments have failed to protect the environment. Several conceded that the courts have done a good job, agreeing that the courts are often more enlightened than the political process; and the public, they added, is ahead of the courts.[13]

The argument that property rights will confer the right to pollute is simply wrong. Property rights have long been governed by the maxim "use your own property so as not to harm another's." As we have seen, property rights in their heyday enabled pollution victims to fight for clean land, air and water. Potential victims and allied environmentalists should have applauded the promised return to a strong property rights regime.

Polluters, in contrast, had good reason to fear the constitutional entrenchment of property rights. A representative of the British Columbia mining industry expressed to a parliamentary committee a sentiment common among his peers with this caution about property rights: "[W]e shouldn't be adding more to the Charter, because the more we add to the Charter the less [*sic*] we take away from the supremacy of Parliament."[14] By and large, polluters favour Parliament's supremacy, preferring government regulation to "regulation" by affected individuals defending their property rights. Industries can capture governments, who rely on them for satisfied voters and funds; governments rarely withhold permission to pollute. Individuals, in contrast, often have nothing to gain from the pollution and resist capture.[15]

It is not property rights but rather their absence that allows resource and manufacturing companies to pollute with impunity. Polluters understand that people armed with strong property rights could enforce trespass and nuisance laws against them. Warned one multinational oil company executive, "If people in Alberta had property rights we'd have to stop most of our drilling. If you let individual property owners decide when we can drill on their land, they'll hold us up to ransom."[16]

While amending the Constitution would provide the surest protection for property rights, it is not the only way to bolster them. Provincial governments, who have jurisdiction over property and civil rights, could implement myriad measures to strengthen property rights.

Provincial legislators could ensure that nothing in provincial acts legalizes nuisances, thus maintaining their citizens' common law rights. Legislators could replace permits granting absolute power to pollute—permits that sanction not just the polluting activity but the necessary consequences of that activity—with those permitting activities on the condition that they do not violate others' property rights.[17]

Such conditions were common in nineteenth-century England, where early sanitation statutes maintained common law rights by specifying that they did not legalize nuisances or other unlawful acts. The Gas Act, which provided that in carrying on their works, gas manufacturers could not injure surrounding land, similarly protected the right of potential victims to sue.[18]

Federal and provincial governments intent on strengthening property rights could also settle legitimate land claims, which are essentially a property rights issue.[19] Aboriginal communities don't just want to *use* their lands and resources; they seek ownership and jurisdiction over them. "Proprietary rights to resources," the Native People's Circle on Environment and Development explained, "provide more real economic benefits than do access rights."[20]

The emphasis on proprietary rights has been reflected in recent land claims. The 1992 Nunavut settlement did not merely give the Inuit the right to manage many resources in the Eastern Arctic; the claimants also secured title to surface rights over 350,000 square kilometres and sub-surface rights over 36,000 square kilometres.[21] And in their claim to 58,000 square kilometres in northwestern B.C., the Gitksan and Wet'suwet'en Indians sought ownership of the land and jurisdiction over its forest, fishing, mining and water resources.[22]

Many native leaders distinguish between individual and collective property rights, favouring the latter. As the Native People's Circle on Environment and Development explained, "The concept of private ownership is foreign to Aboriginal people, who more typically think in terms of community use of land and resources, and territorial boundaries which shift from season to season as patterns of resource use change. Nevertheless, in order to develop healthy economies, Aboriginal people today are looking for ownership of the land base and increased control over resources."[23]

The Crees of Oujé-Bougoumou, Quebec, learned what happens to those who don't own their land. Over a period of 75 years, governments and mining companies pushed their community from one location to another seven times. In 1927, after Quebec granted a mining company rights to land long used by the people of Oujé-Bougoumou, the company destroyed Cree homes while clearing trees from the land. Blasting for a new mine again uprooted the community in 1951. It moved to an island nearby, which mining company clearcuts soon washed away. The community was chased from another home in 1962, when chemicals used in a gold mine poisoned its drinking water. The Crees' next eviction notice came from the Department of Indian Affairs in 1970: insisting that the people were not entitled to a reserve, federal officials burned their homes to the ground. Finally, in 1988, the province provided the community with land on which to build a village. Unlike their kin on reserves, where individual landownership is forbidden, the people of Oujé-Bougoumou purchased their new homes; they understood the importance of establishing property rights in that which they hoped to preserve.[24]

Property rights, to be meaningful, must be enforceable. If a victim can't successfully sue a polluter that has harmed him, his property rights are of little value. To ensure that victims can obtain justice long after companies have ceased doing business, provinces could require polluters to obtain bonds or liability insurance providing adequate funds for clean-up and compensation. Environmental liability insurance, while still limited and expensive, is becoming more common. Some insurers now promise to cover injuries suffered when their polices were in effect, even if the claims are filed after the policies have lapsed.[25]

Requiring polluters to be liable for future pollution costs is not new. British Columbia, Ontario and Quebec require mining companies to provide in advance for site reclamation. Financial assurances range from bonds or letters of credit to cash trust funds. To the degree that the costs of such arrangements reflect a company's environmental liabilities, they encourage environmentally responsible practices. Banks are increasingly demanding environmental audits and management plans from their clients before approving credit; they want to ensure both that their security will not be devalued and that the borrower's cash flow will cover both debt servicing and environmental liability. If insurers become involved, they will inevitably follow suit, using premiums to force companies to operate in a manner minimizing current and future risks.[26]

In addition to entrenching property rights in the Constitution, rescinding laws that legalize nuisances, settling aboriginal land claims, and requiring environmental liability insurance, governments should take one more step towards strengthening property rights: they should curb expropriation by both public and private agencies. Only then will citizens enjoy truly secure property rights.

Notes

1. *Minutes of Proceedings and Evidence of the Standing Committee on Environment*, Issue No. 13, October 24, 1991, 48.

2. Such views were thoroughly aired in parliamentary committee hearings into the effects of the proposed constitutional changes on the environment. They appear throughout the *Minutes of Proceedings and Evidence*, *op. cit.*. See, for example, Issue No. 12, October 23, 1991, A3-4 (featuring the Rawson Academy of Aquatic Science and the Canadian Arctic Resources Committee); Issue No. 17, November 6, 1991, 8, 33, 35 (featuring the Canadian Environmental Law Association, Sierra Club of Canada and Pollution Probe); and Issue No. 13, October 24, 1991, 44-8, 56-7, A32 (featuring the West Coast Environmental Law Association).

For more information on the Canadian Environmental Law Association's position, see the *Globe and Mail*, "Property-rights plan under fire"; echoed in "Debate over property right[s] entrenchment heating up," *Environment Policy & Law*, 313.

For information on the Constitutional Caucus of the Canadian Environmental Network's position, see "Property rights have no place in the charter," *Alternatives*, 25.

3.   Constitutional Caucus of the Canadian Environment Network, *ibid.*, 25. Also see *Minutes of Proceedings and Evidence, op. cit.*, Issue 12, A-4, and Issue 17, 8, 9, 36.

4.   *Minutes of Proceedings and Evidence, op. cit.*, Issue 17, 9. Also see Issue 12, A-4.

Jim Fulton, MP, also claimed that property rights would entrench the right to pollute. *Minutes of Proceedings and Evidence, op. cit.*, Issue No. 13, October 24, 1991, 26.

Similarly, Terence Wade, senior director of legal and governmental affairs for the Canadian Bar Association, argued: "I could easily argue [that] my right to build a slaughterhouse on my property in a residential neighbourhood is a property right—'I can do what I wish with my property'" (*Globe and Mail*, "Property, personal rights could collide").

5.   Canadian Environmental Law Association, "web.announcements topic 130," Announcement on "the Web" (a computer network providing electronic mail and bulletin board services), December 23, 1991.

6.   *Globe and Mail*, "Property rights seen as bargaining ploy."

7.   *Globe and Mail*, Barry Wellar, letter to the editor.

8.   This bias was noted by the Honourable Tom MacMillan, former minister of the Environment, *Minutes of Proceedings and Evidence, op. cit.*, Issue No. 6, September 26, 1991, 31, 34.

9.   *Globe and Mail*, "Canada falls behind U.S."; and the *Hamilton Spectator*, "U.S. environment laws ahead of ours."

10. The Canadian Real Estate Association, *Property Rights*, 15, 64. This study was authored by Gaylord Watkins, former chairman of the Public Interest Advocacy Centre and a lawyer with expertise in constitutional law.

On November 13, 1991, Mr. Watkins told a public forum at Toronto's St. Lawrence Centre that over the past 50 years, the U.S. Supreme Court has not struck down any remedial legislation—including environmental legislation—on the basis of property rights arguments.

Also see "Debate over property right entrenchment heating up,"

Environment Policy & Law, 313; and William Futrell, president, The Environmental Law Institute, *Minutes of Proceedings and Evidence, op. cit.*, Issue 9, 23. Futrell points out that property rights *have* undermined some state or local regulations.

11. In balancing competing interests under Section 1, the Supreme Court has adopted a proportionality test. A measure that violates a right protected by the Charter can be justified only if it is carefully designed to achieve a given objective (one that relates to pressing and substantial concerns), violates the right to the smallest degree possible, and results in effects that are in proportion to the objective (*R* v. *Oakes*, [1986] 1 S.C.R. 103 at 138-9).

12. Gaylord Watkins told the Toronto forum (*op. cit.*) that recent Charter cases demonstrate that Canadian courts are not curbing governments' rights to pass legislation. Entrenching property rights, he suggested, would not stop governments from planning and legislating. It would, however, inspire *better* planning by ensuring fair compensation to those expropriated and by forcing governments to be more accountable.

13. *Minutes of Proceedings and Evidence, op. cit.*, Issue No. 12, 19-21; Issue No. 13, 47, 56-7, A32; Issue No. 16, 43; Issue No. 17, 11, 18.

14. Mr. Melvin H. Smith, public policy consultant, the Mining Association of British Columbia (describing his "own personal inclination"), *Minutes of Proceedings and Evidence, op. cit.*, Issue No. 18, November 7, 1991, 14.

15. For more information on industry's affection for regulation, the ease with which industry captures its regulators, and the adverse effects of regulation's delaying market forces, see Owen and Braeutigam, *The Regulation Game*, 2, 9-11, 18-9, 25.

Also see Dolan and Lindsey, *Economics*, 812-834, for information on the theory of public choice. That theory posits that it is often easier for special interests to capture government than it is for voters to do so. Programs conferring benefits on a minority and dispersing costs widely among many taxpayers or consumers will often gain strong support from the former and indifference or only mild opposition from the latter.

16. Comment made to Lawrence Solomon after his speech to the Canadian Association of Petroleum Landmen, Montreal, Quebec, September 18, 1990.

Indeed, those with property rights may demand a "ransom" for the use of their land. In the United States, where gas pipeline companies do not have the right to cross Indian reserves without a tribe's permission, tribes often negotiate easement fees that are only slightly less than the costs of routing the pipelines around their lands (personal communication with TransCanada Pipelines executive, July 16, 1993). Since such fees—which reflect a legitimate "internalization" of the costs of transporting gas—cut into the pipeline companies' profits, one would expect the industry to be unenthusiastic about the property rights that make them possible.

17. Coase distinguishes between absolute and conditional rights (the latter are those that, in being exercised, may not constitute a nuisance) in "The Problem of Social Cost," 27, where he cites M. B. Cairns, The Law of Tort in Local Government, 1954, 28-32.

18. Brenner, "Nuisance Law and the Industrial Revolution," 423.

One act establishing sewage works is described in *Pride of Derby and Derbyshire Angling Association Ld. and Another* v. *British Celanese Ld. and Others*, [1953] 1 Ch. 149. The 1901 Derby Corporation Act, while establishing sewage disposal works, had specifically prohibited nuisances: "The sewage disposal works constructed . . . shall at all times hereafter be conducted so that the same shall not be a nuisance and in particular the corporation shall not allow any noxious or offensive effluvia to escape therefrom or do or permit or suffer any other act which shall be a nuisance or injurious to the health or reasonable comfort of the inhabitants of Spondon."

The Gas Clauses Act is described in *The Directors, &c., of the Hammersmith and City Railway Company* v. *G. H. Brand and Mary C. Louisa, his Wife* (1869), L. R. 4 171 at 222 (H.L.).

Similarly, an order in connection with England's Electric Lighting Act, specifying that "Nothing in this order shall exonerate the undertakers from any indictment, action, or other proceedings for nuisance in the event of any nuisance being caused by them," is discussed in *Shelfer* v. *City of London Electric Lighting Company* and

Meux's Brewery Company v. *City of London Electric Lighting Company*, [1895] 1 Ch. 287.

19. Some native leaders opposed entrenching property rights in the constitution. The Chief of the Dene Nation warned that stronger property rights could enable individuals to block land-claims negotiations (*Globe and Mail*, "Proposal threatens natives"). And Chief Bill Wilson, the political secretary of the Assembly of First Nations, worried that property rights could emasculate regulations designed to protect property (*Minutes of Proceedings and Evidence, op. cit.*, Issue No. 13, October 24, 1991, 29).

The Canadian Real Estate Association suggests that the protection afforded aboriginal rights under Section 35 of the Constitution is stronger than that which would be afforded by Charter property rights protection, since the former cannot be overridden under Sections 1 and 33 of the Charter (*op. cit.*, 38-40).

20. The Native People's Circle on Environment and Development, *Final Report*, 20.

21. *Financial Post*, "Inuit vote to change face of the Arctic" and "Agreement gives Inuit interest in mining Nunavut's resources."

22. *Globe and Mail*, "Natives win land rights in B.C."; and the *Financial Post*, "B.C. court quashes land claim ruling."

23. The Native People's Circle on Environment and Development, *op. cit.*, 20; also see 33.

Chief Bill Wilson, political secretary of the Assembly of First Nations, explained to the Standing Committee on Environment that the concept of exclusive jurisdiction over property is offensive to his people. He clarified his position as follows: "We know we own the land, we also know that the land owns us" (*Minutes of Proceedings and Evidence, op. cit.*, Issue No. 13, October 24, 1991, 29).

Rosemarie Kuptana, President of the Inuit Tapirisat of Canada, also told the Standing Committee on Environment that the Inuit feel they have collective property rights (*Minutes of Proceedings and Evidence, op. cit.*, Issue No. 8, October 3, 1991, 8).

24. *Globe and Mail*, "A dispossessed people comes home" and "A long and winding road."

25. The market demand for such policies comes in part from U.S. banks; lenders may be liable for pollution costs in the event of a default (*New York Times*, "Insuring Environmental Liabilities"). Also see Canadian Council of Ministers of the Environment, *Contaminated Site Liability Report*, 1.

26. *Financial Post*, "Mining sector wants help for abandoned sites"; personal communication with George Miller, president, Mining Association of Canada, April 7, 1994; and Canadian Council of Ministers of the Environment, *op. cit.*, 4.

Federal and provincial governments are threatening to tap business and consumers in order to establish a fund to pay for the clean-up of "orphaned" contaminated sites—sites whose owners can't be found or are unable to pay for the clean-up themselves. "It's really not fair to ask anybody to pay to clean up a mess made by someone else," admitted one bureaucrat. "But many [stakeholder] workshop participants clearly felt that given that general unfairness, the unfairness should be shared" (Canadian Council of Ministers of the Environment, "Who Should Pay?"; personal communication with Dick Stephens, Manitoba Environment, April 11, 1994).

Under the current program, the federal and provincial governments jointly fund the $250 million National Contaminated Sites Remediation Program, established in 1989 to clean up high risk orphan sites.

Contributions to the current and proposed funds bear no relationship to procedures at a specific site; they therefore provide no accountability mechanisms and no incentives for environmental responsibility.

For more information on banks' role in reducing environmental risk, see Hull, *Valuing the Environment*, 9-10.

12

No Expropriation
Without Full Compensation

The Legislature within its jurisdiction can do everything that is not naturally impossible, and is restrained by no rule human or divine. If it be that the plaintiffs acquired any rights, which I am far from finding, the Legislature had the power to take them away. The prohibition "thou shalt not steal" has no legal force upon a sovereign body. And there would be no necessity for compensation to be given. We have no such restriction upon the power of the Legislature as is found in some States.
Ontario Justice Riddell, 1908[1]

There are some things I prefer not to remember. Property law, for example, is a system of concepts better forgotten.
Bob Rae, future premier of Ontario, 1976[2]

In 1949, Peter Lewington discovered a surveyor's stake on the farm he rented north of London, Ontario. In this way he learned of Imperial Oil's plans to install a pipeline; the company, granted expropriation powers by the federal government, had not bothered to inform him that it would be digging a ditch diagonally across his property. Imperial's secrecy served as a rude introduction to pipeline companies' negligent expropriation practices, preparing the Lewingtons for what was to become a 30-year struggle for environmental responsibility and justice.[3]

Pipelines seemed to follow the Lewingtons. In 1950, the city of London drilled two wells and installed a water pipeline across a wheat field rented by the family, all without asking the Lewingtons' permission or offering compensation. In 1956, Interprovincial Pipe Line Limited (IPL) sought easements for its first oil pipeline in the area. It expropriated a 60-foot strip of land the following year, taking its pipeline through the middle of the Lewingtons' recently purchased Larigmoor Farm. IPL installed a second pipeline in 1967. And in 1975, IPL expropriated an additional 30 feet of working rights to install a larger pipeline.

Construction of the three oil pipelines wreaked havoc on Larigmoor Farm which, as Class I farmland with a pure, shallow well, had been ideally suited both for raising a dairy herd and for growing grain and forage seeds. Excavators breached the aquifer, which had supplied the well and aided underdrainage. Their machines broke and blocked drainage tiles, brought stones to the surface, mixed topsoil with infertile subsoil, and compacted the soil, further damaging crops. Weeds proliferated. Construction debris harmed cattle; open gates and damaged fences led to further livestock losses. Gaping trenches and above-ground pipes blocked the Lewingtons' access to half of their farm.

The Lewingtons were by no means IPL's only victims. Between 1950 and 1974, IPL installed over 5,000 miles of pipeline, at least two-thirds of which crossed agricultural land. Property owners suffered insults ranging from oil spills, which IPL would intentionally ignite, to the incessant noise pollution from nearby pumping stations.

IPL neither denied nor apologized for the harm it caused. Instead, it insisted that it had a right to destroy the environment. "You shall grant us a warrant," the company's senior lawyer told an expropriation judge. "We can go in and make a wasteland of these farms if we want to."

But IPL was not to have the last word. The Lewingtons and their neighbours lobbied the federal government to change the archaic law that allowed pipeline companies to indiscriminately expropriate without consulting affected landowners and without mitigating damage. They pressured the pipeline regulator, the National Energy Board, to introduce environmental guidelines and to more effectively involve the public in route selection. And in 1978, two years after having turned to the courts, they won a suit for damages caused by the most recent pipeline. From then on, pipeline companies who refused to implement environmentally sound practices would have to pay the consequences.

The law enabling IPL to expropriate with impunity was modelled on an early Railway Act, which allowed railroad companies virtually unrestricted access to private property. Governments justified such broad powers in the name of progress: railroads, facilitating resource development, would generate tremendous wealth. But it was personal rather than public wealth that frequently motivated the railroads' parliamentary promoters: many stood to gain financially as participants in the ventures.[4]

Governments continue to benefit from expropriation laws that give them and their agents freedom to act with little regard to costs or consequences. Although both federal and provincial governments have improved laws governing expropriation procedures and compensation, they continue to grant expropriation powers recklessly. According to the Law Reform Commission of Canada, Parliament "has given the power to virtually anyone that in meeting a public need might require land." At the time of the commission's 1976 report, federal legislation had conferred expropriation powers on 29 government entities and 1,234 companies, some of which were under no obligation to follow fair procedures or provide compensation to their victims.[5]

Provincial governments have been even more lavishly irresponsible. In 1968 the Ontario Royal Commission Inquiry into Civil Rights lambasted "the promiscuous manner in which the power is conferred and the methods by which it may be, and often is, exercised." Ontario then boasted 8,017 expropriating authorities, ranging from 241 agricultural societies to 3,238 cemetery owners to a cancer research foundation to 299 public library boards. Such numbers, the commission noted, indicated that "the power to expropriate land has been conferred in Ontario with reckless and unnecessary liberality." The commission criticized expropriation as a civil rights violation: "[T]he mere existence of the power to expropriate property is in itself an encroachment on the rights of an individual in the sense that the security of his rights to property has been diminished." Expropriation is only justified, it suggested, when exercised properly in proper cases—when "inescapably necessary" and truly serving the public interest.[6]

The public interest, however, fails to justify many projects for which land is expropriated—projects such as the casino for which the City of Windsor, Ontario started expropriation proceedings in 1993. Some projects—such as the never-built Pickering Airport for which the federal government expropriated homes and farms in 1973—are unnecessary.[7] Others do extraordinary environmental damage. Hydrodams may poison ecosystems, uproot communities, and destroy traditional ways of life; transmission lines may expose nearby residents to magnetic fields; landfills may contaminate ground water; and myriad other projects may ravage landscapes, tear apart communities, or devalue the property of those living nearby. The environment would clearly benefit if many of these expropriations did not occur, or if they were differently handled.

The guiding principle behind expropriation should be that those who benefit from a project should bear its costs. This principle can be traced back to the *Magna Carta*, the Great Charter of Liberties, signed in 1215, that forbade the king's agents to take a man's timber or horses without his agreement, and provided for compensation in the event of expropriation.[8] If the king benefited from a taking, the king would have to pay.

Likewise, if society benefits, society should pay. Britain's Baron Bramwell advocated such an approach in 1862:

> [T]hat law to my mind is a bad one which, for the public bene-fit, inflicts loss on an individual without compensation. . . . The public consists of all the individuals of it, and a thing is only for the public benefit when it is productive of good to those individuals on the balance of loss and gain to all. So that if all the loss and all the gain were borne and received by one individual, he on the whole would be a gainer. But whenever this is the case,—whenever a thing is for the public benefit, properly understood,—the loss to the individuals of the public who lose will bear compensation out of the gains of those who gain. . . . [U]nless the defendant's profits are enough to compensate this [the plaintiff's loss], I deny that it is for the public benefit he should do what he has done; if they are, he ought to compensate.[9]

Expropriations are fair only if, through compensation, they leave all affected parties as well off as they were before.[10] Just compensation could, for example, enable people to purchase property and rights similar to those which have been taken, and reimburse them for the costs—including the emotional costs and inconvenience—of doing so. If compensation truly leaves owners with their well-being undiminished, they will be indifferent to the expropriation.[11]

The best way to ensure that no one loses is to leave the choice in the hands of those affected—to replace expropriation with voluntary agreements. The experiences of those who have not resorted to expropriation belie the often heard argument that the expropriation process is necessary. Expropriation powers have traditionally been unavailable to real estate developers, who have successfully assembled tracts of land for large developments. Nor have Ontario's independent power producers been able to expropriate; they have instead had to negotiate easements with landowners affected by their generating stations or transmission lines. If they have failed to reach mutually acceptable agreements, so be it; their failures have signified that the projects' benefits could not support their costs.

Those with the power of expropriation threaten dire consequences for society if their privileges be lost. In many cases, however, curbing expropriation would have less dramatic effects. Undoubtedly some projects wouldn't be built, since some people's compensation demands would be prohibitively expensive, and others couldn't be bought out for any price. And some projects would be reconfigured to reduce the costs to those affected.[12] But under certain conditions, giving those affected the right to say no to proposed projects—assigning them firm property rights, in short—would not impede development.

Economist Ronald Coase won a Nobel Prize by demonstrating that if transaction costs are low—if information is readily available and bargaining is easy—the assignment of property rights will not affect resource allocation.[13] The same decisions will be made regardless of which party has the power to decide: whoever values a resource most will end up with it. Of course, transactions may be extremely costly.[14] But secure property rights help minimize transaction costs to the degree that they enhance easy and fast bargaining between buyers and sellers and help assure that agreements can be enforced.

Coase pointed out that while the assignment of rights may not affect the outcome of a proposed project, it will change the distribution of income. If a polluter holds the stronger rights, its victims will have to pay it to stop polluting. If those affected by the pollution hold the stronger rights, the polluter will have to pay them for the right to use their property.

Voluntary exchanges that do occur will reflect both the true value of the lost property and the real cost of the proposed project. Using this knowledge, the parties will make meaningful choices. Rights will be maintained or purchased by those who most value them, leading to the efficient use of resources.[15]

Expropriation need not involve the physical taking of land: it can occur when governments limit owners' uses of their lands or reduce their value through laws and regulations.[16] As with a traditional taking, those benefiting from a regulation whose effect is to expropriate should bear its costs; compensation should leave the regulated party as well off as it would have otherwise been.

Regulations serving the public interest may well be justified. But the fact that the public interest justifies an expropriation should not affect the requirement for compensation. It is critical to distinguish between the public *interest* and the public's *right*: although the public has an interest in many things, it should have a right to expropriate private property only if it pays for it.[17]

Many expropriative regulations are specifically designed to protect the environment. Ontario's 1992 wetlands policy restricted development on designated wetlands and "buffer" lands adjacent to them. Land so designated lost up to 90 per cent of its value, costing provincial landowners hundreds of millions of dollars. Not surprisingly, many property owners objected that the policy expropriated their property rights, forcing them to bear the costs and burdens of achieving a goal that benefited all of society. While not disputing wetlands' importance, they objected to footing the bill to save them.[18]

The Ontario government has also designated thousands of public and private properties as Areas of Natural and Scientific Interest, or ANSIs. Their purpose? To encourage the protection of non-park lands, including eight million acres of privately held property. One landowners' association called the designation "expropriation by stealth and deception"—an arbitrary transfer of control from private property owners to the state without consent or compensation.[19]

The Ministry of Natural Resources first used the ANSI designation in 1990 to prevent property owners from developing their land. John and Sylvia Richards owned 150 acres of land fronting Matchedash Lake, one of Southern Ontario's few remaining wilderness lakes and a designated ANSI. They had, according to MNR, been "outstanding custodians" of the environment for 25 years; on their land could be found numerous rare species of Atlantic coastal plain flora. In the late 1980s they decided to sever six lots for their children and grandchildren. The township amended its official plan and rezoned the area in order to allow the severance. But MNR, wanting to preserve the significant plant species on the Richards' shoreline, opposed any further development; it appealed to the Ontario Municipal Board. The OMB, trying to compromise between the public interest and private property rights, consented to the severing of just two lots, which MNR agreed would not adversely affect the ANSI. Its decision created the strictest cottage development requirements in the province.[20]

Numerous other acts and regulations restrict development in environmentally sensitive areas, violating people's common law property rights to use their property as they wish as long as that use does not violate others' property rights. As Ontario Chief Justice McRuer explained in 1951, "Everyone has a right to use his own property in any way that he may see fit, so long as he does nothing that will be a legal nuisance to his neighbours. That is a common law right. It is a question of liberty that is to be jealously guarded by the Courts, and while one's rights may be affected by proper legislative action, until that is done, one's personal common law rights are to be strictly guarded."[21]

The United States Supreme Court has recognized that restrictive land-use regulations may, due to their expropriative nature, demand compensation. In a series of decisions between 1987 and 1994, the court required governments to pay compensation for "regulatory takings" that deprived landowners of all economically beneficial use of their land, and insisted on a rough proportionality between the regulation and the restricted activity.[22] Canadian courts, unencumbered by a constitutional requirement that expropriation be compensated, have not dealt with the issue to the same extent. Nevertheless, providing compensation has become a legal and legislative convention. Courts have maintained that unless explicitly stated therein, laws are presumed not to condone expropriation without compensation.[23] They have also found that expropriation by regulation can occur and can require compensation.[24]

Clearly not all regulations limiting land use are takings, and not all should be compensated. Regulations benefiting the regulated don't require monetary compensation; the benefits conferred provide compensation in kind, making the regulation a "giving" as well as a taking.[25] Nor should regulations that prevent harm to others be considered takings; since people don't have the right to harm others, government action cannot "take" it from them. Environmental regulations don't take away a polluter's right to pollute when the polluter doesn't have that right in the first place. Likewise, regulations protecting commonly held (or, in some provinces, publicly owned) animals, which no one has the right to destroy, don't constitute takings.[26] On the other hand, government actions that diminish others' rights, or that transfer control of property from private to public hands, do amount to expropriation, and require compensation.

Ironically, expropriation by regulation is generally not the best way to preserve the environment, and is often counterproductive. Just as voluntary agreements are often superior to traditional expropriation, non-coercive schemes appealing either to landowners' consciences or to their pocketbooks have often proven more successful than regulations.[27] Increasing interest in private stewardship has accompanied the public's growing concern about the environment. Property owners hunger for information on how to sustainably manage their lands. According to the Muskoka Heritage Foundation, which promotes stewardship of private lands in south-central Ontario, most landowners who have the necessary information and skills will "do the right thing": they will preserve their natural lands and enhance habitat.[28] Other organizations' experiences confirm that as landowners become aware of the significance of their natural areas many will voluntarily protect them.[29]

Complementing those who protect the environment out of the goodness of their hearts are the myriad others who conserve their lands and resources for economic gain. Property owners are learning that it often pays to create habitat or protect wildlife. Canadian Pacific Resorts and Hotels understands that conservation can be good for the bottom line. Its Kenauk fish and game reserve covers 65,000 acres of hardwood forests and over 70 lakes near Montebello, Quebec. The reserve has been off limits to the general public for centuries: first held by the Bishop of New France in the seventeenth century, it was purchased in 1801 by the Papineau family, who sold it to investors—including CP—in 1929. CP now manages the property for both forestry and tourism. By limiting clearcuts to 100-foot strips in restricted areas, it has succeeded in both retaining an unspoiled beauty and maintaining an impressive density and variety of wildlife. People come from around the world to enjoy the unspoiled wilderness, paying handsomely to hunt or fish on lakes they share with no other guests. Tourism revenues make up for reduced forestry profits, leaving CP with a better overall return than it would realize from unrestrained forestry alone.[30]

In 1991, Abitibi Price started experimenting with managing its privately held forests to enhance conservation and recreation. On the theory that conservation brings financial rewards, the company initiated reforms—ranging from trash removal to more restrained logging practices—on its half-million acres near Thunder Bay, Ontario. Three years later the company signed its first agreement with a tourist outfitter to turn one block of land into a money-making park; it also developed plans to lease cottage lots around remote lakes. "We can market our products—our forests and lakes—better and get more value from them," explained Abitibi's Forestry Systems Supervisor. "We can supply not just sawmills but *lots* of users," he went on, noting that that makes sense financially. "And we're in the business of making money."[31]

If landowners do not independently realize the economic advantages of conservation, environmental groups can intervene, increasing incentives to conserve. Defenders of Wildlife works to increase wolf populations in the American Northwest through programs that shift economic responsibility away from the ranchers who suffer wolf-related damage and toward the people who seek wolf restoration. To overcome ranchers' reluctance to protect animals that may kill their livestock, the environmental group began in 1987 to compensate them for any losses caused by wolves. During the following seven years, it paid over $16,000 to 15 ranchers, effectively neutralizing their opposition to wolves. In 1993, the group decided not just to reduce landowners' liability but to turn what were once liabilities into assets: it offered $5,000 to landowners who allowed wild wolves to rear pup litters on their property. It paid out its inaugural reward in 1994, for the first litter raised in the area in over 30 years.[32]

When all else fails, environmental groups can lease or purchase lands or waters that they wish to preserve. They can outbid their competition if the resources they want to protect are worth more to them than to others. Such is often the case. When other resource users can find satisfactory substitutes for unique environmental tracts, they will find it cheaper to turn elsewhere than to engage in a bidding war with conservationists. Since many industries have grown accustomed to having access to virtually free resources, they may be unable to match even the modest bids of those hoping to preserve the resource.[33]

Some conservation groups, particularly in the United States, purchase "negative covenants"—promises to neighbours binding future as well as current owners—that restrict uses of environmentally important properties. Covenants may include promises to refrain from developing, polluting, or otherwise altering sites. Often, a conservation organization purchases a property, places a covenant on it, and then resells it, confident that future uses will not threaten the environment. Conservation groups also purchase easements that allow them to cross others' properties or to use them in specific ways, such as for hiking.[34]

Land trusts are common in both Europe and the United States. The National Trust, established in 1895 and now supported by more than two million members, is Great Britain's largest private landowner. It owns over 580,000 acres, holds conservation covenants on another 78,000 acres, and has protected 535 miles of coastline from development.[35] A non-government trust owns and manages the Netherlands' largest national park. The United States probably boasts over 1000 trusts.[36]

Trusts can protect water as well as land. Conservation groups regularly buy water rights in the American West, where all too often fisheries, wetlands, and recreational water uses have been compromised by the megaprojects of water bureaucracies and by agricultural and urban users who have demanded more and more water. Trusts have learned that there is no surer way to restore a river's flow than to purchase or lease rights from those who would otherwise remove water from the river. Their efforts have paid off: voluntary transactions between conservationists and water rights holders have provided more water for conservation than have government regulations.[37]

American environmental groups increasingly use the market to protect air quality as well. In 1993, environmentalists joined electric utilities in bidding at the Chicago Board of Trade's first auction of sulphur dioxide pollution permits. In acquiring the rights to emit a specific amount of sulphur dioxide and retiring them unused, they kept them out of the hands of utilities and reduced a primary cause of acid rain.[38]

In Canada, where environmentalists have traditionally relied more on government than on private initiative, private sector conservation is less well established. However, land trusts and other private conservation organizations have grown increasingly important in recent decades, shifting at least some of the costs of conservation to those who most value it.[39]

Since 1962, the Nature Conservancy of Canada has protected more than 115,000 acres of wilderness in 504 nature preserves. The organization purchases threatened natural areas, since, as their executive director explained, "there is no more direct way to protect land than to buy it." Many enthusiastically support this free-market approach to preserving biological diversity: the organization grew exponentially in the early 1990s, when its membership increased nine-fold (to 20,000) and when it raised more money than it had over the course of the previous three decades combined.[40]

Ducks Unlimited—a private conservation organization boasting 700,000 supporters worldwide—has developed or protected over 17 million acres of waterfowl habitat in Canada. The organization often leases or purchases important habitats. Several of its Canadian programs provide technical and financial assistance to farmers who agree to restore waterfowl habitat on their lands. Behind the programs is the organization's belief that farmers should not have to foot the bill for conservation that benefits duck hunters: they are compensated not only for their outlays but also for any agricultural losses incurred.[41]

There is no reason governments can't behave in the same way. Sometimes, in fact, they do. Between 1970 and 1990, Saskatchewan's Fish and Wildlife Development Fund used hunting and trapping licence revenues to purchase 100,000 acres of wildlife habitat; in 1990, Saskatchewan Parks and Renewable Resources also leased 14,000 acres of waterfowl habitat.[42] And Ontario's Minister of Agriculture announced in 1994 that the government would pay fruit farmers to resist development pressures on the Niagara Peninsula. To protect 2,000 acres of unique farmland, the province set aside $18.75 million to purchase covenants that would limit any non-farm uses by current or future owners. The program was strictly voluntary: only farmers who believed they would profit would participate.[43]

Curbing traditional and regulatory expropriation and providing just compensation for that which does occur will protect both property rights and the environment. But even secure property rights will enable people to protect only that which they own outright. It is therefore necessary to broaden property rights to cover resources held in trust—to assign them to some of the resources that now lie in government hands.

Notes

1. Mr. Justice Riddell, Ontario Court of Appeal, *Florence Mining Co. Ltd.* v. *Cobalt Lake Mining Co. Ltd.* (1908), 18 O.L.R. 275 at 279 (C.A.).

2. *Financial Post Magazine*, April 1994.

3. For the following section I have relied solely on Lewington, *No Right of Way*.

4. Lewington, *ibid.*, 43 and 54-5, citing the Law Reform Commission of Canada's (the Hartt Commission's) report on expropriation.

5. Law Reform Commission of Canada, *Report on Expropriation*, 5-8. The Commission listed a number of expropriators in *Working Paper 9: Expropriation*, 78-9.

6. Ontario Royal Commission Inquiry into Civil Rights, *Report Number One*, Volume Three, 960-80.
    Note that the commissioner, the Honourable James McRuer, penned the admirable KVP decision discussed in Chapter Four.

7. In *Paper Juggernaut*, Stewart describes the deeply flawed decision-making process that led the government to turn a thriving community into a 35,000-acre wasteland.

8. *Magna Carta*, Chapters 28, 30, 31, 39, 52. Also see J. C. Holt, *Magna Carta*, 1, 4, 16, 297, 300, 327, 332.

9. Baron Bramwell, *Bamford* v. *Turnley* (1862), 3 B. & S. 66, 122 E.R. 27 at 33.

10. Economists call this the Pareto criterion. Projects are justified as efficient if at least one person is made better off and no one is made worse off. A situation is Pareto-optimal when it is not possible to reallocate resources without making someone worse off.

11. Market value, the conventional determiner of compensation, understates the value to the owner of the expropriated property. As a consequence, "nearly all public acquisition policies leave property owners with their well-being diminished" and cause a "perverse shifting

of losses away from the beneficiaries of the community scheme to individual owners" (Knetsch, *Property Rights and Compensation*, 46, 53). Also see Knetsch and Borcherding, "Expropriation of Private Property and the Basis for Compensation."

The only time most real estate owners can be said to value their property at market prices is when they decide to sell it. At any other time they value their property at higher than market prices, either because of its use value, their emotional attachment to it, or the transactions costs associated with selling it.

12. U.S. courts have recently ruled that electric utilities must compensate people for the economic impacts of their transmission lines, including reductions in property values resulting from "cancerphobia"—the real or perceived health risks associated with electric and magnetic fields (EMF). In response to this reassignment of property rights from utilities to those they affect, many utilities are rerouting and reconfiguring their lines to reduce EMF levels (*Wall Street Journal*, "Power Lines Short-Circuit Sales, Homeowners Claim").

13. Coase, "The Problem of Social Cost."

14. Transactions costs may rise with the number of parties involved. Negotiating with large numbers increases the "holdout" problem—the risk that one or several people will hold out for higher prices and wreck a deal.

Ready availability of alternatives mitigates the holdout problem. Those avariciously holding out for large sums are restrained by the costs of the alternatives. If the holdouts' prices exceed those costs, the negotiator simply looks elsewhere. Thus, those who hold out simply for money have an incentive to keep their demands modest.

Some property owners, in contrast, hold out for higher prices because they truly place a higher value on their property. Their personal valuations should be respected and treated like any other costs—i.e., avoided if possible and paid if unavoidable.

15. For more information regarding the effects of limiting expropriation

and requiring full compensation for those that do occur see Pollot, *Grand Theft and Petit Larceny*, xxix, xxxiii, 120.

16. For more information on expropriation by regulation see Epstein, *Takings*. Epstein suggests that "*All* regulations, *all* taxes, and *all* modifications of liability rules are takings of private property prima facie compensable by the state" (95).

17. For more on the distinction between the public interest and public rights, see Pollot, *op. cit.*, xxii, 61, 64, 80, 81, 99; and Bromley, *Environment and Economy*, 179.

18. *Valley Farmers Forum*, "Wetland designation devaluates property 90%" and "New wetlands regulations cuts off farmer's retirement plan."
    The estimated costs of hundreds of millions are based on projected losses of $17 million in the Ottawa-Carlton region alone.

19. *Markdale Standard*, "GADG survey finds evidence of massive government land grab."

20. *Ministry of Natural Resources* v. *Township of Matchedash Land Division Committee* (1990), 26 OMBR 31.

21. *Re Bridgman and the City of Toronto et al.*, [1951] O.R. 489 at 496.

22. The fifth amendment of the U.S. Constitution prohibits the government from taking private property for public use without paying its owners just compensation. In the 1980s, in a series of decisions including *Keystone Bituminous Coal Assn* v. *DeBenedictis*, *Nollan* v. *California Coastal Commission*, and *First English Lutheran Church* v. *County of Los Angeles*, the U.S. Supreme Court began to protect individuals from regulatory takings. In a 1992 case, *Lucas* v. *South Carolina Coastal Council*, the court held that the government must compensate an owner whom it has deprived of all economically beneficial and productive use of his land unless those uses would constitute nuisances. In 1994, the court found in *Dolan* v. *City of Tigard*

that a city could not condition the grant of a building permit on the surrender of private property for public use without showing that the property owner's sacrifice was roughly proportional to the harm his proposed development might cause.

For more information on recent U.S. court decisions, see Pollot, *op. cit.*; *Wall Street Journal*, "Private Property Rights vs. Public Works" and "Takings Cases Don't Always Favor Takers"; *New York Times*, "Excerpts From Court Ruling Limiting Governments' Power Over Property."

23. In *Manitoba Fisheries Ltd.* v. *The Queen*, the Supreme court cited Lord Radcliffe's 1960 decision in *Belfast Corporation* v. *O.D. Cars Ltd.*: "[T]here would be the general principle, accepted by the legislature and scrupulously defended by the courts, that the title to property or the enjoyment of its possession was not to be compulsorily acquired from a subject unless full compensation was afforded in its place." [1979] 1 S.C.R. 101 at 109-10.

The Supreme Court has several times approvingly cited the House of Lords' 1920 decision in *Attorney-General* v. *De Keyser's Royal Hotel Ltd.*, which established that "The recognized rule for the construction of statutes is that, unless the words of the statute clearly so demand, a statute is not to be construed so as to take away the property of a subject without compensation." See *Manitoba Fisheries Ltd.* v. *The Queen* at 109 and *The Queen* v. *Tener*, [1985] 1 S.C.R. 533 at 559.

The Honourable James McRuer, of the Royal Commission Inquiry into Civil Rights, cited the Judicial Committee of the Privy Council's 1918 decision in *Minister of Railways* v. *Simmer etc. Mines Ltd.* that "general or ambiguous words should not be used to take away legitimate and valuable rights from the subject without compensation," *op. cit.*, 965.

24. In *The Queen* v. *Tener (ibid.)*, the Supreme Court of Canada found that Tener was entitled to compensation for what amounted to expropriation, even though a formal expropriation mechanism had not been invoked. The Teners owned 16 mineral claims on land that had become part of a provincial park; B.C. regulations prevented them from

obtaining park use permits necessary to work their claims. As Madam Justice Wilson explained, "While the grant or refusal of a licence or permit may constitute mere regulation in some instances, it cannot be viewed as mere regulation when it has the effect of defeating the respondents' entire interest in the land. Without access the respondents cannot enjoy the mineral claims granted to them in the only way they can be enjoyed, namely by the exploitation of the minerals. . . . [T]he respondents now have no access to their claims, no ability to develop and realize on them and no ability to sell them to anyone else. They are effectively beyond their reach. They are worthless" (550-1).

25. Regulations limiting land uses but not requiring compensation might include some noise restrictions, zoning requirements, fire regulations (such as those requiring a minimum distance between homes), or other safety regulations (such as rules restricting digging around gas mains).

26. In most provinces, it is the province that owns wildlife. In Ontario, no one owns wildlife, although the provincial government manages it. In contrast, property owners do own the plants on their property. (Personal communication with Jim MacLean, director, Wildlife Policy Branch, Ministry of Natural Resources, May 20, 1994.)

Property rights should not include the right to destroy biological diversity any more than they include the right to pollute commonly held waters. Wildlife users, managers and owners would benefit from the development of a reasonable-use theory similar to that governing water use under a riparian rights regime.

27. Some environmental regulations limiting land use have actually proven to be disincentives to conservation. For information on how the U.S. Endangered Species Act has prompted landowners to destroy both wildlife and habitat in anticipation that a species may be listed as endangered and discovered on their land, see Fisher and Hudson, *Building Economic Incentives Into the Endangered Species Act*, 19, 38, 74, 96, 97.

28. Letter from Donald Gordon, administrator, spring 1993.

29. Reid, *Bringing Trust to Ontario*, 6.

30. Personal communication with Bill Nowell, manager of recreation and fisheries, May 18, 1994; personal communication with R. A. Payne, general manager, May 5, 1994; Kenauk press kit; and the *Globe and Mail*, "Wilderness by the Chateau."

31. Personal communication with Volker Kromm, forestry systems supervisor, May 18, 1994; information on Abitibi's program also obtained from personal communication with Malcolm Squires, divisional forester, May 16, 1994.

32. *Wall Street Journal*, "Wolves in the Marketplace"; and personal communication with Hank Fisher, Defenders of Wildlife's Northern Rockies representative, May 5, 1994.

33. Stroup and Shaw, "The Free Market and the Environment," 41.

34. Findlay and Hillyer, *Here Today, Here Tomorrow*.
Conservation easements are less common in Canada than in the U.S. Laws in Ontario, British Columbia, and Prince Edward Island authorize such easements to some degree, and other provinces are considering following suit (Hilts and Mitchell, "Bucking the Free Market Economy," 21).

35. The National Trust, "Facts and Figures." Also see the Trust's "Annual Report, 1992" and "The National Trust: An Introduction," 1993.

36. Hilts and Mitchell, *op. cit.*, 16. The authors' 1993 estimate of the number of U.S. land trusts considerably exceeds Reid's 1988 estimate of 550 (*op. cit.*, 31). They note a rapid growth in the formation of land trusts between 1988 and 1993.

37. Moore, "Water: The Rights and Wrongs of U.S. Policy," 10; and Smith, "Water Reallocation Through Market Transactions."

38. *Wall Street Journal*, "Environmentalists Vie for Right to Pollute."

39. Hilts and Mitchell, *op. cit.*, 16 ff.

40. Letter from John Eisenhauer, April 1993; The Nature Conservancy of Canada, "Profile"; and personal communication with Sherry Armstrong, Nature Conservancy communications, May 5, 1994.
    In addition to acquiring land for the above-noted preserves, the Nature Conservancy has helped acquire almost 2 million acres of national park land. The organization negotiated the 1993 donation and sale of six resource companies' mineral permits to 670,000 hectares of Yukon land. The companies, inhibited by the local Gwichin community's opposition to mineral exploration on their traditional lands, had long been unable to use their permits. But the federal government could put the lands to "work" immediately: it created Vuntut National Park and the Old Crow Flats Special Management Area. The protected area covers 1.3 million hectares, including habitat for one of the world's largest Porcupine caribou herds and wetlands that support 300,000 nesting—and even greater numbers of staging—waterfowl (*Globe and Mail*, "Six resource firms donate, sell mineral rights for park"; "Yukon land donated," *Canadian Geographic*, 15; and The Nature Conservancy of Canada, "Unrivalled partnership protected outstanding Yukon Lands").

    Land donations supplement the Conservancy's purchases. Shell Canada's 1992 gift of 8,903 undeveloped hectares in southern British Columbia constituted the largest land donation in Canadian history. Shell benefited along with the newly protected elk, bighorn sheep, moose, deer and grizzlies: in addition to buying favourable publicity, the company won a sizable tax credit for the gift (*Globe and Mail*, "Shell donates land: Nature group gets spectacular tract"; and The Nature Conservancy of Canada, "Mount Broadwood Heritage Conservation Area: the largest donation of land in Canadian history").

41. Ducks Unlimited brochures, "Prairie Care: A Conservation Partners Program" and "Ontario Land CARE"; and Ducks Unlimited Canada, 1990 and 1992 Annual Reports.

42. Saskatchewan Parks and Renewable Resources, *Fish & Wildlife Development Fund Activities 1989-1990*, 2, 4.

43. Ontario Ministry of Agriculture, Food and Rural Affairs, "Buchanan announces Niagara tender fruit lands program"; and Elmer Buchanan, Minister of Agriculture, Food and Rural Affairs, speech introducing the program, May 7, 1994.

13

The Gospel According to St. John

The good shepherd giveth his life for the sheep.

But he that is an hireling, and not the shepherd, whose own the sheep are not, seeth the wolf coming, and leaveth the sheep, and fleeth: and the wolf catcheth them, and scattereth the sheep.

The hireling fleeth, because he is an hireling, and careth not for the sheep.

St. John the Divine[1]

In the 1950s, the waters of the River Derwent, in north-central England, flowed unpolluted until they reached the Borough of Derby's two sewer outfalls—one that occasionally released raw sewage and another that routinely discharged inadequately treated effluent from the local sewage treatment works. The river then passed through land owned by British Celanese Ld., whose effluent also polluted and warmed it. Downstream, discharge from the British Electricity Authority's power station further increased the river's temperature.

Because the changes in water quality and temperature killed the river's fish and their food supply, an anglers' club which owned a fishery in the Derwent and an earl who owned land along the river took the upstream polluters to court. The court found all three defendants guilty of nuisance and issued an injunction forbidding them from altering the river's quality or temperature or interfering with the plaintiffs' enjoyment of their fishing rights. The court gave the defendants two years to comply with the injunction.[2]

The Borough of Derby appealed to the court to substitute damages for the injunction. It could not simply rebuild its sewage system at will, it argued; it needed a licence, and, in order to borrow money, the consent of the Minister of Local Government and Planning.

But an injunction, one judge who upheld the lower court ruling countered, was not discretionary: "Anyone who creates an actionable nuisance is a wrongdoer, and the court will *prima facie* restrain him from persisting in his activities." Damages, his colleague added, would be "a wholly inadequate remedy" since the angling club had "not been incorporated in order to fish for monthly sums." An injunction was the best way to meet the fishery owners' demand for clean water, added another judge: "The power of the courts to issue an injunction for nuisance has proved itself to be the best method so far devised of securing the cleanliness of our rivers."[3]

The above scenario has been played out time and again in Britain, where virtually all fisheries are in private hands.[4] There, owners have the legal tools to protect their assets. They also have strong economic incentives to do so. Individuals, fishing clubs, country inns, tourist operators, and other businesses command good prices for the use of their fisheries; the sale of fishing rights also attracts competitive bids. This combination of tools and incentives has succeeded in protecting British rivers, whose salmon and trout populations put their Canadian counterparts to shame.[5]

Many who own or lease threatened fisheries have sought the assistance of the Anglers' Co-operative Association which, through common law court cases, obtains both injunctions to clean up rivers and damages to compensate for losses. The Anglers' Association has argued hundreds of cases since its founding in 1948; it has lost only two.[6] The association has worked on an endless variety of water pollution and withdrawal cases. In the early 1990s its targets included a sewage treatment plant whose phosphate-laced effluent killed fish in a Welsh lake, a water company applying for permission to withdraw water from small streams near Canterbury, and a trout-farm owner who allowed rainbows to escape into a river inhabited by brown trout.[7]

The Anglers' Association stresses that ownership is essential in establishing rights to a healthy fishery. It warns its members, "It must therefore be understood that in case of pollution you cannot bring an action in the Courts unless you: (a) Own the water you fish or (b) Have a legal lease of the water you fish, or an exclusive right to the fishing."[8] Ownership empowers people; legally enforceable property rights invest owners with the authority—and the tools—to protect the fisheries and the waters they control.

One need not look as far as England for models of private ownership of inland fisheries. New Brunswick's riparians enjoy fishing rights to some stretches of rivers. In Quebec, private clubs hold fishing rights on a number of salmon rivers. And before European settlement of North America, aboriginal families frequently established fishing rights in defined geographical areas. The Pacific Coast Kwakiutl Indians, for example, assigned exclusive territorial fishing rights to kinship groups; some held private rights to fish over designated halibut banks, while others owned entire salmon streams.[9]

Ownership doesn't only facilitate stewardship; in a system of secure property rights, ownership also *promotes* stewardship. Like St. John's shepherd, fisheries' owners tend to behave more responsibly than their managers. And although they may not lay down their lives to protect their fish, they have proven far more reliable than their non-propertied counterparts. Individual, corporate, or community owners have incentives to maximize their resources' value, taking into account not just their current worth but their future value as well. As one economist pointed out, "you don't have to be an economist to know that it doesn't pay to kill the goose that lays the golden egg."[10] Investment, conservation, and efficient use are in owners' self-interest; it is they who reap the rewards.[11]

Self-interest likewise motivates the politicians and bureaucrats who are paid to manage common resources. But for them, personal gain often results not from protecting resources but from increasing their budgets, putting people to work, and ensuring reelection—incentives, as illustrated earlier, that have ravaged our forests.

The guardian of Canada's fisheries—the federal government—has likewise overseen that resource's destruction. It has allowed pollution to devastate the Great Lakes' once vigorous commercial fisheries. It has permitted hydroelectric dams to destroy valuable river habitats. Communities, firms and individuals who relied on—but did not own—these fisheries have been powerless to save them.

Nowhere is the government's failure to protect fisheries more evident than on Canada's East Coast. Major federal involvement there began in the 1970s in response to a series of crises in the fishing industry. The government, in keeping with international agreements, extended its jurisdiction to 200 miles from the shore and introduced a number of regulations and licensing schemes.[12]

According to the 1982 Task Force on the Atlantic Fisheries, in the late 1970s "[a]n attitude quickly developed that any financial problem in the industry could be solved by a greater volume of production."[13] The government's self-described "expansionist development philosophy"[14] enabled the fishing industry to increase while catches steadily decreased. More and larger boats pursued fewer and fewer fish, until several fisheries—most notably northern cod, haddock and other groundfish—collapsed.[15]

While the fish disaster brewed, keeping people employed dominated the government's concerns. Managers based catch limits not just on what they thought the fishery could bear but also on the economic needs of fishing communities.[16] A 1982 report noted the consideration of "community dependence" in resource allocation decisions and included maximizing employment as a policy objective.[17] Such concerns prompted ongoing assistance—including construction and insurance subsidies, tax breaks, loan guarantees, and unemployment insurance benefits—for fishermen, boat owners and processors.[18] Essentially, the government was paying people to destroy a valuable resource by enabling them to enter and stay in an industry that couldn't support them; it was encouraging ecologically destructive and economically inefficient expansion.

Not surprisingly, such perverse policies had disastrous effects. The collapse of the cod fishery led in 1992 to a moratorium, expanded the following year and expected to last throughout the decade, that left 30,000 fishermen and plant workers without jobs. The loss of the cod, worth $700 million to the Newfoundland fishery just three years earlier, devastated an entire society and left the government trying to wean people from an industry on which it had so long encouraged dependence.[19]

Historically, property rights have evolved in response to growing demand, be it for agricultural land, minerals, timber or fish. As long as there has been plenty to spare, there has been no need for property rights. As resources have grown scarce (and increasingly valuable), property rights have become needed and resource users have become more willing to bear the costs of establishing and enforcing them.[20]

In the seventeenth century, aboriginal people in what is now Quebec and Labrador owned neither land nor wildlife, both of which were plentiful. As the development of the commercial fur trade increased fur's scarcity and value, it became economic to husband fur-bearing animals. Husbandry depended in part on being able to prevent others from hunting the animals; thus, private property rights in land developed. By the early eighteenth century, Algonquin and Iroquois families had developed exclusive hunting and trapping territories; they practised conservation and retaliated against trespassers.[21]

Increasing scarcity invites the establishment of long-term, tradable property rights in Canada's fisheries.[22] A number of countries have assigned property rights to inland and ocean fisheries. In some of the most successful ocean fisheries cases, the rights have taken the form of individual transferable quotas (ITQs) that allocate to individual fishermen a percentage of a total allowable catch. ITQs provide a number of incentives to use resources efficiently. Confident that their rights to fish are secure, fishermen need not waste money building bigger boats and equipping them with more advanced gear in a race to catch fish. And those who are unable to use their quotas efficiently can sell them to others who can put them to better use. ITQs also promote conservation. With valuable assets tied up in their property rights to a percentage of the catch, fishermen have an economic interest in conserving fish stocks and in keeping out interlopers: it is they who will capture the benefits of such activities.

In New Zealand, which introduced ITQs in the mid-1980s, the system now governs 32 different fisheries. More efficient fishermen have bought out their less efficient counterparts, eliminating the excess capacity that had previously characterized the fleet. And with economic incentives to preserve and enhance the fishery, quota holders are financing research, exploration, enhancement, and policing measures.[23]

Ideally, government-regulated ITQ regimes for harvesting fish are just one stage in the evolution of private ownership of the fisheries. Although governments frequently set total allowable catches, ITQ systems can become completely self-regulating, with an association of all ITQ holders setting catches and taking on other management responsibilities. Such a shift in responsibility occurred in several New Zealand fisheries in the early 1990s.[24] A further evolution could entail outright ownership of fisheries, removing owners' obligation to utilize their resources exclusively as fisheries when conservation, tourism or other uses proved more valuable.

Technological advances, by facilitating the enforcement of property rights, spur their development. In the mid-nineteenth century, cattlemen in the American West didn't have sufficient stone or timber to fence the vast acres of prairie shortgrass required for cattle. Initially, there was plenty of land to go around. But as land grew scarcer and more valuable, it became increasingly important to define and enforce property rights. Brand registries were established and fine-tuned. Numerous attempts were made to restrict entry onto land that had previously been held in common. Governments passed laws to restrict grazing on public lands. But it wasn't until the 1870s, when barbed wire became available, that private landowners could start fencing their land and effectively enforcing their property rights. Sales of barbed wire leapt from 10 thousand to 8.5 million pounds between 1874 and 1880.[25]

As increasing scarcity makes the establishment of property rights in the fisheries more pressing, technological developments will make their enforcement increasingly feasible. Satellite technology is a case in point. Assigning property rights to ocean fisheries has traditionally been hindered by the difficulty of keeping out trespassers. Satellites make "fencing" the ocean possible. In the United States, NASA has experimented in policing the oceans with satellites that can identify boats by the unique "fingerprints" in their exhaust.[26] Similar technology may likewise enable owners to monitor their fishing zones, and to enforce their property rights in fisheries.[27]

Broader property rights in fisheries, as in other resources, would be a two-edged sword. Inevitably, some owners would—either through error or ignorance—deplete their stocks.[28] As long as their activities did not violate others' property rights, the law would permit them. But with the removal of governments' perverse incentives to harvest resources uneconomically, the destruction of private property would occur less frequently. That which did occur would be modest compared to the wholesale environmental devastation wrought directly or abetted by governments.

What is true for fisheries is equally true for many other resources: secure, enforceable property rights would empower citizens or communities to protect forests, waters and minerals. With the limits of today's technology, property rights cannot be assigned to all resources; the atmosphere, for example, remains "unfence-able." While property rights cannot be assigned to the atmosphere, however, they can be assigned to the atmosphere's assimilative capacity, or to its capacity to absorb wastes. Under a system of tradable emissions permits—such as that used to control sulphur dioxide emissions in the United States—governments establish a cap on allowable emissions in a particular airshed and then allocate shares of that cap to polluters. Polluters who reduce their emissions may sell their excess allocations to others, including environmental groups wishing to retire them in order to bring emissions below the government cap.[29]

Whenever property rights cannot be clearly assigned, they will fail as tools for environmental protection and second-best measures must be relied upon. In such cases, attempts to compensate through government regulations or other mechanisms are essential. But the more precisely property rights can be defined, and the greater the extent to which they are assigned to specific groups and individuals, the better the environment will fare. If given the proper tools, owners will protect their resources. As observed more than two centuries ago by the celebrated English author on agriculture, politics and economics, Arthur Young, "Give a man the secure possession of bleak rock, and he will turn it into a garden; give him nine years lease of a garden, and he will convert it to a desert. . . . The magic of property turns sand into gold."[30]

Notes

1.   The Gospel According to St. John, *The Holy Bible*, King James Version, Chapter 10, verses 11-13.

2.   *Pride of Derby and Derbyshire Angling Association Ld. and Another* v. *British Celanese Ld. and Others*, [1953] 1 Ch. 149.

3.   *Ibid.* at 194, 181, and 192 respectively.

4.   In Britain, only the fisheries in public reservoirs are not privately owned (Dales, *Pollution, Property & Prices*, 68, citing Douglas Clark, "Fisheries and Wildlife Values in Pollution").

5. Peter Pearse notes that in England's *Country Life* magazine, the owners of fishing rights advertise fishing opportunities (personal communication, September 21, 1994). According to Clark, fisheries change hands at high prices (cited by Dales, *ibid.*, 68).

Clark, *ibid.*, maintains that Britain's fine game fisheries are superior to those in any accessible part of Canada, while Pearse notes that some Canadian sportfishermen search out Britain's salmon and trout ("Property Rights and the Development of Natural Resource Policies in Canada," 315).

6. Personal communication with Anglers' Co-operative Association staffer, June 16, 1994. The ACA had 30 cases underway at the time.

According to Clark, the ACA investigated almost 700 pollution cases in its first 19 years (cited by Dales, *op. cit.*, 68).

7. Anglers' Co-operative Association, *ACA Review*.

8. Anglers' Co-operative Association, "What to do in case of pollution."

9. Pearse, "Property Rights and the Development of Natural Resource Policies in Canada," 315; Pearse, *Rising to the Challenge*, 47, 62, 136; Anderson and Leal, *Free Market Environmentalism*, 128; Higgs, "Legally Induced Technical Regress in the Washington Salmon Fishery"; and Johnsen, "The Formation and Protection of Property Rights Among the Southern Kwakiutl Indians."

10. Dales, *op. cit.*, 64.

11. In Aristotle's words, "what is common to many is taken least care of; for all men regard more what is their own than what others share with them in" (*A Treatise on Government*, Book 2, 29).

For more information on the ways in which property ownership promotes good stewardship see Bromley, *Environment and Economy*, 23-8, 148-9; Pearse, *op. cit.*; Demsetz, "Toward a Theory of Property Rights," 355-6; and Fox, "The Pricing of Environmental Goods: A

Praxeological Critique of Contingent Valuation," "Ownership and Stewardship of Natural Resources," and "Free Market Environmentalism."

For information on the adverse economic and environmental consequences of the absence of property rights in resources see Hardin, "The Tragedy of the Commons," Sweeney et al., "Market Failure, the Common-Pool Problem, and Ocean Resource Exploitation," and Gordon, "The Economic Theory of a Common-Property Resource."

12. For information on the crisis besetting the Atlantic fisheries and the introduction of federal regulation, see Sinclair, "Regulating the fisheries." Scott and Neher detail the considerable extent of federal fisheries regulations in *Public Regulation of Commercial Fisheries*.

13. Canada, Task Force on Atlantic Fisheries, *Navigating Troubled Waters*, 13.

14. Canada, Department of Fisheries and Oceans, *Policy for Canada's Atlantic Fisheries in the 1980s*, v.

15. For an overview of historically low groundfish stock levels, see Canada, Department of Fisheries and Oceans, *Report on the Status of Groundfish Stocks in the Canadian Northwest Atlantic*, 7-8.

16. Canada, Department of Fisheries and Oceans, *Policy for Canada's Atlantic Fisheries in the 1980s*, 23.

17. Canada, Task Force on Atlantic Fisheries, *op. cit.*, 138 and 14-5 respectively.

18. Ironically, even when the fishery was at its peak, it couldn't provide an adequate living for all involved (Canada, Department of Fisheries and Oceans, Task Force on Incomes and Adjustment in the Atlantic Fishery, *Charting a New Course*, 10). Fishermen and processors have long relied on unemployment insurance to supplement their incomes, inflating their numbers and creating even more capacity in the industry and greater pressure on the fishery.

For an overview of federal assistance to fishermen and processors, see Scott and Neher, *op. cit.*, 59-60.

19. *Globe and Mail*, "Fish on wane despite effort to save them."

The Conference Board of Canada's Hull notes the disastrous consequences of government subsidies to the east coast fishing industry in his discussion entitled "Perverse Side-Effects of Government Initiatives" in *Valuing the Environment*, 4.

20. Demsetz, *op. cit.*, 350-7; Pearse, "Scarcity of Natural Resources and the Implications for Sustainable Development," 10-13; and Anderson and Leal, *op. cit.*, 7, 26-34, 38, 45, 65.

21. Fur trading on the West Coast also prompted the emergence of private hunting rights that could be passed from one generation to the next (Demsetz, *op. cit.*, 351-3, citing Eleanor Leacock, *American Anthropologist*, Volume 56, No. 5, Part 2, Memoir No. 78, 15, and Frank G. Speck, "The Basis of American Indian Ownership of Land," *Old Penn Weekly Review*, January 16, 1915, 491-95). For more information on the evolution of property rights in aboriginal communities see Political Economy Research Center, *PERC Reports*.

22. Scott and Neher advocate a system of specific, marketable rights in *Public Regulation of Commerical Fisheries*, 41-4. Also see Scott, "The Fishery."

23. For information on ITQs in New Zealand see Pearse, "Developing Property Rights as Instruments of Natural Resources Policy," 115-20. For other examples of ITQ systems, see Anderson and Leal, *op. cit.*, 130-2; and "Fresh angle," *The Economist*.

24. Scott, "Development of Property in the Fishery" and "Obstacles to Fishery Self-Government"; and Pearse, personal communication, September 21, 1994.

25. Anderson and Leal, *op. cit.*, 27-31.

26. Miller, "Land of the Free," 70.

In another development, in July 1994 the U.S. Coast Guard started requiring oil tankers in Alaska's Prince William Sound to carry black boxes that would enable satellites to monitor their positions ("The July Almanac: Environment," *The Atlantic Monthly*, 12).

27. Pearse notes that transponders on fishing boats can provide a continuous reading—regardless of darkness or fog—on the location of every vessel in every fleet. Fishermen can also use the devices to transmit information about their catch (personal communication, September 21, 1994).

Technological advances of a different sort may eventually help solve problems associated with establishing property rights in sea life that is by nature mobile, and doesn't respect boundaries. Owners may soon be able to identify far-ranging species, such as whales, with radio tracking devices. University of Chicago economist Robert Taylor recommends conserving whales through private ownership—and tracking them as noted above—in his 1992 paper, "The Market and the Environment" (*Daily Telegraph*, "'Save the Whales by Privatisation' Call").

What Taylor suggests for whales has already occurred with wildlife. Red wolves in South Carolina wear radio-activated collars that inject them with tranquilizer if they wander too far afield. Alternatively, wolves could wear collars similar to those worn by dogs restrained by invisible fencing; they would receive a shock if they approached a boundary line (Anderson and Leal, *op. cit.*, 34).

28. Charles Hurwitz's threat to log ancient redwoods provides one of the most egregious examples of an owner's willingness to destroy a precious resource. In 1993, the financier demanded $600 million from the government in exchange for leaving 4,500 acres of trees standing in the United States' largest privately owned redwood forest. His company had earlier logged the country's second-largest private redwood stand, home to the rare marbled murrelet, in a challenge to wildlife regulations that it claimed violated its property rights (*Wall Street Journal*, "Cutting Costs: For Takeover Baron, Redwood Forests Are Just One More Deal").

29. Governments' incentives to establish politically popular emissions caps, to raise the caps once established, or to lower them more slowly than planned could limit the effectiveness of tradable pollution permit systems. Some industries—particularly inefficient newcomers—would lobby for higher caps. But many industries would join environmentalists in lobbying for lower caps. Depending on how the government set the caps, and to whom it distributed shares, those working to keep caps low (and to keep the value of pollution shares high) could include efficient industries (new or established) that would suffer less than their inefficient competitors from higher pollution costs, and established industries wanting to avoid competition, to avoid putting up money to purchase additional shares, to avoid any devaluation of their investments in pollution abatement, and to avoid a dilution of the valuable assets that their shares represent.

For a seminal book on tradable emissions permits, see Dales, *op. cit.*, Chapter 6. For a more current look at how a tradable emissions system could be used to reduce sulphur dioxide emissions in Canada, see Economic Instruments Collaborative, "Controlling Acid Deposition Through Emission Trading," in *Achieving Atmospheric Quality Objectives Through the Use of Economic Instruments.*

30. Arthur Young, *Travels*, Volume 1, 1787, cited by Nancie Marzulla, "Property Rights as a 'Central Organizing Principle.'"

Appendices

Wisdom of the Ages

A

Trespass Case Summaries

1903: Sammons v. Gloversville[1]
Sewer filth, accumulating on a river bank, constitutes a trespass.

At the turn of the century, a very polluted Cayadutta Creek flowed through Sampson Sammons' New York farm. Upstream, the city of Gloversville emptied its sewers and drains into the creek, fouling its waters and depositing filth on its beds and along its banks. So, too, did the city of Johnstown, along with several tanneries. Mr. Sammons went to court to restrain Gloversville from further polluting the creek or its banks. The trial court found that city's sewage disposal practices amounted to a continuing trespass that substantially injured Mr. Sammons' property rights. It issued an injunction, to take effect after one year, prohibiting Gloversville from fouling Mr. Sammons' premises by discharging its sewage into the creek. The court retained the right to extend the injunction if it took longer than a year for the city to establish a different sewage system or to obtain legislative relief. Both the Appellate Division and the Court of Appeals affirmed the decision.

Gloversville opposed the injunction, arguing that since its sewage constituted only one of several sources of pollution, enjoining it would not clean up the creek. The trial judge responded:

> It is true that the injury to plaintiff will not be wholly obviated by restraining the defendant alone, but, if the plaintiff suffers substantial damages from one, he has the right, I think, to stop that, notwithstanding the fact that he may suffer also from another source. He could sue all and thus obtain entire relief; but he has the right, also, to sue the persons who injure him separately, and, if he proves substantial injury from that source, he has the right to have that part of the injury cease. He can take the others in their order, if he sees fit, and thus relieve himself entirely, or he can waive the injury by not asking to be relieved.[2]

Nor did the courts accept Gloversville's defence that it had statutory authority to pollute. According to the Court of Appeals judge, the city's legislative permission to construct sewers implied neither the right to appropriate property nor the right to commit a nuisance: "[T]he discretion of the municipal authorities in maintaining a system of sewage should be exercised in conformity with private rights."[3]

Whether the city acted for the public benefit was of no consequence. As the trial judge explained, it was uniform practice in New York to enjoin trespass, regardless of the public necessity of the offending works or the great inconvenience that could result from their restraint.

1959: *Fairview Farms* v. *Reynolds Metals and Martin* v. *Reynolds Metals*[4]

Invisible matter or energy may constitute a trespass.

Fairview Farms had operated a dairy farm near Troutdale, Oregon, since 1935. Since its construction in 1942, the aluminum reduction plant next door had emitted fluorides in the form of fumes, gases and particulates, which settled on Fairview's grasses and forage crops, rendering them unfit for feed. Periodically, Fairview had to refrain from pasturing its cows on contaminated fields; at those times it purchased hay and other forage, for which the aluminum plant paid in periodic settlements.

Despite years of promises, the aluminum plant failed to control its emissions. Fairview finally sued for trespass. Although the court (believing that damages would make the dairy farm "whole" again) refused to issue the requested injunction, it did find that the plant's emissions, which physically entered upon Fairview's lands, injuring cows and decreasing milk production, constituted a trespass.

The District Court judge who heard the case acknowledged that traditionally, trespass concerned direct physical invasions by tangible matter—intrusions visible to the naked eye. But the times, he noted, were changing: "One of these changes is scientific development which today allows the court, with the aid of scientific detecting methods, to determine the existence of a physical entry of tangible matter, which in turn gives rise to a cause of action in trespass under the Oregon Court's holding that every unauthorized entry upon land of another constitutes actionable trespass."[5] The fluoride emissions that Fairview Farms complained of, while invisible to the naked eye, could be accurately measured; the resulting toxic contamination could be determined in a laboratory.

Running concurrently with the Fairview Farms case was another case against Reynolds Metals, this one heard first by the Circuit Court and then by the Supreme Court of Oregon. Here, too, farmers had sued the aluminum company for trespass by fluoride compounds that made their land and water unfit for raising livestock. And here, too, the court found that invisible matter may constitute a trespass.

Justice O'Connell, for the Supreme Court, rejected the "dimensional test" proposed by the aluminum company. He explained that in the past, extremely small objects (such as gun shot, lead particles, a spray of water, and soot) had constituted trespasses. Modern science could now detect direct invasions by unseen instruments: "In fact, the now famous equation $E=mc^2$ has taught us that mass and energy are equivalents and that our concept of 'things' must be reframed."[6] The judge concluded, "[W]e may define trespass as any intrusion which invades the possessor's protected interest in exclusive possession, whether that intrusion is by visible or invisible pieces of matter or by energy which can be measured only by the mathematical language of the physicist."[7]

Justice O'Connell acknowledged that such a definition could require courts to treat trespasses more like nuisances in that they would have to decline to deal with trifling intrusions: "[T]here is a point where the entry is so lacking in substance that the law will refuse to recognize it, applying the maxim de minimis no curat lex [the law does not concern itself about trifles]."[8]

1976: Kerr v. Revelstoke[9]
A lumber company may not pollute its neighbours' property with fly ash or sawdust.

James and Florence Kerr, attracted by the site's tranquility and scenic beauty, purchased 160 acres of farm land in southwestern Alberta. There they built the Chinook Motel, opening it in 1951 and enlarging it over the next several years.

In 1958, Revelstoke Building Materials Ltd. commenced business across the road. The lumber company expanded its operations (thanks in part to government incentives) until, by 1971, it ran a sawmill, planer, and teepee burner, along with chipper and debarker operations, at the site.

The business generated a tremendous amount of smoke, sawdust, fly ash, and noise, eventually causing the Kerrs to close their motel. They went to court, alleging trespass, nuisance, and negligence.

Justice Shannon, of the Alberta Supreme Court's Trial Division, agreed that the physical invasion of fly ash and sawdust from the lumber company constituted a trespass. He cited the 1765 decision in *Entick* v. *Carrington*: "'Every invasion of property, be it ever so minute, is a trespass.'"[10] He also referred to Salmond on Torts: "'It is a trespass to place any chattel upon the plaintiff's land, or to cause any physical object or noxious substance to cross the boundary of the plaintiff's land. . . .'"[11] A trespass is a trespass, the judge noted, regardless of whether it causes any damage: "Trespass is actionable without proof of damages."[12]

The judge also found that the lumber company interfered with the Kerr's use and enjoyment of their property—"the essence of private nuisance."[13] Its operations generated concern, anxiety and discomfort, not only for the Kerrs but also for their clients, who couldn't even carry on normal conversations, let alone sleep at night, what with the machinery's ear-piercing squealing and clanking.

For reasons that he did not explain, the judge decided that "in these circumstances an injunction would not be an appropriate remedy."[14] He may have been influenced by the fact that the motel had been closed for five years. Or he may have been sensitive to the federal government's efforts to encourage industry to locate in this depressed economic area—something he commented on in his judgment. Whatever his rationale, instead of granting an injunction he awarded general damages of $30,000.

1978: *Friesen* v. *Forest Protection*[15]
It is unlawful to spray pesticides onto another's land.

Abram Friesen, a professor at the University of New Brunswick, lived with his wife and four children on a farm in Island View, just west of Fredericton, New Brunswick. On the evening of May 21, 1976, Dr. and Mrs. Friesen were picking fiddleheads near a brook on their farm when planes flew directly overhead, emitting a cloud of spray that descended on them, burning their cheeks, causing their eyes to water, and making them cough. The Friesens, organic farmers who shunned pesticides, were furious. They knew that as part of New Brunswick's spruce budworm control program, Forest Protection Limited was spraying a pesticide formulation containing fenitrothion—a highly toxic organophosphate. Just one week earlier, Dr. Friesen had asked the company not to spray his property.

During the following weeks Dr. and Mrs. Friesen experienced a variety of physical ailments, which they attributed to fenitrothion poisoning. Their 12-year-old son suffered a protracted asthmatic attack, which the Friesens blamed on inhalation of drifting spray. The spraying company, in contrast, called the boy's attack a response to the emotional distress suffered by his parents; similarly, it judged the adults' symptoms psychosomatic. The Friesens also found several hundred dead bees near their hives, and lost two cows, a pony, and two sheep; no evidence, however, linked these deaths to the spraying.

The Friesens sued Forest Protection Limited for damages under trespass and nuisance. The court awarded them $1,328.20 plus taxed costs.

Mr. Justice Dickson determined that Forest Protection Limited had indeed trespassed:

> To throw a foreign substance on the property of another, and particularly in doing so to disturb his enjoyment of his property, is an unlawful act. The spray deposited here must be considered such a foreign substance, and its deposit unquestionably amounted to a disturbance, however slight it may have been, of the owners' enjoyment of their property. I therefore must conclude that the defendant, in depositing the spray did in fact commit what would, in the absence of statutory authority, be considered a trespass. This of course does not involve any question of whether or not the spray may have been toxic or non-toxic, because even to have thrown water, or garbage, or snow, or earth tippings, or any substance on the property would equally have amounted to an act of trespass.[16]

Mr. Justice Dickson also found Forest Protection Limited guilty of nuisance: "[A]t the same time the spraying by the defendant constituted what in law must be considered a private nuisance. Such a nuisance has been defined as an act or omission which causes damage to another person in connexion with the latter's use of land or interference with the enjoyment of land or of some right connected with land."[17]

In his judgment, Mr. Justice Dickson considered at great length the question of whether the defendant had statutory authority to commit a trespass or nuisance. Forest Protection Limited contended that New Brunswick's Forest Service Act authorized the protection of provincial forests from insects and diseases, that the Lieutenant-Governor in Council had approved its aerial spraying program and indemnified it with respect to damage claims, and that the Minister of Natural Resources had delegated to it "whatever authority is necessary . . . to effectually carry out the above program."[18]

After a lengthy review of scholars and cases on the issue of statutory authority, the judge concluded that Forest Protection Limited could not avail itself of the defence. Nothing in the Forest Service Act "authorizes either the Lieutenant-Governor in Council or the Minister to place spray, at least without consent, on private lands to the detriment of private rights of the owner. . . . Nowhere in the Act is given to the Minister the authority to enter, for the purpose of combatting forest insects or disease, upon private property either by spraying or otherwise."[19]

1988: Didow v. Alberta Power[20]

Transmission lines constitute a trespass of airspace.

Fifty feet off the ground, the cross-arms of an Alberta Power transmission line protruded six feet over the Didows' farm. The Didows objected that in addition to being unsightly, the cross-arms and the lines attached to them would interfere with aerial spraying and seeding operations, the use of tall machinery, and tree planting in the area.

Relying on the thirteenth-century Latin maxim *cujus est solum, ejus est usque ad coelum et ad inferos* (to whomsoever the soil belongs, he owns also to the sky and to the depths), the Didows argued that the cross-arms constituted a trespass of their air space. The Alberta Court of Appeal agreed.

In his judgment for the court, Justice Haddad explored the extent to which a landowner has rights to the airspace above his land. Early common law cases confirming the Latin maxim had determined that signs, telegraph wires, eaves, or any other artificial or permanent structures hanging over another's land should be forbidden as trespasses. That the owner was not using his land, and was therefore not damaged by the trespass, was irrelevant: "[A] landowner is entitled to freedom from permanent structures which in any way impinge upon the actual or potential use and enjoyment of his land."[21]

On the other hand, as the utility had argued, some recent cases regarding airlines had demonstrated that airspace is public domain. The judge concluded that such decisions would not apply to transmission lines: air traffic generally takes place much further from the ground, is transient, and does not directly interfere with the use of one's property. And a low-flying aircraft, he noted, might indeed commit a trespass.

The utility also argued that public policy considerations should permit it to intrude over private property. Furthermore, it noted, "tens of thousands of miles of transmission lines across Alberta occupy private property."[22] But the court was not swayed: "[I]f there are many miles of transmission lines already trespassing the air space above private property without any leave or licence, they will not transform an unlawful practice into a lawful one."[23]

Notes

1. *Sammons* v. *City of Gloversville*, 34 Misc. Rep. 459, 70 N.Y. Supp. 284 (Sup. Ct. 1901), aff'd 67 App. Div. 628, 74 N.Y. Supp. 1145, 175 N.Y. 346, 67 N.E. 622 (1903).

2. *Ibid.* at 285-6.

3. *Ibid.* at 624.

4. *Fairview Farms, Inc.* v. *Reynolds Metals Company*, 176 F. Supp. 178 (D. Or. 1959); *Paul Martin et al.* v. *Reynolds Metals Company*, 342 P. 2d 790 (Or. 1959), cert. denied, 362 U.S. 918 (1960).

5.   *Ibid.* at 186.

6.   *Paul Martin et al.* v. *Reynolds Metals Company, op. cit.* at 793.

7.   *Ibid.* at 794.

8.   *Ibid.* at 795.

9.   *Kerr et al.* v. *Revelstoke Building Materials Ltd.* (1976), 71 D.L.R. (3d) 134 (Alta. S.C.).

10.   *Ibid.* at 136, citing *Entick* v. *Carrington* (1765), 19 St. Tr. 1030.

11.   *Ibid.* at 137, citing *Salmond on the Law of Torts*, 15th ed. (1969) at p. 53.

12.   *Ibid.* at 138.

13.   *Ibid.* at 137.

14.   *Ibid.* at 138.

15.   *Friesen et al.* v. *Forest Protection Limited* (1978), 22 N.B.R. (2d) 146 (Q.B.).

16.   *Ibid.* at 162.

17.   *Ibid.* at 162.

18.   *Ibid.* at 164.

19.   *Ibid.* at 167.

20.   *Didow et al.* v. *Alberta Power Limited*, [1988] 5 W.W.R. 606 (Alta. C.A.).

21. *Ibid.* at 616.

22. *Ibid.* at 612.

23. *Ibid.* at 612.

B

Private Nuisance Case Summaries

1851: *Walter* v. *Selfe*[1]
A brick-maker is forbidden to violate his neighbour's right to unpolluted and untainted air.

Shortly after Mr. Selfe began manufacturing bricks on his property in the English countryside, the owner and tenant of the neighbouring house and garden took him to court. They sought an injunction against the burning process, objecting that the resulting smoke, vapour, and "floating substances" caused inconvenience and discomfort.

Knight Bruce, the Vice-Chancellor who heard the case, determined that the brick burning constituted a nuisance and issued an injunction prohibiting any burning that damaged or annoyed the plaintiffs or injured their garden. The plaintiffs, he said, were entitled to "unpolluted and untainted air," which he described as "air not rendered to an important degree less compatible, or at least not rendered incompatible, with the physical comfort of human existence—a phrase to be understood of course with reference to the climate and habits of England."[2]

Knight Bruce found it unnecessary to determine whether the smoke from Mr. Selfe's brick burner threatened human or animal health. Suffice it to say that it was "an inconvenience materially interfering with the ordinary comfort physically of human existence, not merely according to elegant or dainty modes and habits of living, but according to plain, sober and simple notions among English people."[3]

Mr. Selfe tried without success to defend his brick burning on the grounds that others also polluted the local air. But, the Vice-Chancellor responded, the plaintiffs had not objected to these more remote operations. And even if they were nuisances, they would "not form a reason why the defendant should set up an additional nuisance. There is no ground, I think, for inferring a licence to him."[4]

Nor did Mr. Selfe's argument that he was merely using his land in a common and useful way sway the Vice-Chancellor, who noted that otherwise lawful uses of one's property would be forbidden if they interfered with others' property rights: "There are notorious instances of various kinds in which the rights of neighbouring occupiers or a neighbouring proprietor prevent a man from using his land as, but for those rights, he properly and lawfully might use it. A man may be disabled from building on his own land as he may wish, by reason of his neighbour's rights."[5]

1858: The Attorney General v. The Borough of Birmingham[6]

A city may not discharge raw sewage into a river, even if doing so serves the national interest.

Mr. Adderley owned a large estate on the Tame River, seven miles below its convergence with the Rea River. Although the town of Birmingham had long drained sewers into the Rea, until the 1850s they were sufficiently small and disperse, and the sewage sufficiently purified by filtration, as to not interfere with downstream water quality. Following the passage of the Birmingham Improvement Act of 1851, however, the town council constructed one large main public sewer disgorging into the Tame River, polluting it badly. The pollution aggravated disease, killed fish, and prevented cattle from drinking from the river and sheep from being washed in it. After four years of empty assurances that the town council would soon stop polluting, Mr. Adderley turned to the courts, requesting an interim injunction preventing the opening of additional sewers and an undertaking that Birmingham would, within a specified period, abate the existing nuisance.

The defendants did "not deny that the evil complained of is highly offensive."[7] They argued, however, that the court should allow continued pollution in the name of the public good. "[T]he evil that must ensue if the Court should interfere would be incalculable," they maintained. "The deluge of filth will cause a plague, which will not be confined to the 250,000 inhabitants of Birmingham, but will spread over the entire valley and become a national calamity. The increase of population, inseparable from the progress of a nation in industry and wealth, is attended of necessity by inconvenience to individuals against which it is in vain to struggle. In such cases private interests must bend to those of the country at large."[8]

Vice-Chancellor Sir Page Wood dismissed the argument as an "extreme position . . . of remarkable novelty." He was not, he explained, a public safety committee; his function was simply to interpret the law and to define who has what rights. Once the plaintiff's right to enjoy a clean river was established, the court should grant an injunction, regardless of its consequences: "[I]t is a matter of almost absolute indifference whether the decision will affect a population of 25,000 or a single individual carrying on a manufactory for his own benefit."[9] Sir Page added that if an injunction would produce considerable injury, the court would, "by way of indulgence," give the defendant an opportunity to stop its nuisance before enjoining its activity. But if the defendant failed to stop the nuisance, it would be up to Parliament—rather than the court—to allow it to continue: "If, after all possible experiments, they cannot drain Birmingham without invading the Plaintiff's private rights, they must apply to Parliament for power to invade his rights."[10]

The defendants also argued that pollution should be permitted on the grounds that Birmingham residents had a prescriptive right to pollute (meaning a right to carry on a longstanding activity). Sir Page answered that whether or not such a right had existed, previous sewage disposal had not polluted the river as it was now doing. Previous rights would therefore no longer apply.

Lastly, the defendants claimed that the Birmingham council operated under legislative authority. Again, Sir Page rejected this argument. His review of the act governing the matter indicated that it preserved people's common law rights respecting nuisances. It is clear, he concluded, that "nothing in this Act contained has given the Defendants any right so to interfere with the river as to produce the nuisance of which the Plaintiff complains."[11]

1859: *Imperial Gas Light and Coke* v. *Broadbent*[12]
Once a plaintiff's rights have been established, a judge will, as a matter of course, issue an injunction against a nuisance.

Samuel Broadbent had leased market gardens near Fulham, England, for 15 years when, in 1851, the Imperial Gas Light and Coke Company constructed a large retort house 40 feet from his grounds. The noxious gasses emitted from the building injured his flowers, fruits and vegetables. After one legal action in which he obtained damages but following which the gas company erected another retort house, aggravating the nuisance, Mr. Broadbent returned to court, this time seeking an injunction. A series of courts, culminating in the House of Lords, heard his case; all agreed that an injunction was the appropriate remedy for this ongoing nuisance.

The gas company argued that the "balance of convenience" was in its favour: while its activities merely inconvenienced Mr. Broadbent with "trifling damage," an injunction would stop the making of gas and greatly injure the public. In response, Lord Kingsdown pointed out that, in principle, the size of the damage makes no difference. He spelled out the rules governing injunctions as follows:

> The rule I take to be clearly this: if a Plaintiff applies for an injunction to restrain a violation of a common law right, if either the existence of the right or the fact of its violation be disputed, he must establish that right at law; but when he has established his right at law, I apprehend that unless there be something special in the case, he is entitled as of course to an injunction to prevent the recurrence of that violation.[13]

Lord Campbell agreed that once a plaintiff's right has been established, it is a judge's duty to grant an injunction if a nuisance continues; he would do so as a matter of course. Damages, he explained, would be insufficient: "How can he prove to a jury the exact quantity of pecuniary loss that he may have sustained? He may be able to show the value of the flowers and trees that have been destroyed, but how can he show the irreparable injury done to his trade by his customers leaving him, whom he may find it most difficult or impossible to get back?"[14]

Lord Campbell noted that conducting one's works in a manner that injures another violates the maxim, *Sic utere tuo ut alienum non laedas* (use your own property so as not to harm another's). He explained, "The Appellants are at liberty, under the injunction, to carry on their works so that they do not injure the Plaintiff, and they must either find out some mode by which they can carry on their works without that injury, or they must limit the quantity of gas to that which they made before this new retort was constructed."[15]

1865: St. Helen's Smelting v. Tipping[16]

Nuisances resulting in material injury or financial harm cannot be excused, regardless of the character of the neighbourhood in which they occur.

In June 1860, William Tipping purchased the Bold Hall manor house, along with 1300 acres of surrounding land. Three months later, operations began at the nearby St. Helen's Copper Smelting Company (Limited). The works emitted noxious gases and vapours which damaged Mr. Tipping's hedges and trees, sickened his cattle, adversely affected people, reduced the land's value, and generally interfered with his beneficial use of land. Mr. Tipping sued St. Helen's directors and shareholders to recover damages for injuries done to his trees and shrubs.

The first trial concluded that the smelting operations constituted a nuisance. Although the business was "an ordinary business, and conducted in a proper manner," it was not carried on in a proper place. Mr. Tipping was awarded damages of £361.

St. Helen's appealed the decision, arguing that the judge had misdirected the jury. The presence of many other manufactories and chimneys in the neighbourhood, it claimed, made it a suitable place to carry on its business. It cited the judgment in *Hole* v. *Barlow*: "The right of the owner of a house to have the air unpolluted is subject to this qualification, that necessities may arise for an interference with that right *pro bono publico*, to this extent, that such interference be in respect of a matter essential to the business of life, and be conducted in a reasonable and proper manner, and in a reasonable and proper place."[17]

The House of Lords rejected St. Helen's argument and refused to grant a new trial.

In his judgment, which future courts would frequently cite, Lord Westbury distinguished between alleged nuisances resulting in personal discomfort and those resulting in material injury or financial harm. Courts should consider the character of the neighbourhood only in the former cases:

> My Lords, in matters of this description it appears to me that it is a very desirable thing to mark the difference between an action brought for a nuisance upon the ground that the alleged nuisance produces material injury to the property, and an action brought for a nuisance on the ground that the thing alleged to be a nuisance is productive of sensible personal discomfort. With regard to the latter, namely, the personal inconvenience and interference with one's enjoyment, one's quiet, one's personal freedom, anything that discomposes or

injuriously affects the senses or the nerves, whether that may or may not be denominated a nuisance, must undoubtedly depend greatly on the circumstances of the place where the thing complained of actually occurs. If a man lives in a town, it is necessary that he should subject himself to the consequences of those operations of trade which may be carried on in his immediate locality, which are actually necessary for trade and commerce, and also for the enjoyment of property, and for the benefit of the inhabitants of the town and of the public at large. If a man lives in a street where there are numerous shops, and a shop is opened next door to him, which is carried on in a fair and reasonable way, he has no ground for complaint, because to himself individually there may arise much discomfort from the trade carried on in that shop. But when an occupation is carried on by one person in the neighbourhood of another, and the result of that trade, or occupation, or business, is a material injury to property, then there unquestionably arises a very different consideration. I think, my Lords, that in a case of that description, the submission which is required from persons living in society to that amount of discomfort which may be necessary for the legitimate and free exercise of the trade of their neighbours, would not apply to circumstances the immediate result of which is sensible injury to the value of the property.[18]

Lord Wensleydale's judgment stressed that trifling inconveniences are not grounds for nuisance. In a county "where great works have been created and carried on, and are the means of developing the national wealth, you must not stand on extreme rights and allow a person to say, 'I will bring an action against you for this and that, and so on.' Business could not go on if that were so. Everything must be looked at from a reasonable point of view; therefore the law does not regard trifling and small inconveniences, but only regards sensible inconveniences, injuries which sensibly diminish the comfort, enjoyment or value of the property which is affected."[19]

1866: Dent v. Auction Mart[20]
Property rights include the right to light and air.

Dent, Palmer, & Co. had leased its London premises for ten years when Auction Mart Company, Limited, purchased a number of neighbouring houses, pulled them down, and started to rebuild. Dent objected that the new structures—both higher than the old and closer to its premises— would block its light and air flow. As one witness explained, "The result would be . . . to place the staircase windows of Messrs. Dent's house in a dismal stagnant well of small size and great depth."[21]

Dent offered not to oppose the construction if Auction Mart paid it £2000 in damages and installed light-reflecting enamelled tiles on the new wall. When these negotiations failed, Dent sought an injunction. The court issued "a perpetual injunction restraining the Defendants from erecting any building so as to darken, hinder, or obstruct the free access of light and air to the ancient windows of the Plaintiffs."[22]

In his judgment, Vice-Chancellor Sir Page Wood noted the increasing frequency of such disputes as people built higher buildings that were more likely to affect their neighbours. He acknowledged that many cases, such as those causing simple annoyance or damages amounting to a few pounds, did not warrant injunctions. Two circumstances would, however, call for an injunction: a substantial interference with comfort and/or a substantial diminution of light for carrying on work. These criteria applied to the case at hand.

Sir Page extensively cited *Yates* v. *Jack*, a recent case in which the court prohibited the raising by 50 per cent of a building thirty feet from the plaintiffs' premises. The plaintiffs, it found, had "'an absolute indefeasible right to the enjoyment of the light, without reference to the purpose for which it has been used.'"[23] In that case, Sir Page noted, "it was no answer to a Plaintiff complaining that his light had been obstructed to shew that other persons had been able to carry on trade successfully with less light than would remain to the complaining party after the obstruction had been set up."[24] Accordingly, he dismissed Auction Mart's contention that its construction would leave Dent with as much light as others would find sufficient for the same purposes.

Sir Page rejected the defendant's argument that, in this case, the plaintiff should be entitled only to damages. A damage award, he explained, would amount to giving the defendant the right to purchase the plaintiff's property at a price set by a jury: "His comfort is to be taken away, not at his own estimate, but at the value which a jury might put on it."[25] Rather, it is the property owner who should decide whether or not he wants "to sell his comfort and ease," and at what price:

> [I]t cannot be contended that those who are minded to erect a building that will inflict an injury upon their neighbour have a right to purchase him out without any Act of Parliament for that purpose having been obtained. It appears to me it cannot safely be held that this Court will allow parties so to exercise the rights which they may have in their soil as to inflict an injury on their neighbour, if the neighbour is unwilling to take any compensation; or even though he be willing to take compensation, if he is not ready to submit to the valuation of a jury, but insists on his own right to determine what the value of his property is.[26]

1875: Smith v. Smith[27]
Awarding damages in lieu of injunctions may amount to forcing people to sell their property rights.

The plaintiff and defendant owned and occupied adjoining properties, separated in the back by a nine-foot-high party wall. The windows of the plaintiff's kitchen, scullery, and workshop faced the wall from a distance of eight feet. In 1875, the defendant added on to his home, raising the wall from nine feet to 26 feet and obscuring the light and air flow that the plaintiff had enjoyed for 46 years. The addition darkened the plaintiff's kitchen, scullery, and workshop, necessitating the use of gaslight. It rendered the workshop useless for the plaintiff's cabinet-making and upholstering—work which required good light. Furthermore, it affected his family's health, obliging his wife and daughter to leave the home. The plaintiff filed suit, requesting damages and an injunction.

The defendant did not deny obstructing the light. He argued, however, that the court should exercise its power to substitute damages for an injunction on the grounds that the plaintiff's delay in filing suit had led him to spend a considerable sum on construction.

Regardless, Sir George Jessel issued a mandatory injunction for removal of the addition. He explained that the court must exercise its powers "in such a way as to prevent the Defendant doing a wrongful act, and thinking that he could pay damages for it."[28] One cannot force another to sell his property rights:

> In granting a mandatory injunction, the Court did not mean that the man injured could not be compensated by damages, but that the case was one in which it was difficult to assess damages, and in which, if it were not granted, the Defendant would be allowed practically to deprive the Plaintiff of the enjoyment of his property if he would give him a price for it. When, therefore, money could not adequately reinstate the person injured, the Court said, . . . "We will put you in the same position as before the injury was done."[29]

Sir George suggested that a defendant's intentions could affect the remedy chosen by the court. Ignorance of wrong could justify the substitution of damages for an injunction. However, ignorance could not justify the defendant's behaviour in this case: it was inconceivable that the defendant did not know that he was blocking the plaintiff's light.

1894: Shelfer v. City of London Electric Lighting Company[30]
An injunction is the appropriate remedy for nuisance unless the damages are small, easily estimated, and can be adequately compensated by money.

In 1891, the City of London Electric Lighting Company acquired land adjacent to the Waterman's Arms, a public house on the River Thames. It excavated, erected buildings, and installed large electricity generators—some as close as 30 feet from the public house.

The generating station showered its neighbours with clouds of steam. Its engines' noise and vibrations shook the Waterman's Arms' rooms and furniture, disturbing people's sleep, interfering with their comfort, and even making some of them sick. The public house began to list, and a two-inch-wide crack appeared in one wall.

Victualler and innkeeper William Shelfer, along with Meux's Brewery Company, from whom he leased the Waterman's Arms, brought actions for injunctions and damages. Although the lower court found that the power generation constituted a nuisance, it awarded damages instead of an injunction on the grounds that the nuisance had not decreased the public house's profitability and that an injunction would cause great inconvenience. The plaintiffs appealed the decision and obtained from the Chancery Division an injunction restraining the continuance of the nuisance.

In the chancery hearing, the electric company fought an injunction on the grounds that it would harm the public interest. It argued that the court "ought not to grant an injunction to restrain a work which is for the benefit of the whole City of London, in which many of the main streets and public buildings would be left in darkness if the company's works were stopped."[31]

Lord Justice Lindley explained that, regardless of the public inconvenience, before the passage of Lord Cairns' Act Mr. Shelfer would have been entitled to an injunction to prevent the continuation of the nuisance. The judgment in *Imperial Gas Light and Coke Company* v. *Broadbent* had articulated the principle that "an injunction would not be refused on the ground that the public might be inconvenienced if an injunction were granted."[32]

Although Lord Cairns' Act had empowered the courts to substitute damages for injunctions, Lord Justice Lindley insisted that the act had not prompted them to consider the public good when choosing remedies: "Neither has the circumstance that the wrongdoer is in some sense a public benefactor (*e.g.*, a gas or water company or a sewer authority) ever been considered a sufficient reason for refusing to protect by injunction an individual whose rights are being persistently infringed. . . . Courts of Justice are not like Parliament, which considers whether proposed works will be so beneficial to the public as to justify exceptional legislation, and the deprivation of people of their rights with or without compensation."[33]

All three chancery judges agreed that substituting damages for an injunction would amount to expropriation. Lord Halsbury noted that refusing an injunction would "enable a company who could afford it to drive a neighbouring proprietor to sell, whether he would or no, by continuing a nuisance, and simply paying damages for its continuance."[34] Lord Justice Lindley added, "[E]ver since Lord Cairns' Act was passed the Court of Chancery has repudiated the notion that the Legislature intended to turn that Court into a tribunal for legalizing wrongful acts; or in other words, the Court has always protested against the notion that it ought to allow a wrong to continue simply because the wrongdoer is able and willing to pay for the injury he may inflict."[35] Finally, Lord Justice Smith explained, "a person by committing a wrongful act (whether it be a public company for public purposes or a private individual) is not thereby entitled to ask the Court to sanction his doing so by purchasing his neighbour's rights, by assessing damages in that behalf, leaving his neighbour with the nuisance."[36]

Lord Justice Smith, whose judgment would be frequently cited in future cases, offered the following guidelines for the substitution of damages for an injunction:

> [I]t may be stated as a good working rule that—
> (1.) If the injury to the plaintiff's legal rights is small,
> (2.) And is one which is capable of being estimated in money,
> (3.) And is one which can be adequately compensated by a small money payment,
> (4.) And the case is one in which it would be oppressive to the defendant to grant an injunction:—
> then damages in substitution for an injunction may be given.[37]

As Mr. Shelfer's injury clearly did not fit the above description, an injunction was the appropriate remedy.

The electric company argued that legislation permitted—even required—it to create nuisances. It had to construct its works in the densely populated area that it supplied with electricity. Since houses surrounded every available spot, it could not avoid causing offence to someone. In short, it could not supply electricity without statutory protection.

The lower court had denied the electric company's claim that it had statutory authority to commit nuisances: "It is well settled that power to do a particular thing . . . does not justify the undertakers . . . in doing that thing so as to commit a nuisance, unless by express language or by necessary implication."[38] The higher court's Lord Justice Lindley also rejected the electric company's argument that an injunction could prevent it from carrying on its business. It could, he said, avoid committing nuisances by increasing the number of its stations and decreasing the size of the generators at each one.

1896: Drysdale v. Dugas[39]

A stable, although modern and well-run, constitutes a nuisance in a residential neighbourhood.

In 1891, William Drysdale constructed a livery stable on Montreal's primarily residential St. Denis Street. The stable was 25 feet away from C. A. Dugas's home, and immediately adjacent to another house that Mr. Dugas would soon purchase. The stable smelled, and its 30 noisy horses disturbed Mr. Dugas and his tenant. Mr. Dugas brought a successful nuisance action for damages, both for his own discomfort and for reductions in his tenant's rent.

In his appeal to the Supreme Court of Canada, Mr. Drysdale argued that stables were indispensable in a large city, and that this one had been constructed using the best possible drainage and ventilation methods. One judge agreed, saying that a judgment against Mr. Drysdale's impeccable operations would make it virtually impossible to maintain a stable in Montreal. The other Supreme Court judges, however, upheld the lower courts' decisions to grant damages.

In his judgment, Chief Justice Sir Henry Strong rejected the defences of necessity and reasonable use. Regarding the former, he cited *Broder* v. *Saillard*, a similar case dealing with the noises made by horses in a stable. There, he explained, the courts repelled the argument that the stable was both necessary and reasonable.[40] In dismissing the defence of reasonable use, Sir Henry also cited *Bamford* v. *Turnley*, a case demonstrating that the argument that extreme care and caution could justify an offensive action was "entirely without foundation."[41]

Sir Henry's decision dealt extensively with the issue of locality, or the character of the neighbourhood. He explained that one must pay heed to a property's surroundings when determining whether a nuisance exists: "It would be of course absurd to say that one who establishes a manufactory in the use of which great quantities of smoke are emitted, next door to a precisely similar manufactory maintained by his neighbour, whose works also emit smoke, commits a nuisance as regards the latter, though if he established his factory immediately adjoining a mansion in a residential quarter of a large city, he would beyond question be liable for damages for a wrongful use of his property to the detriment of his neighbour."[42] The character of the neighbourhood, however, remains a limited defence. Sir Henry explained that the decision in *Bamford* v. *Turnley* included important comments on the locality rule. In that decision, the court had determined: "Whenever, taking all the circumstances into consideration including the nature and extent of the plaintiff's enjoyment before the acts complained of, the annoyance is sufficiently great to amount to a nuisance according to the ordinary rule of law, an action will lie whatever the locality may be."[43]

Sir Henry also addressed the extent to which Mr. Drysdale was free to use his own property. He explained that even the most absolute proprietary rights "must, according to the general principles of all systems of law, be subject to certain restrictions subordinating the exercise of acts of ownership to the rights of neighbouring proprietors; *sic utere tuo ut alienum non laedas* is as much a rule of the French law of the province of Quebec as of the common law of England."[44]

The issue of "coming to a nuisance" also arose. Mr. Drysdale had objected that since Mr. Dugas had acquired the neighbouring property after the stable's construction, he had no right to complain. Sir Henry dismissed this argument: "This circumstance as to the date of the respondent's acquisition of title can make no difference in his rights to object to the nuisance. In *Tipping* v. *St. Helen's Smelting* . . . the facts were that the plaintiff had come to the nuisance (*i.e.* acquired his property) with a knowledge of the existence of the nuisance, and it was nevertheless held that he was entitled, not merely to damages, but to an injunction to restrain the further commission of the acts complained of."[45]

1901: Hopkin v. Hamilton Electric Light[46]

An electric company's licence to produce and sell power does not confer upon it any authority to create a nuisance.

The Hopkin family had lived on Victoria Avenue North, in Hamilton, Ontario, for 26 years when, in 1900, the Hamilton Electric Light and Cataract Power Company built a transformer and distribution station next door. The station, just 13 feet from the Hopkins' home, included three large engines that vibrated vigorously. Although the vibrations did not structurally damage the Hopkins' house, they reduced its value. In fact, they made it virtually uninhabitable—so unhealthy and uncomfortable as to cause the Hopkins to move out. Mrs. Hopkin went to court, where the judge found that the electric company had created a serious nuisance. He awarded damages and issued an injunction, effective three months later, restraining the company from operating on its works so as to occasion a nuisance.

In considering the electric company's claim that statutory authority exempted it from liability for its nuisance, Mr. Justice Street reviewed a number of cases on the subject and summarized his findings:

> It is well established . . . on the one hand that a company obliged by law to serve the public—as a common carrier, for instance—clothed by statute with authority to do certain things, may do them at the place and in the manner authorized by the statute, without being liable to be charged with a nuisance necessarily created and without paying any compensation other than that provided by statute to persons who may be injured thereby. . . .
>
> On the other hand, it is equally clearly settled that a body, whether public or private, possessed of powers which are strictly permissive—that is to say, which the law will not compel it to execute, those powers being such as are capable of execution without the creation of a nuisance, and conferred without any provision being made for compensating persons injured by their exercise—is only authorized to execute them in such a manner as not to create a nuisance.[47]

The judge concluded that while the government had granted the electric company the power "to construct, maintain, complete, and operate works for the production, sale, and distribution of electricity," it had not compelled it to operate in such a location and manner as to create a nuisance. Nor had the government provided for compensation for injuries caused by the company's operations. Such a company, he said, must act so as not to create a nuisance. And if nuisance were an inevitable result of its activities, it would have to be restrained. Regardless, the judge noted, the work in question could very likely have been carried on in a less injurious way. Had the company been willing to spend more money, it could have avoided the nuisance by dividing its work amongst several stations or purchasing more land for its operations.

1916: *Beamish* v. *Glenn*[48]
Courts should issue injunctions against nuisances as a matter of course, unless they cause only slight or temporary damage.

In 1911, Mr. Beamish purchased a lot on Toronto's Boston Avenue, and there erected a home. The neighbourhood featured a mix of residences, factories, and shops; Carlaw Avenue, to the west, was primarily industrial, while to the east, houses lined Pape Avenue. When, four years later, Mr. Glenn tried to purchase the adjoining lot for a blacksmith shop, Mr. Beamish actively opposed the plan. Despite receiving negative petitions and deputations, City Council's Property Committee granted a permit for the proposed smithy. Mr. Glenn constructed his shop and began the noisy, smelly, smoky work of shoeing horses and setting tires on wagons. The persistent clanging of the hammer on the anvil and the odour of singed hoofs offended Mr. Beamish and compelled him to close his doors and windows even in very warm weather. He sued Mr. Glenn, accusing him of committing a nuisance and preventing him and his family from enjoying their property.

The trial judge, Mr. Justice Sutherland, found that the blacksmith business did indeed constitute a nuisance, despite the presence of other noisy, smoky factories in the neighbourhood. Echoing the judgment in *Appleby* v. *Erie Tobacco Co.*, he explained that the noise, smoke, and odours "'cause material discomfort and annoyance and render the plaintiff's premises less fit for the ordinary purposes of life, even making all possible allowances for the local standard of the neighbourhood.'"[49]

The fact that the defendant did his work "in a usual and reasonable fashion" did not influence the judge: "If the defendant has caused a nuisance to the plaintiff, it is of course no defence to say that he is making a reasonable use of his premises in the carrying on of a lawful occupation." On appeal, Mr. Justice Riddell agreed. "It is," he said, "of no importance."[50]

Nor could a city permit exonerate the blacksmith. The trial judge explained that the permit conferred no authority to commit a nuisance. Upon hearing the appeal, Chief Justice Meredith elaborated: "The power of cities to regulate and control the location, erection, and use of buildings . . . is a restrictive power, not one under which the right can be given to any one man to injure the property of another, or so to deprive another of any of his property or other rights."[51]

Mr. Justice Sutherland discussed the circumstances warranting an injunction. The court, he explained, will not normally enjoin an activity if it causes slight or temporary damage. Otherwise, an injunction would be the rule. The judge cited the decision in *Attorney-General* v. *Cole & Son*: "'if it really is a nuisance, then it seems almost to follow as a matter of course that it is a nuisance which ought to be restrained, assuming that it is not of a trifling or a passing character.'"[52]

In this case, the blacksmith shop nuisance would not pass; Mr. Glenn intended to carry on his business as before. So Mr. Justice Sutherland chose an injunction as the appropriate remedy. The Divisional Court, after hearing the defendant's appeal, upheld the original judgment. Chief Justice Meredith explained, "[T]he carrying on of the defendant's business, even in an ordinary, careful and proper manner, cannot be continued there. The business ought to go elsewhere, in the defendant's own interests."[53]

1949: *Walker* v. *McKinnon Industries*[54]

In causing sensible, visible, and material damage to a neighbouring florist, a foundry's emissions constitute a nuisance.

Mr. Walker had been growing flowers commercially since 1905, when he built his first greenhouse in St. Catharines, Ontario. The 1925 start-up of the McKinnon foundry to the southwest of his property didn't interfere with his business. But 15 years later, after the steel and iron products manufacturer built a forge-shop, enlarged the foundry, and changed its smelting process to one using cupolas, problems abounded. Oily fumes, soot, fly ash, and iron oxide from the new works formed a film on the glass of Mr. Walker's greenhouses, blocking the sunlight. A film coated his plants, interfering with photosynthesis and growth. Sulphur dioxide in the foundry's fumes further injured the plants.

During the war years, Mr. Walker refrained from suing the foundry, believing that the courts were unlikely to restrain a company that manufactured urgently needed munitions. Instead, the two parties reached agreements regarding damages and temporary easements for the pollution. Once the war ended, however, Mr. Walker launched a court action for both damages and an injunction.

Chief Justice McRuer, who heard the case in the Ontario High Court, found that the deposit on the greenhouse glass and the injury to the plants materially injured Mr. Walker and constituted a nuisance. He ordered damages and issued an injunction, to take effect in four and a half months, against the discharge of any damaging substance. Two higher courts affirmed his judgment.

In his decision, Chief Justice McRuer extensively reviewed the law of nuisance. He started with Blackstone, who in 1769 had broadly (*too* broadly, thought the Chief Justice) defined private nuisance as "any thing done to the hurt or annoyance of the lands, tenements, or hereditaments of another."[55]

In narrowing the definition of nuisance, the Chief Justice suggested that the injury should be sensible, visible, and material. He cited *Bamford* v. *Turnley* for the first criterion: "[W]hat makes life less comfortable and causes sensible discomfort and annoyance is a proper subject of injunction."[56]

Regarding the second criterion—the visibility of injury—the Chief Justice cited *Salvin* v. *North Brancepeth Coal Co.*, in which the distinction was made between injuries apparent to "ordinary persons conversant with the subject-matter" and injuries merely predicted by scientists with microscopes: "[A]lthough when you once establish the fact of actual substantial damage it is quite right and legitimate to have recourse to scientific evidence as to the causes of that damage, still if you are obliged to start with scientific evidence, such as the microscope of the naturalist, or the tests of the chemist, for the purposes of establishing the damage itself, that evidence will not suffice. The damage must be such as can be shewn by a plain witness to a plain common juryman."[57]

Lastly, in regards to the materiality of the injury, the Chief Justice distinguished between material injury to property and sensible personal discomfort, referring to the decision in *St. Helen's Smelting Co.* v. *Tipping*.

Chief Justice McRuer proceeded to reject three common defences to pollution: the existence of other pollution and the economic and social burdens imposed by stopping it. Other pollution, the Chief Justice explained, is no defence: "[E]ven if others are in some degree polluting the air, that is no defence if the defendant contributes to the pollution so that the plaintiff is materially injured. It is no defence even if the act of the defendant would not amount to a nuisance were it not for others acting independently of it doing the same thing at the same time."[58]

Nor can a polluter defend himself on the basis of economic considerations: "The cases well establish that economic considerations do not enter into the matter, and I am not called upon to weigh the economic disadvantages to the defendant."[59] Nor should a judge weigh the *social* costs of shutting down a polluting industry. In *Bamford* v. *Turnley*, the Chief Justice remembered, "Baron Bramwell in cogent language disposes of any argument that 'the public benefit' of the works complained of may be taken into consideration."[60]

1952: *Russell Transport* v. *Ontario Malleable Iron*[61]
The operations of a long-established foundry become a nuisance when a business starts up on previously vacant neighbouring land.

In 1949 and 1950, the Russells purchased vacant land in Oshawa, Ontario, which they used for their new vehicle-transport business. They would pick up cars and trucks from General Motors and other manufacturers, sort and store them in their marshalling yard, and then deliver them to distributors across Ontario. Business went well until the autumn of 1951, when a distributor noticed damage to the finish of vehicles stored by Russell Transport. Inspections revealed that many of the cars in the marshalling yard were pitted and corroded. General Motors ordered the removal of all of its products from the yard.

Russell Transport traced the problem to Ontario Malleable Iron Co. Ltd., whose foundry was located just west of the marshalling yard. Charging nuisance, they went to court. Chief Justice McRuer, who heard the case in the Ontario High Court, determined that the iron and iron-oxide particles emitted from the foundry rendered the transport company's property unfit for its intended purpose and caused the company material damage. He ordered damages and an injunction, to take effect in six months, prohibiting damaging discharges.

Ontario Malleable Iron Co. argued that over the years it had acquired a right to pollute: it had been doing business since 1907, and its predecessors had operated a foundry on the property since 1876. Chief Justice McRuer denied that the plaintiff had such prescriptive rights, both because the nature and extent of the operations had changed considerably over the years and because any pollution that the foundry had emitted would not have amounted to a nuisance against the formerly vacant land. "The defendant," he explained, "must not only show that it has exercised the right to deposit the substances herein complained of on the plaintiffs' lands, for the prescribed period, but that the exercise of the right amounted to a nuisance actionable at the instance of the plaintiffs and their predecessors in title for the full period of 20 years."[62]

The Chief Justice also refused to consider that the transport company had "come to the nuisance." Only after two years in business did it become aware of the nuisance. And regardless, according to *Salmond on Torts*, "It is no defence that the plaintiffs themselves came to the nuisance."[63] On this subject the Chief Justice also cited *Fleming* v. *Hislop*: "[W]hether the man went to the nuisance or the nuisance came to the man, the rights are the same. . . ."[64]

Chief Justice McRuer devoted much attention to the question of reasonable use, introducing his discussion with another reference to

Salmond on Torts: "It is no defence that all possible care and skill are being used to prevent the operation complained of from amounting to a nuisance. . . . He who causes a nuisance cannot avail himself of the defence that he is merely making a reasonable use of his own property. No use of property is reasonable which causes substantial discomfort to others or is a source of damage to their property."[65]

The foundry had relied on *Sturges* v. *Bridgman*, where the court had held that "whether anything is a nuisance or not is a question to be determined, not merely by an abstract consideration of the thing itself, but in reference to its circumstances; what would be a nuisance in Belgrave Square would not necessarily be so in Bermondsey. . . ."[66] Chief Justice McRuer commented that that case, which had dealt with noise and vibration, had been cautiously applied to some situations that produced personal discomfort rather than those resulting in material injury to property. For more on that distinction, he referred to the judgment in *St. Helen's Smelting Co.* v. *Tipping*, which had determined that the character of the neighbourhood cannot justify a nuisance that causes material injury to another's property.

The Chief Justice also explained that although taking reasonable care is no defence against nuisance, the failure to take reasonable care can jeopardize the defence of reasonable use: "[I]f the defendant has taken no reasonable precautions to protect his neighbour from injury by reason of operations of his own property the defence of reasonable user is of little avail."[67] He determined that the defendant, having "adopted no method of modern smoke or fume control," had not taken such precautions.

1972: Newman v. Conair Aviation[68]

It is a nuisance to spray an insecticide which, drifting over the property line, frightens and distresses a neighbour.

Patricia Newman was in her yard in Delta, British Columbia, when a low-flying aircraft sprayed her neighbour's pea crop with a dilution of the insecticide Cygon 4E. Although the plane sprayed only up to the fence line, the insecticide drifted over the property line and enveloped

Ms. Newman in a bitter cloud. Ms. Newman, who thought the spray was poisonous, developed a stomach ache and a headache, from which she suffered for the next week. Her horse, who had been terrified by the plane's roar, also seemed sick for several days. When Patricia's elderly mother, Margaret Newman, arrived home shortly thereafter, the plane passed again and she, too, was enveloped in spray, which caused itching, burning, headaches and nausea. The Newmans sued for damages, targeting both their neighbour and the company he had hired to spray his crop.

Chief Justice Wilson of the British Columbia Supreme Court found both the farmer and the spraying company liable for damages. He agreed with their contention that the diluted spray could not have harmed human or animal health, or that of trees or vegetables. But he explained that it was a nuisance nonetheless, for it interfered with the Newmans' enjoyment of their property. Their fear and subsequent illness, he said, was normal: "The reaction of an ordinary person, disturbed by a threatening noise and enveloped in a moist mist of what he knows is a toxic spray, must be one of fright, perhaps of terror, and nausea, without actual poisoning, may reasonably follow. The groundling, sprayed without warning, is not to be expected to know that the mist which covers his body and enters his nose and mouth is poisonous only to insects."[69]

The Chief Justice also pointed out that the women's ordeal could have easily been avoided. The farmer could have sprayed the area near his property line by hand; furthermore, he could have warned his neighbours that a loud airplane would be spraying a harmless spray.

1981: *Schenck v. Ontario*[70]
The application of road salt which damages fruit trees along the highway constitutes a nuisance.

Louis Schenck operated a peach farm near St. Catharines, Ontario. Michael Rokeby grew apples on his farm near Aylmer, Ontario. Fruit trees on both farms suffered from salt sprayed by traffic on highways bordering their orchards; the salt dessicated the trees, causing severe die-back and reducing crop yields. Both farmers sought compensation from the province for their economic losses; both were denied. In 1978, both sued. Mr. Justice Robins, of the Supreme Court of Ontario, ordered that the two cases be tried together.

Mr. Justice Robins found that while the application of salt was neither unreasonable nor negligent, it was nonetheless a nuisance, since it had interfered with the farmers' use of their lands and caused them material injury. Although the government enjoyed immunity from injunctions (thanks to the Proceedings Against the Crown Act), it could not escape liability for damages.

In its defence, the government argued that the use of road salt was in the public interest. Mr. Justice Robins countered that taxpayers should bear the costs of socially useful activities: "I do not agree that the plaintiffs' property interests may be infringed with impunity. . . . In reality, [the farmers'] injury is a cost of highway maintenance and the harm suffered by them is greater than they should be required to bear in the circumstances, at least without compensation. Fairness between the citizen and the state demands that the burden imposed be borne by the public generally and not by the plaintiff fruit farmers alone."[71]

The government also argued that it had legislative authority to pollute. But it failed to persuade Mr. Justice Robins that damage from road salt was the inevitable result of its exercising the duty imposed upon it by the Public Transportation and Highway Improvement Act, which required it to maintain the province's highways. The legislation neither contemplated such a nuisance nor provided for compensation. "An acceptance of the government's position," the judge concluded, "is tantamount to permitting expropriation without compensation"[72]— something that the legislation could not justify.

Furthermore, the legislation governing highway maintenance was permissive, rather than mandatory; under it, the province could have chosen to use harmless, but more expensive, de-icing agents. On this issue the judge cited a recent House of Lords decision: "[I]t is 'for the defendant to establish that any proved nuisance was wholly unavoidable and this quite regardless of the expense that might necessarily be involved in its avoidance.'"[73]

1986: Desrosiers v. Sullivan Farms[74]

A piggery may not discharge odours that interfere with its neighbours' enjoyment of their property.

When Terrance Sullivan expanded his Charlo, New Brunswick pig farm in 1980, his neighbours complained. His pigs produced 260 cubic feet of liquid manure each day, which, channelled into a manure lagoon for storage and decomposition, created an unbearable stench. The community, a judge later said, was "in a state of siege by smell."[75] Children could not play outdoors; families could not barbecue, air their laundry, or even leave their windows open. Some complained of nausea, others of sleeplessness and stress.

The community battled the pig farm on many fronts. Residents complained to the village council and to three provincial departments, with no avail. They even organized a protest parade. Finally, 25 neighbours went to court, seeking damages and an injunction.

Mr. Justice Stevenson, who heard the case at the trial division, found that the pig farm's offensive odours constituted an intolerable nuisance: they interfered with the plaintiffs' reasonable enjoyment of their properties. He awarded damages totalling $30,500. The judge did not grant an injunction, explaining that he could not enjoin something that didn't exist. Since a 1984 fire had destroyed Sullivan's barn and 1214 animals, and since the manure lagoon had been pumped out and covered a year later, the nuisance had ceased. The judge noted, however, that had the nuisance continued, he would have had no alternative but to issue an injunction. And if the operations were to resume (as was threatened by the presence of a new barn and lagoon on the property) they could face an injunction in a new lawsuit. Thirteen months later, the Court of Appeal upheld Mr. Justice Stevenson's decision.

In his defence, Mr. Sullivan argued that he had complied with the requirements of the provincial departments of health, agriculture, and environment. Mr. Justice Stevenson rejected the argument. "Compliance with rules and regulations contained in or authorized by legislation," he explained, "does not relieve one from the common law rule that he must conduct his activities in such a way as not to create a nuisance."[76] Justice of Appeal Hoyt agreed. He explained that provincial certificates of compliance "demonstrate Mr. Sullivan's good intentions in attempting to construct a piggery in accordance with approved practices. The evidence discloses that Mr. Sullivan sought and usually followed the advice of officials in the Departments of Agriculture and Environment. But, of course, he could not, at least in 1980, obtain a licence to create a nuisance."[77]

1990: 340909 Ontario Ltd. v. Huron Steel Products[78]
Noise and vibrations, even those in mixed-use or industrial neighbour-hoods, may constitute nuisances.

Soon after Huron Steel Products installed a new 800-tonne press at its Windsor, Ontario, stamping plant in 1979, Douglas Kenney complained to both the company and the Ministry of the Environment. As president of a corporation called 340909 Ontario Ltd., which owned an apartment building near the plant, he was concerned that the noise and vibrations resulting from the press's operation were causing his tenants to leave and making it difficult to rent apartments, thus reducing his rental income and the value of his building.

But Mr. Kenney could not get the government to enforce its noise regulations. Although tests conducted by the Ministry of the Environment indicated that the press exceeded provincial noise guidelines, and despite assurances from Huron Steel that it would improve the situation, the plant continued its noisy operations. Frustrated by the lack of progress, Mr. Kenney's company launched a nuisance case in which it sought damages and an injunction.

At the trial before the High Court of Justice in 1990, several former and current residents of the neighbourhood testified that the press's noise made falling asleep difficult, and that its vibrations shook furniture, disturbed pictures, and rattled glasses in their cupboards. This testimony, along with that of expert witnesses who described the degree to which the plant exceeded provincial noise guidelines, convinced Mr. Justice Potts that the press's noise and vibration were excessive.

The judge determined that the Environmental Protection Act required the press to have a certificate of approval from the Ministry of the Environment. "I do not know why this process was not strictly adhered to by the Ministry for the #1 press," he mused. "Possibly the Ministry was trying to persuade rather than compel Huron Steel and other existing industries to comply with the guideline levels."[79]

The court acted where the government would not. Mr. Justice Potts found that Huron Steel's operations unreasonably interfered with its neighbour's use and enjoyment of its property, thus constituting a nuisance. He awarded $71,427 damages for lost rental revenue and reduction in the value of the apartment building. He also ordered that if Huron Steel failed to complete remedial work within four and a half months, it would be prohibited from operating its press.

Mr. Justice Potts's decision included a discussion of three issues put forward by Huron Steel in its defence: reasonable use, the character of the neighbourhood, and the public good. The steel company had argued that its operations were reasonable in that particular neighbourhood. The judge responded that the presence of other industrial activity in the mixed-use neighbourhood could not justify the nuisance, which would offend the typical resident: "'Unreasonableness' in nuisance law is when the interference in question would not be tolerated by the ordinary occupier."[80] The judge cited Fleming's *The Law of Torts*: "Legal intervention is warranted only when an excessive use of property causes inconvenience beyond what other occupiers in the vicinity can be expected to bear, having regard to the prevailing standard of comfort of the time and place. . . . It is not enough to ask: Is the defendant using his property in what would be a reasonable manner if he had no neighbour? The question is, Is he using it reasonably, having regard to the fact that he has a neighbour?"[81]

The judge noted that activities in even industrial neighbourhoods can constitute nuisances. *Rushmer* v. *Polsue & Alfieri Ltd.*, for example, "stands for the proposition that the addition of a fresh noise may give rise to a nuisance no matter what the character of the locale."[82] And in *Oakley* v. *Webb* it had been determined, "There is a local standard applicable in each particular district, but, though the local standard may be higher in some districts than in others, yet the question in each case ultimately reduces itself to the fact of nuisance or no nuisance, having regard to all the surrounding circumstances."[83]

In discussing the question of the public good, Mr. Justice Potts noted that the Huron Steel plant employed 200 people, whose jobs could be imperilled by any requirement for extensive structural changes to reduce noise. While acknowledging that "[t]he importance of the defendant's enterprise and its value to the community is a factor in determining if the defendant's conduct is unreasonable," the judge observed that "this tends to go to the leniency of the remedy, rather than liability itself."[84]

Notes

1. *Walter* v. *Selfe* (1851), 29 L.J.R. (20 N.S.) 433 (Ch.).

2. *Ibid.* at 434.

3. *Ibid.* at 435.

4. *Ibid.* at 435.

5. *Ibid.* at 436.

6. *The Attorney-General* v. *The Council of the Borough of Birmingham* (1858), 4 K. &. J. 528, 70 E.R. 220.

7. *Ibid.* at 223.

8. *Ibid.* at 224.

9. *Ibid.* at 225.

10. *Ibid.* at 226.

11. *Ibid.* at 226.

12. *The Directors, &c., of the Imperial Gas Light and Coke Company*

v. *Samuel Broadbent* (1859), 7 H.L.C. 600, 11 E.R. 239.

13. *Ibid.* at 244.

14. *Ibid.* at 243.

15. *Ibid.* at 244.

16. *The Directors, etc. of the St. Helen's Smelting Co.* v. *William Tipping* (1865), 11 H.L.C. 642, 11 E.R. 1483.

17. *Ibid.* at 1485, citing *Hole* v. *Barlow* (1858), 4 C. B. (N.S.) 334.

18. *Ibid.* at 1486.

19. *Ibid.* at 1487-8.

20. *Dent* v. *Auction Mart Company; Pilgrim* v. *The Same; Mercers' Company* v. *The Same* (1866), L.R. 2 Eq. 238.

21. *Ibid.* at 240.

22. *Ibid.* at 255.

23. *Ibid.* at 250, citing *Yates* v. *Jack* (1866), L.R. 1 Ch. 295.

24. *Ibid.* at 249.

25. *Ibid.* at 247.

26. *Ibid.* at 246.

27. *Smith* v. *Smith* (1875), L.R. 20 Eq. 500.

28. *Ibid.* at 505.

29. *Ibid.* at 504.

30. *Shelfer* v. *City of London Electric Lighting Company* and *Meux's Brewery Company* v. *City of London Electric Lighting Company*, [1895] 1 Ch. 287.

31. *Ibid.* at 294.

32. *Ibid.* at 315.

33. *Ibid.* at 316.

34. *Ibid.* at 311.

35. *Ibid.* at 315-6.

36. *Ibid.* at 322.

37. *Ibid.* at 322-3.

38. *Ibid.* at 295-6.

39. *William Drysdale* v. *C.A. Dugas* (1896), 26 S.C.R. 20.
Although this case originated in Quebec, the Chief Justice of the Supreme Court of Canada cited another justice's observation that "the English and French law on the subject of nuisance are exactly alike" (at 23).

40. *Ibid.* at 25, citing *Broder* v. *Saillard* (1876), 2 Ch.D. 692.

41. *Ibid.* at 26, citing *Bamford* v. *Turnley* (1860), 3 B. &. S. 62, 122 E.R. 25.

42. *Ibid.* at 23-4.

43. *Ibid.* at 24.

44. *Ibid.* at 23.

45. *Ibid.* at 25.

46. *Hopkin* v. *Hamilton Electric Light and Cataract Power Co.* (1901), 2 O.L.R. 240.

47. *Ibid.* at 244.

48. *Beamish* v. *Glenn* (1916), 36 O.L.R. 10.

49. *Ibid.* at 14, citing *Appleby* v. *Erie Tobacco Co.* (1910), 22 O.L.R. 533.

50. *Ibid.* at 13, 18.

51. *Ibid.* at 17.

52. *Ibid.* at 14, citing *Attorney-General* v. *Cole & Son*, [1901] 1 Ch. 205 at 206.

53. *Ibid.* at 16.

54. *Walker* v. *McKinnon Industries Ltd.*, [1949] 4 D.L.R. 739 (Ont. H.C.), aff'd [1950] 3 D.L.R. 159 (Ont. C.A.), aff'd [1951] 3 D.L.R. 577 (P.C.).

55. *Ibid.* at 763.

56. *Ibid.* at 764; quote cited by Lord Halsbury in *Fleming* v. *Hislop* (1886), 11 App. Cas. 686.

57. *Ibid.* at 765-6, citing James, L. J., who was commenting on Sir George Jessel, M.R. in *Salvin* v. *North Brancepeth Coal Co.* (1874), L.R. 9 Ch. 705.

58. *Ibid.* at 767.

59. *Ibid.* at 769.

60. *Ibid.* at 765, referring to *Bamford* v. *Turnley, op. cit.*

61. *Russell Transport Ltd. et al.* v. *Ontario Malleable Iron Co. Ltd.*, [1952] O.R. 621 (H.C).

62. *Ibid.* at 734.

63. *Ibid.* at 728, citing *Salmond on Torts*, 10th ed., pp. 228-31.

64. *Ibid.* at 729, citing *Fleming* v. *Hislop, op. cit.*

65. *Ibid.* at 728.

66. *Ibid.* at 729, citing *Sturges* v. *Bridgman* (1879), 11 Ch.D. 852 at 865.

67. *Ibid.* at 731.

68. *Newman et al.* v. *Conair Aviation Ltd. et al.* (1972), 33 D.L.R. (3d) 474 (B.C.S.C.).

69. *Ibid.* at 477.

70. *Schenck et al.* v. *Her Majesty the Queen in Right of Ontario; Rokeby* v. *Her Majesty the Queen in Right of Ontario* (1981), 11 C.E.L.R. 1 (Ont. H.C.J.).

71. *Ibid.* at 8-9.

72. *Ibid.* at 11.

73. *Ibid.* at 11, citing *Allen* v. *Gulf Oil Refining Ltd*, [1981] 1 All E.R. 353 (H.L.).

74. *Desrosiers et al.* v. *Sullivan and Sullivan Farms Ltd.* (1986), 66 N.B.R. (2d) 243 (Q.B.). *Sullivan and Sullivan Farms Ltd.* v. *Desrosiers et al.* (1987), 76 N.B.R. (2d) 271 (C.A.).

75. *Ibid.* at 246.

76. *Ibid.* at 249.

77. *Ibid.* at 274-5.

78. *340909 Ontario Ltd.* v. *Huron Steel Products (Windsor) Inc. and Huron Steel Products* (1990), 73 O.R. (2d) 641 (H.C.J.), aff'd (1992), 10 O.R. (3d) 95.

79. *Ibid.* at 648.

80. *Ibid.* at 645.

81. *Ibid.* at 644.

82. *Ibid.* at 654.

83. *Ibid.* at 644.

84. *Ibid.* at 655.

C

Riparian Rights Case Summaries

1858: *Miner* v. *Gilmour*[1]
An upstream tanner may not block a river's flow to a downstream miller.

Harlow Miner owned a tannery beside the River Yamaska, in Lower Canada. Francis Gilmour owned land across the river, along with a grist mill downstream. Between the two men's property stretched a dam, the operation of which they disputed. Mr. Miner preferred the gate in the dam to remain closed, increasing the amount of water available to propel his tannery's wheels and machinery. But Mr. Gilmour insisted on keeping the gate open, causing more water to flow downstream to his mill.

In 1853, Mr. Miner commenced legal proceedings against his neighbour. Mr. Gilmour responded that in dry weather, it would be impossible to operate his waterpower-driven mill without opening the upstream gate. Without the additional water he would have to shut down for several months a year, causing great inconvenience.

The case went all the way to the Privy Council in England, which determined that the disputed dam violated Mr. Gilmour's riparian rights by interrupting the river's flow; he would be fully justified in opening the gates.

In his judgment for the Privy Council, Lord Kingsdown summarized the riparian law:

> By the general law applicable to running streams, every riparian proprietor has a right to what may be called the ordinary use of the water flowing past his land; for instance, to the reasonable use of the water for his domestic purposes and for his cattle, and this without regard to the effect which such use may have, in case of a deficiency, upon proprietors lower down the stream. But further, he has a right to the use of it for any purpose, or what may be deemed the extraordinary use of it, provided that he does not thereby interfere with the rights of other proprietors, either above or below him. Subject to this condition, he may dam up the stream for the purpose of a mill, or divert the water for the purpose of irrigation. But, he has no right to interrupt the regular flow of the stream, if he thereby interferes with the lawful use of the water by other proprietors, and inflicts upon them a sensible injury.[2]

1875: *Swindon Waterworks* v. *Wilts and Berks Canal*[3]

A waterworks company has no right to divert water from a stream in order to supply a nearby town.

The English Wilts and Berks Canal Company operated a navigation canal, which it supplied with water from Wroughton Stream, on which it owned property. In 1866, the Swindon Waterworks Company purchased land on a tributary of Wroughton Stream, there building a reservoir into which it diverted the tributary's water, which it then supplied to the town of Swindon.

The canal company complained that the diversion diminished its water supply. In a year of drought, having had to refuse heavy barge traffic because of insufficient water in the canal, it filed a suit requesting an injunction. After being heard by two lower courts, the case went to the House of Lords. The law lords found that the canal company was entitled to the flow of Wroughton Stream and its tributaries; it forbade the waterworks company from diverting this flow into its reservoir.

Lord Cairns, in a decision that was said to have settled—indeed, almost codified—riparian law,[4] distinguished between ordinary uses, such as washing and drinking, and extraordinary uses. The latter, he said, were allowed only if connected with the riparian land. Since the waterworks company provided water to Swindon, it did not meet this criterion:

> [T]his is not a user of the stream which could be called a reasonable user by the upper owner; it is a confiscation of the rights of the lower owner; it is an annihilation, so far as he is concerned, of that portion of the stream which is used for those purposes, and that is done, not for the sake of the tenement of the upper owner, but that the upper owner may make gains by alienating the water to other parties, who have no connection whatever with any part of the stream.[5]

Lord Cairns also noted that a riparian whose rights had been violated need not prove damages. Whether or not an injury had been sustained was "quite immaterial." A lower riparian could protect his rights in order to prevent an upper riparian from obtaining a prescriptive right (a right to carry on longstanding activities) to an extraordinary water use.

1877: *Pennington* v. *Brinsop Hall Coal*[6]
A mill owner's right to clean water takes precedence over keeping 500 people employed by a polluting colliery.

Richard Pennington and his son owned and operated a cotton mill beside Borsdane Brook, near Wigan, England. Water from the brook had supplied the mill for over 40 years when, in 1875, the Penningtons complained that the Brinsop Hall Coal Company, owner of a colliery located two and a half miles upstream, was pumping contaminated water from its mines into the brook. The water, impregnated with sulphuric acid, corroded the mill's iron boilers and other machines, requiring the Penningtons to clean and repair them far more frequently than they had in the past. The Penningtons filed suit, requesting damages and an injunction.

The coal company urged the court to limit any decision against it to damages, explaining that an injunction would force it to shut the colliery (representing a £190,000 capital investment) and throw 500 men out of work. But the court refused to balance the economic and social costs of an injunction against the plaintiffs' legal rights. In his decision, Mr. Justice Fry noted that he knew of no riparian case in which damages had been awarded in lieu of an injunction. He also explained that damages could compensate the Penningtons for past injuries only; future injuries, which would vary depending on unforeseeable uses, could not be estimated in advance. He forbade the pollution perpetually.[7]

1893: *Young* v. *Bankier Distillery*[8]
Miners have no right to alter the quality of a stream—not even to merely harden its still pure waters.

For 60 years, the Bankier Distillery Company, in the Scottish county of Sterling, operated beside a stream known as the Doups Burn, whose pure soft water perfectly suited the distillation of whiskey. Then John Young and Company, lessors of the upstream Banknock Colliery, started pumping water out of their coal mines and discharging it into the Doups Burn. The water, although pure and drinkable, was very hard, and rendered the stream unfit for the distillery's use.

The proprietors of the Bankier Distillery sought an injunction and damages on the grounds that their riparian rights had been violated. In 1893, the House of Lords upheld a lower court's judgment prohibiting the discharge of mine waters into the stream. As Lord Shand so succinctly said, "[T]he lower owner is entitled to have the water transmitted to him with its natural qualities unimpaired."[9] Lord Macnaghten similarly explained that, subject to upper riparians' ordinary and reasonable uses, a lower riparian is "entitled to the water of his stream, in its natural flow, without sensible diminution or increase and without sensible alteration in its character or quality. . . . [T]he appellants have no more right to pour into the burn foreign water which has the effect of changing its natural quality than they would have to put into it some chemical substance which would produce a similar alteration."[10]

The law lords rejected the colliery's argument that it could alter the quality of the stream as long as it didn't affect ordinary (or primary) uses, such as drinking and washing. Lord Watson explained, "I am not satisfied that a riparian owner is entitled to use water for secondary purposes, except upon the condition that he shall return it to the stream practically undiminished in volume and with its natural qualities unimpaired. I am not satisfied that in returning the water in a state fit for primary uses he has any right to alter its natural character, and so make it unfit for uses to which it had been put, or might be put, by a riparian proprietor below."[11] Lord Shand concurred: "I fully share the doubts which have been expressed as to the right of any upper proprietor so to use the water of a stream as to affect injuriously its natural quality as restored to the bed to the prejudice of the lower riparian owner, even though the water restored should be fit for ordinary domestic purposes."[12]

That the mining company was using its property in a natural and proper way was irrelevant. As Lord Macnaghten noted, "[I]t is not permissible in such a case for a man to use his own property so as to injure the property of his neighbour."[13]

1900: Weston Paper v. Pope[14]

In choosing a site, a paper mill underestimates its potential environmental effects at its own peril.

In 1894, the Weston Paper Company began manufacturing paper and other products from straw at its new mill near Greenfield, Indiana. It discharged its wastes into Brandywine Creek, which, three miles downstream, flowed through farmland belonging to Sarah Pope and others. These lower riparians had farmed and raised animals on their land for over 30 years, and had watered their livestock and fished for their dinners from Brandywine Creek. The new mill's wastes obstructed and polluted the creek, killed fish, destroyed grass when the creek overflowed, and reduced the farmland's value. The stench emanating from the wastes required the farmers to shut their doors and windows during hot weather, and caused much inconvenience and discomfort. The farmers went to court, where they obtained damages and an injunction restraining the discharge of the "putrescible and fermentable or otherwise deleterious waste."[15]

In affirming the lower court's decision to stop the pollution, the state Supreme Court refused to weigh the paper mill's $90,000 construction costs against the plaintiffs' material damages, which amounted to just $250. Judge Hadley noted that the creek's condition constituted a nuisance which caused damages "immeasurable by a pecuniary standard."[16] In this context, the size of the company's investment was irrelevant:

> The fact that [the] appellant has expended a large sum of money in the construction of its plant, and that it conducts its business in a careful manner and without malice, can make no difference in its rights to the stream. Before locating the plant the owners were bound to know that every riparian proprietor is entitled to have the waters of the stream that washes his land come to it without obstruction, diversion, or corruption, subject only to the reasonable use of the water, by those similarly entitled, for such domestic purposes as are inseparable from and necessary for the free use of their land; and they were bound, also, to know the character of their proposed business,

and to take notice of the size, course, and capacity of the stream, and to determine for themselves, and at their own peril, whether they should be able to conduct their business upon a stream of the size and character of Brandywine creek without injury to their neighbors; and the magnitude of their investment and their freedom from malice furnish no reason why they should escape the consequences of their own folly.[17]

As no public necessity required the mill to operate at its chosen location, Judge Hadley, echoing Blackstone, concluded that the business could be "carried on elsewhere less injuriously to the rights of others."[18]

The court similarly refused to consider the argument that the paper company had simply contributed to an already existing problem. That Greenfield's sewage disposal practices bore some responsibility for the creek's pollution was irrelevant. As Judge Hadley explained, "It is no defense that the city of Greenfield empties its sewage into the stream, whereby it is polluted. The fact that a water course is already contaminated from various causes does not entitle others to add thereto, nor preclude persons through whose land the water flows from obtaining relief by injunction against its further pollution."[19]

1900: Strobel v. Kerr Salt[20]
The rights of small businessmen may take precedence over a region's leading industry.

In 1886, the Kerr Salt Company founded a salt manufacturing business on Oatka Creek in western New York. It sunk seven 2,000-foot-deep wells into rock salt beds, into which it pumped 150,000 gallons of water daily. Bringing the brine to the surface, purifying the solution, and evaporating the water left the company with 860 barrels of pure white salt each day. But the process both depleted the creek's flow and littered the land with salt, which then washed into the creek.

After six years, William Strobel and 13 other downstream riparians asked the court to restrain the salt company from diverting or polluting the creek. The plaintiffs had operated mills and factories downstream of the salt works for over half a century. Now, especially during the dry season, they lacked sufficient water to run their mills. Furthermore, the salty water, formerly pure, rusted boilers, machinery, and pipes. It killed fish and vegetation. Cows and horses refused to drink it.

The lower court dismissed the action, and the Appellate Division affirmed the judgment. Seven of the plaintiffs then appealed to the Court of Appeals of New York, which reversed the earlier judgments.

In delivering the opinion for the Court of Appeals, Judge Vann noted the tension between an upper riparian's right to use water and a lower riparian's right to receive water:

> A riparian owner is entitled to a reasonable use of the water flowing by his premises in a natural stream . . . and to have it transmitted to him without sensible alteration in quality or unreasonable diminution in quantity. . . . As all other owners upon the same stream have the same right, the right of no one is absolute, but is qualified by the right of the others to have the stream substantially preserved in its natural size, flow, and purity, and to the protection against material diversion or pollution. This is the common right of all, which must not be interfered with by any. The use by each must . . . be consistent with the rights of the others, and the maxim of 'Sic utere tuo' observed by all.[21]

Reasonable use could not be strictly defined; it might include watering cattle, temporarily detaining water behind dams in order to run machinery, or irrigating land, and would vary depending on the stream, prescriptive rights, the damage done, and other local circumstances. But the Kerr Salt Company's water use—new, extraordinary, and destructive—could not be considered reasonable.

The Kerr Salt Company claimed that manufacturing salt was a proper, necessary, and reasonable use of Oatka Creek's water. Salt was the valley's leading industry. Kerr alone employed more than 100 men and women. To shut it down—to say nothing of the dozen other salt mines on Oatka Creek that might be subject to similar actions—would harm the public interest. Although such arguments had persuaded the lower courts, the Court of Appeals disagreed. Judge Vann objected to the trial judge's approving citation of a judgment regarding "'a case in which the interest and convenience of the individual must give way to the general good.'" "This," he warned, "would amount to a virtual confiscation of the property of small owners in the interest of a strong combination of capital."[22] In defending individual rights against the interests of industry Judge Vann cited an early decision in *Coal Co.* v. *Sanderson*[23]:

> It was urged that the law should be adjusted to the exigencies of the great industrial interests of the commonwealth, and that the production of an indispensable mineral . . . should not be crippled and endangered by adopting a rule that would make colliers answerable in damages for corrupting a stream into which mine water would naturally run. . . . The consequences that would flow from the adoption of the doctrine contended for could be readily foretold. Relaxation of legal liabilities and remission of legal duties to meet the current needs of great business organizations, in one direction, would logically be followed by the same relaxation and remission, on the same grounds, in all other directions. One invasion of individual right would follow another, and it might be only a question of time when, under the operations of even a single colliery, a whole countryside would be depopulated.[24]

Judge Vann then launched into his own passionate defence of individual rights:

> The lower riparian owners are entitled to a fair participation in the use of the water, and their rights cannot be cut down by the convenience or necessity of the defendant's business. . . . While the courts will not overlook the needs of important manufacturing interests, nor hamper them for trifling causes, they will not permit substantial injury to neighboring property, with a small but long-established business, for the purpose of enabling a new and great industry to flourish. They will not change the law relating to the ownership and use of property in order to accommodate a great business enterprise. According to the old and familiar rule, every man must so use his own property as not to injure that of his neighbor; and the fact that

he has invested much money and employs many men in carrying on a lawful and useful business upon his own land does not change the rule. . . .[25]

Lastly, Judge Vann addressed the fact that the dozen other salt works along Oatka Creek, similarly operated, also diminished and polluted the flow. Their contribution to the problem in no way diminished the Kerr Salt Company's obligation; if anything, it enhanced it: "The fact that other salt manufacturers are doing the same thing as the defendant, instead of preventing relief, may require it. 'Where there is a large number of persons mining on a small stream, if each should deteriorate the water a little, although the injury from the act of one might be small, the combined result of the acts of all might render the water utterly unfit for further use; and, if each could successfully defend an action on the ground that his act alone did not materially affect the water, the prior appropriator might be deprived of its use, and at the same time be without a remedy.'"[26]

1903: *Warren* v. *Gloversville*[27]
Neither the requirements of great industries nor a country's need to develop its natural resources can justify violating a riparian's rights.

John Warren owned a house and a meat market on land bordering the canal running through Johnstown, New York. The canal flowed from the Cayudetta Creek, which, four miles upstream, passed through the city of Gloversville. Gloversville had been discharging its 18,000 inhabitants' sewage into the creek since 1890, rendering downstream waters "foul, noxious, and filthy" and permeating Mr. Warren's buildings with "unwholesome, offensive, and deleterious odors arising therefrom." Mr. Warren sued for damages and an injunction, receiving only the former from the trial court. He successfully appealed.

The Appellate Division's Judge Chase explained that since Mr. Warren had suffered substantial damage, he was entitled to an injunction, regardless of its impact on the general good. (He then suspended the injunction, which prohibited the city from fouling Mr. Warren's land, for one year and reserved the right to further postpone its operation if necessary.) In his defence of individual rights over those of municipalities or industries, the judge reviewed *Strobel* v. *Kerr Salt* and the nuisance case of *Sammons* v. *Gloversville*. He concluded:

> An equity court is not bound to issue an injunction, when it will produce great public or private mischief, merely for the purpose of protecting a technical or unsubstantial right. . . . When, however, the damages are substantial, the fact that an injunction would interfere with great industries, the development of natural resources, or with the plans of a great city for drainage, is not a sufficient reason for relaxing the ordinary rules governing the rights of riparian owners of land. . . . Where wrongful interference with the waters of a stream causes substantial injury, an injunction to the person so substantially injured is a matter of right.[28]

1912: *Crowther* v. *Cobourg*[29]

A town may not discharge any sewage into a stream, even if it is odourless and apparently threatens no one's health.

In the early part of this century, the town of Cobourg, Ontario, constructed a sewer that emptied into Factory Creek. The owners of a large hotel, the grounds of which Factory Creek crossed, objected that some of the nine houses served by the new sewer discharged human waste into it—waste that went untreated into the creek. They sued the town.

In its defence, Cobourg argued that the pollution from its sewer wasn't serious as it neither smelled nor was likely to produce disease. Mr. Justice Middleton, who heard the case in the Ontario High Court, agreed that the creek was not "an offence to the eye or the nose" (although he cautioned that in the summer's heat it could become annoying and dangerous, especially in the event of disease in one of the houses connected to the sewer). But the degree of dilution and the sewage's innocuousness weren't relevant issues, he concluded, for the town had "no right to pollute this stream in the smallest degree."[30] In support of his position, the judge cited *Young* v. *Bankier Distillery*, which, he said, showed that "nuisance or no nuisance is not the question, but the right to the water in its natural condition."[31] The judge therefore issued an injunction "restraining the defendants from in any way polluting the stream in question by discharging or permitting to be discharged through the drain in question any sewage or other foul or noxious matter."[32]

In his decision, Mr. Justice Middleton defended individual rights over collective rights. The municipality had argued against an injunction on the ground that it would create a hardship for it. This, the judge noted, "ignores the fact that the plaintiff's right to this stream is a property right, and the municipality have no right to take or destroy the property of an individual without compensation. Many an individual has had to suffer from a failure to recognise this elementary principle, and the only difference in the case of a municipality is, that it is given the power to expropriate."[33]

Mr. Justice Middleton approvingly noted the respect paid to individual rights in the nuisance case, *Attorney-General* v. *Corporation of Birmingham*, along with the following passage from the decision in *Roberts* v. *Gwyrfai District Council*:

> I know of no duty of the Court which it is more important to observe and no power of the Court which it is more important to enforce than its power of keeping public bodies within their rights. The moment public bodies exceed their rights, they do so to the injury and oppression of private individuals, and those persons are entitled to be protected from injury arising from the operations of public bodies.[34]

1913: Whalen v. Union Bag & Paper[35]
A pulp mill may not pollute already foul water.

Robert Whalen owned a 255-acre farm on Kayaderosseras Creek, near Albany, New York. A few miles upstream, the Union Bag & Paper Company operated its pulp mill, which represented an investment of over a million dollars and employed between 400 and 500 people. The mill's sulphurous effluent and wood waste materials polluted Kayaderosseras Creek, interfering with Mr. Whalen's use of his farm and diminishing its value. Mr. Whalen went to court, first obtaining an injunction (to be suspended for one year) against the pollution from the trial court, then losing it in the Appellate Division, and finally regaining it in the New York Court of Appeals.

In his dissenting opinion at the appellate level, Judge Betts objected to his colleagues' having noted that since other industries also fouled Kayaderosseras Creek, enjoining Union Bag & Paper would not purify the water. It would be absurd to allow pollution on the grounds of other pollution, and prevent only contamination of pure water: "Of course, this provision substantially defeats itself, as the other wrongdoers if brought to court by plaintiff can point to this defendant (claimed to be the chief offender) and insist that while it, the defendant, is not restrained they should not be, so that this judgment, if it remain, renders plaintiff impotent to obtain an injunction against any defiler of this stream."[36] He cited the decision in *Sammons* v. *Gloversville* to support his arguments on this subject.

Judge Betts also vigorously objected to his colleagues' having balanced the burdens and benefits of an injunction. Citing *Strobel* v. *Kerr Salt* and *Warren* v. *Gloversville*, he explained, "It has always been the boast of equity that any substantial injustice might be corrected by it to even the humblest suitor, and that the financial size of such a suitor's antagonist was not important."[37]

In summary, Judge Betts protested that his colleagues had made "a new departure in riparian law,"[38] and recommended that the lower court's decision to grant an injunction be affirmed.

Two years later, the Court of Appeals did indeed affirm the earlier injunction. In his judgment for the Court of Appeals, Justice Werner noted that the lower court had weighed the injunction's great cost to the pulp mill against Mr. Whalen's relatively small injury. In reinstating the injunction, Justice Werner maintained that such a balancing of injuries was unjustified: "Although the damage to the plaintiff may be slight as compared with the defendant's expense of abating the condition, that is not a good reason for refusing an injunction. Neither courts of equity nor law can be guided by such a rule, for if followed to its logical conclusion it would deprive the poor litigant of his little property by giving it to those already rich."[39]

Justice Werner referred to Pomeroy's discussion of the injustice of substituting damages for an injunction. "[D]enying the injunction," Pomeroy had said, "puts the hardship on the party in whose favor the legal right exists, instead of on the wrongdoer. . . . The weight of authority is against allowing a balancing of injury as a means of determining the propriety of issuing an injunction."[40] Justice Werner also cited the decision in *Weston Paper* v. *Pope* as one that aptly expressed the rule to be applied to the case at hand.

1913: *Nepisiquit Real Estate and Fishing* v. *Canadian Iron*[41]
Downstream fishermen may prevent an iron mine from discolouring a river.

The Nepisiquit Real Estate and Fishing Company owned a number of lots along the last 20 miles of New Brunswick's Nepisiquit River, where its members fished for salmon and trout. During the summer of 1912, the upstream Canadian Iron Corporation discoloured the river's waters while grinding up and washing its iron ore—a process that caused leakage into one of the river's tributaries.

The fishing company went to court, claiming that the pollution injured spawning grounds and practically destroyed its fishing privileges. The iron company denied the charges. But Mr. Justice McLeod had visited the site and seen the dirtied, muddied water. A riparian, he said (citing *Young* v. *Bankier Distillery*, among others), "has the right to the full flow of the water in its natural state, without any diminution or pollution."[42] Clearly the iron mill had altered the Nepisiquit's natural condition.

The judge accordingly restrained the iron company from polluting the river. As a concession to the company's importance, however, he allowed it a four-month grace period in which to make necessary changes.

1914: *Watson* v. *Jackson*[43]
A riparian may not divert water for use off riparian lands.

In the early part of this century, numerous dams and ponds could be found along Ontario's Don River. Some were used to generate power, others ran mills, and others had fallen into disrepair. In 1912, W. H. Jackson acquired one of the latter—an old mill and tannery site that had been out of commission since a section of the dam had broken away 34 years earlier. He rebuilt the dam and created a pond to generate power and to supply the village of Thornhill and a nearby sanitarium with water.

Mr. Watson, who lived downstream, objected to any interference with the river's flow. The Don, "a strong, live stream," wound through his property; had it not been for the river, he would not have purchased that land. He went to court, seeking an injunction.

In his judgment for the Appellate Division of the Ontario Supreme Court, Mr. Justice Clute noted that extraordinary water uses must be connected with riparian land, a principle articulated by Lord Cairns in *Swindon Waterworks* v. *Wilts and Berks Canal*. To divert water off riparian land and to consume it for purposes unconnected with that land "would be, not only an unreasonable use of the water, but would be a use altogether outside and beyond the right of the riparian proprietor to use the water."[44] The judge therefore forbade Mr. Jackson to divert the Don's water to the sanitarium, Thornhill, or the surrounding country.

1918: *Stollmeyer* v. *Trinidad Lake Petroleum*[45]

An oil company may not divert or pollute a river, even if in so doing it harms no one.

Trinidad's Vessigny River flowed through jungle lands owned by the Trinidad Lake Petroleum Company Limited. The company dammed the river and a tributary, creating two reservoirs that would provide its own petroleum fields with a plentiful and uniform water supply and enable it to pump water to its subsidiaries' distant oil wells. In addition to diverting the river, the company polluted it by returning to it used, oil-impregnated water.

Charles Stollmeyer, who owned 100 acres of unused land at the river's mouth, took his case against the upstream oil company through

Trinidad's court system and, ultimately, to the British Privy Council, which recognized his riparian right to the natural flow of the river.

In establishing a riparian's right to an undiminished and unpolluted flow, the Privy Council's Lord Sumner cited Lord Macnaghten's judgement in *Young* v. *Bankier Distillery*. He proceeded to find that the oil company, first in filling its reservoir and then in sending water to other properties, sensibly diminished the river's flow; it had no entitlement to do so. Nor had the company any entitlement to pollute the river. The fact that Mr. Stollmeyer had suffered no damages affected neither his rights nor the company's obligations.

The oil company urged the court to spare it an injunction on the grounds that the injury to it and to the local economy would outweigh the benefit to the plaintiff. That argument had convinced the Trinidadian trial judge, who had dismissed Mr. Stollmeyer's action in part because it would harm the district's only industry. But it didn't sway the Privy Council. Lord Sumner explained:

> There can be no doubt that if the respondents have caused such sensible diminution and this violated the appellants' rights, they cannot excuse or defend their wrong by showing how disproportionate is the loss which they will suffer by being restrained to any loss which the appellants have suffered or are likely to suffer by their wrongful acts, or by dwelling on the general importance of the enterprises, which, if they cannot obtain a supply of water, must promptly come to an end. These considerations may be relevant to the form of remedy, especially to the time and opportunities which should be given them for finding some way out of their difficulty, but they cannot operate to deprive the appellants of their right to have their wrong redressed, if wrong has been done them.[46]

The court did indeed grant the oil company ample time to find a way out of its difficulty: it allowed it two years to implement necessary works, after which time Mr. Stollmeyer would be at liberty to apply for an injunction.

1928: Groat v. Edmonton[47]

A city's environmental obligations limit its property rights.

A deep ravine traversed the Groats' land in Edmonton, Alberta. Although the stream flowing through the ravine to the Saskatchewan River was once pure and healthy, and used for drinking and supplying livestock, it had become "grossly polluted." The Groats blamed the pollution on several factors, including the construction of a large storm sewer which discharged surface water, horse droppings, street sweepings, and other filth from Edmonton's streets into the ravine, especially in the spring, when the city flushed the winter's accumulated filth from the sewer.

The Groats took legal action against Edmonton, which ultimately resulted in a 1928 Supreme Court of Canada ruling that the city had violated the Groats' riparian rights, entitling them to damages and an injunction, which would take effect after two years, against continued nuisances.

Citing *Young* v. *Bankier Distillery* and *Stollmeyer* v. *Trinidad Lake Petroleum*, Mr. Justice Lamont explained that although the city, as an upper riparian, had the right to drain its land, it did not have the right to collect pollution in a sewer and then flush it into a stream. The city's obligations restricted its rights: it could not discharge its filth onto neighbours' lands. As Lord Lindley had said in *Ballard* v. *Tomlinson*:

> *Prima facie* no man has a right to use his own land in such a way as to be a nuisance to his neighbour, and whether the nuisance is effected by sending filth on to his neighbour's land, or by putting poisonous matter on his own land and allowing it to escape on his neighbour's land, or whether the nuisance is effected by poisoning the air which his neighbour breathes, or the water which he drinks, appears to me wholly immaterial. If a man chooses to put filth on his own land he must take care not to let it escape on to his neighbour's land.[48]

Several of the judges rejected Edmonton's claim that it had statutory authority to pollute. According to Mr. Justice Rinfret, "So far as statutory powers are concerned, they should not be understood as authorizing the creation of a private nuisance—unless indeed the statute expressly so states."[49] While the city charter provided for the construction and management of a sewer system, it did not expressly authorize pollution. Nor was pollution a necessary result of the works that had been approved; even the city engineer admitted that it could be prevented.

Mr. Justice Rinfret acknowledged that the city represented the collective rights of its ratepayers, who required sewers. "But these rights," he explained, "are necessarily restricted by correlative obligations. Although held by the municipalities for the benefit of all the inhabitants, they must not—except upon the basis of due compensation—be exercised by them to the prejudice of an individual ratepayer."[50]

The judge echoed the decision in the nuisance case of *Attorney-General* v. *Birmingham*: "But, whatever the consequences, and much as the result may cause inconvenience, the principle must be upheld that, unless Parliament otherwise decrees, 'public works must be so executed as not to interfere with private rights of individuals.'"[51]

1953: Pride of Derby and Derbyshire Angling v. British Celanese[52]
A fishing club may save a river from upstream industries.

The waters of the River Derwent, in north-central England, flowed unpolluted until they reached the Borough of Derby's sewer outfalls—one that discharged storm water overflow and untreated sewage during flood conditions and another that discharged inadequately treated effluent from the local sewage treatment works. The river then passed through land owned by British Celanese Ld., whose effluent polluted and warmed it. Downstream, discharge from the British Electricity Authority's power station further increased the river's temperature.

Because the changes in water quality and temperature killed the river's fish and their food supply, the Pride of Derby and Derbyshire Angling Association Ld., a fishing club that owned a fishery in the Derwent, and the Earl of Harrington, who owned land along the river, took the three upstream polluters to court. In 1952, the court issued an injunction restraining the defendants from altering the river's quality or temperature or interfering with the plaintiffs' enjoyment of their fishing rights; it then suspended the injunction's operation for two years. The Chancery Division, upon appeal by two of the defendants, confirmed the decision.

Master-of-the-Rolls Evershed rejected the Borough of Derby's argument that it had statutory authority to pollute. For that defence to work, he explained, the nuisance would have to be expressly authorized by an act of Parliament or, alternatively, be the inevitable consequence of that which an act did authorize. While the 1901 Derby Corporation Act had established sewage disposal works, it had not authorized pumping untreated sewage into the river. In fact, it had specifically prohibited nuisances: "The sewage disposal works constructed . . . shall at all times hereafter be conducted so that the same shall not be a nuisance and in particular the corporation shall not allow any noxious or offensive effluvia to escape therefrom or do or permit or suffer any other act which shall be a nuisance or injurious to the health or reasonable comfort of the inhabitants of Spondon. . . ."[53] The language, Master Evershed concluded, seemed "almost too plain for argument"; the act did not exempt Derby from liability.

The Borough of Derby also argued that when it had built its sewage system at the turn of the century it had been sufficient for the local population. Subsequent population growth—a circumstance beyond its control—rendered it inadequate. Lord Justice Denning protested that if local authorities, under the Planning Acts, have control over development in their district, they should be responsible for its consequences: "They know (or ought to know) that the increase in building will cause the existing sewers to overflow, and yet they allow it to go on without enlarging the capacity of the sewerage system. By so doing, they themselves are helping to fill the system beyond its capacity, and are guilty of nuisance.[54]

The Borough of Derby urged the court to substitute damages for an injunction. Damages would be a sufficient remedy. And an injunction, it maintained, would be improper. It could not simply rebuild its sewage system at will; it needed a licence, and, in order to borrow money, the consent of the Minister of Local Government and Planning.

But awarding damages, Master Evershed noted, would require the plaintiffs to return to the courts again and again—an extremely costly process. Furthermore, an injunction was not purely discretionary:

> It is, I think, well settled that if A proves that his proprietary rights are being wrongfully interfered with by B, and that B intends to continue his wrong, then A is prima facie entitled to an injunction, and he will be deprived of that remedy only if special circumstances exist, including the circumstance that damages are an adequate remedy for the wrong that he has suffered. In the present case it is plain that damages would be a wholly inadequate remedy for the first-named plaintiffs, who have not been incorporated in order to fish for monthly sums.[55]

Lord Justice Romer agreed: "Anyone who creates an actionable nuisance is a wrongdoer, and the court will prima facie restrain him from persisting in his activities."[56]

1967: Rugby v. Walters[57]
Spray irrigation, being evaporative, is not an acceptable riparian water use.

John Walters owned a 200-acre farm on the south bank of the River Avon near Rugby, England. In 1959 he installed and began using a spray irrigation system, drawing water sometimes from the river, and other times from a reservoir on his property. Some summer days he would spray his crops with up to 60,000 gallons, most of which evaporated instead of returning to the river. Despite its large volume, Mr. Walters' water use had no visible or measurable effect on the river; while it peaked at 10.8 per cent of the daily flow, it usually comprised less than 1 per cent of the monthly flow.

The Rugby Joint Water Board objected to Mr. Walters' spraying operations. The Avon was Rugby's principal source of water supply and the board, as a riparian owner, was entitled to receive the river's full flow downstream of Mr. Walter's farm. The board filed suit in 1964.

In his 1966 judgment, Mr. Justice Buckley reviewed many familiar cases (including *Miner* v. *Gilmour, Swindon Waterworks* v. *Wilts & Berks Canal,* and *Young* v. *Bankier Distillery*) and concluded that "a riparian owner is not entitled to take water from a stream for extraordinary purposes without returning it to the stream substantially undiminished in quantity."[58] Withdrawing water from the Avon for large-scale spray irrigation could not qualify as an ordinary water use; nor would it be a justifiable extraordinary use, since the water would not return to the stream.[59] The judge therefore forbade Mr. Walters from withdrawing water from the river for that purpose.

1970: Gauthier v. Naneff[60]
A charity's honourable intentions cannot justify possible pollution.

In April 1970, the Parks and Recreation Commission, in Sudbury, Ontario, approved the use of Bell Park for the Ontario Outboard Championships—a speed boat regatta to be held on Lake Ramsay in September by the Sudbury Rotary Club.

In August, Hazen Gauthier learned of the proposed races from an article in the *Sudbury Star*. He worried that the 60 motorboats competing in the regatta would contaminate Lake Ramsay, Sudbury's principal source of water. After trying unsuccessfully to persuade the Rotary Club to abandon its plans, he asked the Ontario Water Resources Commission to intervene on his behalf. Ontario's Minister of Energy and Resources Management refused, explaining that "the local authorities had made the decision to hold the regatta and no interference by the Commission seemed warranted."[61]

Mr. Gauthier, along with three other Sudbury residents, then launched an action for a restraining order. One of the plaintiffs, Rita Glenn Dixon, owned land on Lake Ramsay. Citing Ms. Dixon's riparian rights, Judge Dunlap issued an injunction prohibiting the planned races.

In his decision, Judge Dunlap relied on Chief Justice McRuer's judgment in *McKie* v. *K.V.P.* (see Chapter Four), along with its numerous historical references. He concluded that Ms. Dixon's riparian rights entitled her "to the flow of water through or by her land in its natural state."[62] Were the planned races to proceed, there would be "a reasonable apprehension of the impairment to some degree" of Ms. Dixon's rights.[63] In such cases, as Lord Kingsdown had stated in the nuisance case, *Imperial Gas Light & Coke* v. *Broadbent*, injunctions should be granted as a matter of course.

Explaining that Ms. Dixon need not prove damages to obtain an injunction, Judge Dunlap cited *Kerr on Injunctions*:

> Where a defendant claims the right to use the water of a stream in [an] unreasonable manner, it is not necessary for the plaintiff to show that he has sustained actual injury in order to obtain an injunction. . . . A riparian owner is entitled to the flow of water past his land, in its natural state of purity undeteriorated by noxious matter discharged into it by others, and anyone who fouls the water infringes a right of property of the riparian owner, who can maintain an action against the wrongdoer without proving that the pollution has caused him actual damage. . . . In the case of injury to riparian rights from the pollution of water, the Court does not, except in special cases, award damages in lieu of an injunction.[64]

Judge Dunlap refused to consider the motives of the defendants or the impact that an injunction would have upon them:

> It is trite law that economic necessities of the defendants are irrelevant in a case of this character. It is unfortunate that in the circumstances of this case the rights of a riparian land proprietor come into conflict with the laudable objects of a charitable pursuit formulated and prosecuted with sincerity and dedication. . . . None the less, the most honourable of intentions alone at no time can justify the expropriation of common law rights of riparian owners. . . .
>
> It was urged upon me by counsel for the defendants that the financial commitments of the defendants were such as to tilt the scales of convenience in support of the rejection of this application. While I am in sympathy with this submission for the reason already expressed, I cannot yield to same in violation of the rights already acknowledged.[65]

Notes

1. *Miner* v. *Gilmour* (1858), 12 Moo. P.C. 131, 14 E.R. 861.

2. *Ibid.* at 870.

3. *The Directors, etc. of the Swindon Waterworks Company Limited* v. *The Proprietors of the Wilts and Berks Canal Navigation Company* (1875), L.R. 7 H.L. 697.

4. Lord Halsbury, in *McCartney* v. *Londonderry & Lough Swilly Railway Co. Ltd.*, [1904] A.C. 301 (H.L.).

5. *Swindon Waterworks* v. *Wilts and Berks, op. cit.* at 705.

6. *Pennington* v. *Brinsop Hall Coal Company* (1877), 5 Ch. D. 769.

7. The judge awarded "a perpetual injunction . . . to restrain the Defendants from discharging water from their mines and colliery into the stream so as to cause an injury to the Plaintiffs' mill, engine, boilers, and works . . . or so as to cause the stream to flow to the Plaintiffs' mill and premises in a state less pure than that in which it flowed thither previously to the commencement of the Defendants' pumping." He suspended the injunction for three months (*Ibid.* at 774).

8. *John Young and Company* v. *The Bankier Distillery Company and Others*, [1893] A.C. 691 (H.L.).

9. *Ibid.* at 700.

10. *Ibid.* at 698-9.

11. *Ibid.* at 696.

12. *Ibid.* at 700.

13. *Ibid.* at 699.

14. *Weston Paper Co.* v. *Pope et al.*, 155 Ind. 394, 57 N.E. 719, 56 L.R.A. 899 (1900).

15. *Ibid.* at 720.

16. *Ibid.* at 720.

17. *Ibid.* at 721.

18. *Ibid.* at 721.

19. *Ibid.* at 721.

20. *Strobel et al.* v. *Kerr Salt Co.*, 164 N.Y. 303, 320, 58 N.E. 142, 147, 51 L.R.A. 687, 79 Am. St. Rep. 643 (N.Y. Ct. App. 1900).

21. *Ibid.* at 147.

22. *Ibid.* at 145.

23. 1878 trial decision, overturned in 113 Pa. St. 126, 6 Atl. 453 (1886).

24. Cited in *Strobel et al.* v. *Kerr Salt Co.*, *op. cit.* at 146. Judge Vann acknowledged that a higher court had, in the name of the community interest in natural resource development, overturned this decision, but noted that "[c]ourts of the highest standing have refused to follow the Sanderson Case" and that "its doctrine was finally limited by the court which announced it" (at 147).

25. *Ibid.* at 147-8.

26. *Ibid.* at 148, citing *Hill* v. *Smith*, 32 Cal. 166.

27. *Warren* v. *City of Gloversville*, 81 App. Div., 291, 293, 80 N.Y.

Supp. 912, 913 (N.Y. Ct. App. 1903).

28. *Ibid.* at 913-4.

29. *Crowther* v. *Town of Cobourg* (1912), 1 D.L.R. 40 (Ont. H.C.).

30. *Ibid.* at 42.

31. *Ibid.* at 42.

32. *Ibid.* at 43.

33. *Ibid.* at 42.

34. *Ibid.* at 43, citing *Roberts* v. *Gwyrfai District Council*, [1899] 2 Ch. D. 608.

35. *Whalen* v. *Union Bag & Paper Co.* First appeal: 145 App. Div. 1, 129 N.Y. Supp. 391, (1911); Second appeal: 208 N.Y. 1, 5, 101 N.E. 805, 806, (N.Y. Ct. App. 1913).

36. *Ibid.* at 393.

37. *Ibid.* at 393.

38. *Ibid.* at 395.

39. 101 N.E. 806.

40. *Ibid.* at 806, citing Eq. Juris. Volume 5.

41. *Nepisiquit Real Estate and Fishing Company, Limited* v. *Canadian Iron Corporation, Limited* (1913), 42 N.B.R. 387 (Ch.D.).

42. *Ibid.* at 392.

43. *Watson* v. *Jackson* (1914), 19 D.L.R. 733 (Ont. S.C.).

44. *Ibid.* at 745.

45. *Stollmeyer and Others* v. *Trinidad Lake Petroleum Company Limited, and Others*, [1918] A.C. 485 (P.C.).

46. *Ibid.* at 494.

47. *Malcolm Forbes Groat and Walter S. Groat* v. *The Mayor, Aldermen and Burgesses, being the Corporation of the City of Edmonton*, [1928] S.C.R. 522.

48. *Ibid.* at 537-8, citing *Ballard* v. *Tomlinson* (1885), 29 Ch. D. 115 at 126.

49. *Ibid.* at 533.

50. *Ibid.* at 533.

51. *Ibid.* at 534.

52. *Pride of Derby and Derbyshire Angling Association Ld. and Another* v. *British Celanese Ld. and Others*, [1953] 1 Ch. 149.

53. *Ibid.* at 164.

54. *Ibid.* at 190.

55. *Ibid.* at 181.

56. *Ibid.* at 194.

57. *Rugby Joint Water Board* v. *Walters*, [1967] 1 Ch. 397.

58. *Ibid.* at 422.

59. It is interesting to compare this case with *Embrey and Another* v. *Owen*, in which conventional irrigation that neither perceptibly diminished the stream nor impeded the operation of downstream mills was deemed to be a reasonable water use (1851), 6 Exch. 353, 155 E.R. 586.

60. *Gauthier et al.* v. *Naneff et al.* (1970), [1971] 1 O.R. 97 (H.C.J.).

61. *Ibid.* at 99.

62. *Ibid.* at 101.

63. *Ibid.* at 103.

64. *Ibid.* at 101-2, citing 6th ed., pp. 216-8 and 239-40.

65. *Ibid.* at 103.

Works Cited

Albion, Robert G. *Forests and Sea Power: The Timber Problem of the Royal Navy 1652-1862*. Cambridge: Harvard University Press, 1926.

Anderson, Terry, and Donald Leal. *Free Market Environmentalism*. San Francisco: Pacific Research Institute for Public Policy and Westview Press, 1991.

Angler's Co-operative Association. *ACA Review* (Summer 1993).

—————. "What to do in case of pollution." Undated brochure.

Anisman, Philip. "Water Pollution Control in Ontario." *Ottawa Law Review* 5: 342-410.

Aristotle. *A Treatise on Government, or, The Politics of Aristotle*. London: J. M. Dent; New York: E. P. Dutton, 1912.

Armstrong, Frederick H. *City in the Making: Progress, People and Perils in Victorian Toronto*. Toronto: Dundurn Press, 1988.

—————. *Toronto: The Place of Meeting*. Windsor Publications, 1983.

Bardach, Eugene, and Robert A. Kagan. *Going By the Book: The Problem of Regulatory Unreasonableness*. Philadelphia: Temple University Press, 1982.

Blackstone, Sir William. *The Commentaries on the Laws of England. (London: 1765-9). Adapted to the Present State of the Law by Robert Malcolm Kerr*. London: John Murray, 1876.

Block, Walter. "Economists and Environmentalists: Friends or Foes?" Lecture presented to the Faculty of Forestry, University of Toronto, November 7, 1990.

—————. "Environmental Problems, Private Property Rights Solutions." In *Economics and the Environment: A Reconciliation*, edited by Walter Block, 281-332. Vancouver: The Fraser Institute, 1990.

Brenner, Joel Franklin. "Nuisance Law and the Industrial Revolution." *The Journal of Legal Studies* 3, no. 2 (June 1974): 403-33.

Bromley, Daniel W. *Environment and Economy: Property Rights and Public Policy*. Cambridge: Blackwell, 1991.

Buchanan, Elmer (Ontario Minister of Agriculture, Food and Rural Affairs). "Introducing the Niagara Tender Fruit Lands Program." Speech delivered in Niagara-on-the-Lake, Ontario, May 7, 1994.

Campbell, Richard S., Peter H. Pearse, Anthony Scott, and Milan Uzelac. "Water Management in Ontario—An Economic Evaluation of Public Policy." *Osgoode Hall Law Journal* 12, no. 3 (December 1974): 475-526.

Canada. Department of Fisheries and Oceans, Task Force on Incomes and Adjustment in the Atlantic Fishery. *Charting a New Course: Towards the Fishery of the Future*. November 1993.

———. Department of Fisheries and Oceans. *Policy for Canada's Atlantic Fisheries in the 1980s: A Discussion Paper*. Introduced by Roméo LeBlanc. June 1981.

———. Department of Fisheries and Oceans, Atlantic Stock Assessment Secretariat Science Branch. *Report on the Status of Groundfish Stocks in the Canadian Northwest Atlantic*. June 1994.

———. Forestry Canada. *Forestry Facts*. Revised May 1990.

———. House of Commons. *Debates*. February 6, 1970.

———. House of Commons. *Minutes of Proceedings and Evidence of the Standing Committee on Environment*. Issue No. 6, September 26, 1991; Issue No. 8, October 3, 1991; Issue No. 9, October 8, 1991; Issue No. 12, October 23, 1991; Issue No. 13, October 24, 1991; Issue No. 16, November 5, 1991; Issue No. 17, November 6, 1991; Issue No. 18, November 7, 1991.

———. Task Force on Atlantic Fisheries, Michael J. L. Kirby, Chair. *Navigating Troubled Waters: A New Policy for the Atlantic Fisheries*. 1983.

Canadian Council of Ministers of the Environment. *Contaminated Site Liability Report: Recommended Principles for a Consistent Approach Across Canada*. Prepared by the Core Group on Contaminated Site Liability. March 25, 1993.

———. "Who Should Pay? Financing the Clean-up of Orphan Contaminated Sites." *Envirogram* 3, no. 1 (March 1994): 1, 5.

Canadian Environmental Law Association. "web.announcements topic 130." Announcement on "the Web" computer network, December 23, 1991.

Canadian Environmental Law Research Foundation. "An Overview of Canadian Law and Policy Governing Great Lakes Water Quantity Management." *Case Western Reserve Journal of International Law* 18, no. 67 (1986): 109-53.

The Canadian Real Estate Association. *Property Rights: The Flawed Charter. The Case for an Amendment to the Charter of Rights and Freedoms*. October 1991.

Careless, J. M. S. *Toronto to 1918: An Illustrated History*. Toronto: James Lorimer & Co., 1984.

Clover, Glen Edward. "Torts: Trespass, Nuisance, and $E=mc^2$." *Oklahoma Law Review* 19 (1966): 117-22.

Coase, Ronald H. "The Problem of Social Cost." *The Journal of Law & Economics* 3 (October 1960): 1-44.

Constitutional Caucus of the Canadian Environment Network. "Property rights have no place in the Charter." *Alternatives* 18, no. 4 (1992): 25.

Cooperman, Jim. "Cutting Down Canada." In *Clearcut: The Tragedy of Industrial Forestry*, edited by Bill Devall, 55-63. San Francisco: Sierra Club Books and Earth Island Press, 1993.

Crocker, Thomas D., and A. J. Rogers. *Environmental Economics*. Hinsdale, Ill.: Dryden Press, 1971.

Daily Telegraph. Moore, Toby. "'Save the Whales by Privatisation' Call." January 27, 1992.

Dales, J. H. *Pollution, Property & Prices: An Essay in Policy-Making and Economics*. Toronto: University of Toronto Press, 1968.

"Debate over property right entrenchment heating up." *Environment Policy & Law* (November 1991): 313.

Demsetz, Harold. "Toward a Theory of Property Rights." *The American Economic Review* 57, no. 2 (May 1967): 347-59.

Denhez, Marc. *You Can't Give It Away: Tax Aspects of Ecologically Sensitive Lands*. Sustaining Wetlands Issues Paper No. 1992-4. Ottawa: North American Wetlands Conservation Council (Canada), 1992.

"Deposit of Gaseous and Invisible Solid Industrial Wastes Held to Constitute Trespass." *Columbia Law Review* 60 (1960): 877-82.

Dewees, Donald N. "The Comparative Efficacy of Tort Law and Regulation for Environmental Protection." University of Toronto Law and Economics Working Paper Series, no. 12. November, 1991.

Dewees, D. N. with Michael Halewood. "The Efficiency of the Common Law: Sulphur Dioxide Emissions in Sudbury." *University of Toronto Law Journal* 42 (1992): 1-21.

Dolan, Edwin G. and David E. Lindsey. *Economics*. 6th ed. Chicago: The Dryden Press, 1991.

Drushka, Ken. *Stumped: The Forest Industry in Transition*. Vancouver: Douglas and McIntyre, 1985.

Ducks Unlimited Canada. *1990 Annual Report*.

————. *1992 Annual Report.*

————. "Ontario Land CARE," Brochure. August 1993.

————. "Prairie Care: A Conservation Partners Program." Undated brochure.

Economic Instruments Collaborative. *Achieving Atmospheric Quality Objectives Through the Use of Economic Instruments.* Ottawa: The National Round Table on the Environment and the Economy, 1993.

Ellickson, Robert C. "Alternatives to Zoning: Covenants, Nuisance Rules, and Fines as Land Use Controls." *The University of Chicago Law Review* 40, no. 4 (Summer 1973): 681-781.

Epstein, Richard. *Takings: Private Property and the Power of Eminent Domain.* Cambridge: Harvard University Press, 1985.

————. "The Social Consequences of Common Law Rules." *Harvard Law Review* 95, no. 8 (June 1982): 1717-1751.

Estrin, David, and John Swaigen. *Environment on Trial: A Guide to Ontario Environmental Law and Policy.* 3rd ed. A project of the Canadian Institute for Environmental Law and Policy. Toronto: Edmond Montgomery Publications Limited, 1993.

Financial Post. Crawford, Michael. "Bracing for environmental rights bill." May 26, 1992.

————. Ficner, Charles. "Confiscating Ontario private property." September 23, 1991.

————. Fletcher, Anne. "Carmanah no winner for MB?" November 24-6, 1990.

————. Joyce, Greg. "B.C. court quashes land claim ruling." June 26, 1993.

————. Kennedy, Peter. "Mining sector wants help for abandoned sites." February 24, 1994.

————. Kinross, Louise. "Inuit vote to change face of the Arctic" and "Agreement gives Inuit interest in mining Nunavut's resources." November 17, 1992.

————. "Conservationists blast 'nature tax,'" March 16, 1994.

————. "Logging gets OK in spotted owl area," May 15, 1992.

————. "Then and Now: Bob Rae." *The Financial Post Magazine*, April 1994.

Findlay, Barbara, and Ann Hillyer. *Here Today, Here Tomorrow: Legal Tools for the Voluntary Protection of Private Land in British Columbia.* Vancouver: West Coast Environmental Law Research Foundation, January 1994.

"Fingering pollution." *The Economist*, November 27, 1993, 91-2.

Fisher, Hank, and Wendy E. Hudson. *Building Economic Incentives Into the Endangered Species Act.* 2nd ed. Washington D.C.: Defenders of Wildlife, December 1993.

Flaherty, David H. "Writing Canadian Legal History: An Introduction." In *Essays in the History of Canadian Law*, edited by David H. Flaherty. Toronto: The University of Toronto Press and The Osgoode Society, 1981.

Fox, Glenn. "Free Market Environmentalism." Paper presented at Economic Rights and the Canadian Constitution, a conference sponsored by the Ontario Committee for Economic Education, June 6-7, 1992.

———. "Ownership and Stewardship of Natural Resources." Paper presented at Liberty '92, the convention of the Ontario Libertarian Party, November 28, 1992.

———. "The Pricing of Environmental Goods: A Praxeological Critique of Contingent Valuation." November 15, 1992.

"Fresh angle." *The Economist*, June 11, 1994, 85.

Fridman, G. H. L. *Introduction to the Law of Torts.* Toronto: Butterworths, 1978.

Gall, Gerald L. *The Canadian Legal System.* Toronto: The Carswell Company Limited, 1977.

Gimpel, Jean. *The Medieval Machine: The Industrial Revolution of the Middle Ages.* 2nd ed. Aldershot: Wildwood House, 1988.

Glazebrook, G. P. de T. *The Story of Toronto.* Toronto: University of Toronto Press, 1971.

Globe and Mail. Cox, Kevin. "Fish on wane despite effort to save them." June 29, 1994.

———. Fine, Sean and Jeff Sallot. "Property, personal rights could collide." September 25, 1991.

———. Loverseed, Helga. "Wilderness by the Chateau." January 6, 1993.

———. Lush, Patricia. "Shell donates land: Nature group gets spectacular tract." December 3, 1992.

———. Mahood, Casey. "Canada falls behind U.S." June 8, 1993.

———. McLaren, Christie. "Carmanah logging called poor investment." November 23, 1990.

———. Mittelstaedt, Martin. "Private Ontario woodlots under a tax." September 26, 1994.

———. Mittelstaedt, Martin. "Property-rights plan under fire." October 2,

1991. Echoed in "Debate over property right entrenchment heating up." *Environment Policy & Law* (November 1991): 313.

———. Motherwell, Cathryn. "Six resource firms donate, sell mineral rights for park." July 20, 1993.

———. Picard, André. "A dispossessed people comes home" and "A long and winding road." December 4, 1993.

———. Platiel, Rudy. "Proposal threatens natives." September 30, 1991.

———. Wellar, Barry. Letter to the editor. November 19, 1991.

———. Wilson, Deborah and Robert Matas. "Natives win land rights in B.C." June 26, 1993.

———. York, Geoffrey. "Property rights seen as bargaining ploy." September 26, 1991.

———. Articles about the British Columbia government's decision to log parts of Clayoquot Sound dated April 14, May 1, May 3, and May 12, 1993.

Gordon, H. Scott. "The Economic Theory of a Common Property Resource: The Fishery." *The Journal of Political Economy* 62 (April 1954): 124-42.

Grumbine, R. Edward. "Policy in the Woods." In *Clearcut: The Tragedy of Industrial Forestry*, edited by Bill Devall, 253-61. San Francisco: Sierra Club Books and Earth Island Press, 1993.

Halsbury's Laws of England. 4th ed. London: Butterworths, 1984-5.

The Halton Region Conservation Authority. "Submission to Fair Tax Commission." May 31, 1993.

Hamilton Spectator. Solomon, Lawrence. "U.S. environment laws ahead of ours." June 7, 1986. (This article also appeared in the *Kingston Whig-Standard*, June 14, 1986 and *Brandon Sun*, June 14, 1986.)

Hardin, Garrett. "The Tragedy of the Commons." *Science* 162 (December 13, 1968): 1243-8.

Harvey, Christopher. "Riparian Water Rights: Not Dead Yet." *The Advocate* 48, pt. 4 (July 1990): 517-24.

Heuston, R. F. V., and R. A. Buckley. *Salmond and Heuston on the Law of Torts.* 19th ed. London: Sweet & Maxwell, 1987.

Higgs, Robert. "Legally Induced Technical Regress in the Washington Salmon Fishery." *Research in Economic History* 7 (1982): 55-86.

Hilts, Stewart, and Peter Mitchell. "Bucking the Free Market Economy: Using Land Trusts for Conservation and Community-Building." *Alternatives* 19, no. 3 (1993): 16-23.

Hogue, Arthur R. *Origins of the Common Law.* Bloomington: Indiana University Press, 1966. Reprint. Indianapolis: Liberty Fund, 1985.

Holt, J. C. *Magna Carta.* 2nd ed. Cambridge: Cambridge University Press, 1992.

The Holy Bible, King James Version, John, chapter 10.

Horwitz, Morton J. *The Transformation of American Law 1780-1860.* New York: Oxford University Press, 1992.

Hoskins, W. G. *The Making of the English Landscape.* London: Hodder and Stoughton Ltd., 1955.

Hull, Brian. *Valuing the Environment: Full-Cost Pricing—an Inquiry and a Goal.* The Conference Board of Canada Report 103-93.

Johnsen, D. Bruce. "The Formation and Protection of Property Rights Among the Southern Kwakiutl Indians." *The Journal of Legal Studies* 15 (January 1986): 41-67.

"The July Almanac: Environment." *The Atlantic Monthly,* July 1994, 12.

Kenauk: La seigneurie de Montebello. Undated press kit.

Kerr, Donald, and Jacob Spelt. *The Changing Face of Toronto: A Study in Urban Geography.* Ottawa: Geographical Branch, Mines & Technical Surveys, 1965.

Kluckner, Michael. *Toronto: The Way It Was.* Toronto: Whitecap Books, 1988.

Knetsch, Jack. *Property Rights and Compensation: Compulsory Acquisition and Other Losses.* Toronto: Butterworths, 1983.

Knetsch, Jack, and Thomas E. Borcherding. "Expropriation of Private Property and the Basis for Compensation." *University of Toronto Law Journal* 29 (1979): 237-52.

Lambert, Richard S., with Paul Pross. *Renewing Nature's Wealth: A Centennial History of the Public Management of Lands, Forests & Wildlife in Ontario, 1763-1967.* Ontario: Ontario Department of Lands and Forests, 1967.

Lauer, T. E. "The Common Law Background of the Riparian Doctrine." *The Missouri Law Review* 28, no. 1 (Winter 1963): 60-107.

Law Reform Commission of Canada, the Hon. E. Patrick Hartt, Chairman. *Report on Expropriation.* March 1976.

———. *Working Paper 9: Expropriation.* 1975.

Lewington, Peter. *No Right of Way: How Democracy Came to the Oil Patch.* Ames: Iowa State University Press, 1991.

Lucas, Alastair R. *Security of Title in Canadian Water Rights.* Calgary:

Canadian Institute of Resources Law, 1990.

Magna Carta. 1215. Reprinted as Appendix 6 in Holt, J. C. *Magna Carta.* 2nd ed. Cambridge: Cambridge University Press, 1992.

Magnet, Joseph Eliot. "Intentional Interference with Land." In *Studies in Canadian Tort Law*, edited by Lewis Klar, 287-323. Toronto: Butterworths, 1977.

Markdale Standard. "GADG survey finds evidence of massive government land grab." November 24, 1993.

Marzulla, Nancie. "Property Rights as a 'Central Organizing Principle.'" *Free Perspectives*, Summer 1993, 9.

McLaren, John P. S. "The Common Law Nuisance Actions and the Environmental Battle—Well-Tempered Swords or Broken Reeds?" *Osgoode Hall Law Journal* 10, no. 3 (December 1972): 505-61.

———. "Nuisance Law and the Industrial Revolution—Some Lessons from Social History." In *Issues in Tort Law*, edited by Freda Steel and Sanda Rogers-Magnet, 313-375. Toronto: The Carswell Company Ltd., 1983.

———. "The Tribulations of Antoine Ratté: A Case Study of the Environmental Regulation of the Canadian Lumbering Industry in the Nineteenth Century." *University of New Brunswick Law Journal* 33 (1984): 203-59.

McNeil, Kent, and Patrick Macklem. *Aboriginal, Treaty and Riparian Rights in the Moose River Basin: The Potential Impact of the Ontario Hydraulic Plan . . . Task Five: Riparian Rights in the Moose River Basin.* A report prepared for the Moose River/James Bay Coalition and submitted as evidence in the Environmental Assessment Hearing into Ontario Hydro's Demand Supply Plan, December 1992.

M'Gonigle, Michael, and Ben Parfitt. *Forestopia: A Practical Guide to the New Forest Economy.* Madeira Park: Harbour Publishing, 1994.

Middleton, Jesse Edgar. *Municipality of Toronto Canada: A History.* Toronto: Dominion Publishing, 1923.

Miller, John. "Land of the Free." *Policy Review* (Winter 1993): 66-70.

Mississauga News. Stewart, John. "Developer denuding land for tax break." February 17, 1994.

———. "Stop the axes." Editorial, February 17, 1994.

Moore, Deborah. "Water: The Rights and Wrongs of US Policy." *World Rivers Review* 7, no. 1 (January/February 1992): 8-11.

Morrison, George R. *Espanola on the Spanish.* 1989.

Mulvany, C. Pelham. *Toronto: Past and Present: A Handbook of the City.* Toronto: W. E. Caiger, 1884.

Mussell, Al. "Property Rights in the Development of Ontario Forest Tenures." Unpublished paper produced at the University of Guelph's Department of Agricultural Economics and Business, December 1992.

The National Trust. "Annual Report, 1992."

———. "Facts and Figures." Undated pamphlet.

———. "The National Trust: An Introduction." Pamphlet. 1993.

The Native People's Circle on Environment and Development, Louis (Smokey) Bruyere, Chair. *Final Report*. Ontario Round Table on Environment and Economy, April 30, 1990.

The Nature Conservancy of Canada. "Mount Broadwood Heritage Conservation Area: the largest donation of land in Canadian history." *The Ark* (Spring 1993).

———. "Profile." *The Ark* (Fall 1993).

———. "Unrivalled partnership protected outstanding Yukon Lands." *The Ark* (Fall 1993).

Nautiyal, Jagdish. "Forest Tenure Structure in Ontario." *The Forestry Chronicle* 53, no. 1 (February 1977): 20-5.

Nedelsky, Jennifer. "Judicial Conservatism in an Age of Innovation." *Essays in the History of Canadian Law*, edited by David H. Flaherty. Toronto: The University of Toronto Press and The Osgoode Society, 1981.

Nelles, H. V. *The Politics of Development: Forests, Mines & Hydro-electric Power in Ontario, 1849-1941*. Toronto: Macmillan of Canada, 1974.

New York Times. Cushman, John. "Choice of Chief Upsets Ranks of Forest Service." October 27, 1993.

———. Cushman, John. "Property Tax Changes Are Urged to Help Preserve Northeast Forest." March 4, 1994.

———. Hilts, Philip. "Cells May Bear Mark Of Each Cancer Agent." January 18, 1994.

———. Nasar, Sylvia. "A Talent for Rewriting History." October 13, 1993.

———. Passell, Peter. "Economic Scene." October 21, 1993.

———. Quint, Michael. "Insuring Environmental Liabilities." February 17, 1994.

———. Salpukas, Agis. "A New Slant on Exxon Valdez Spill." December 1, 1993.

———. "Excerpts From Court Ruling Limiting Governments' Power Over Property." June 25, 1994.

————. "White House Seeking to Ease Ban on Logging in Owl Areas." February 15, 1994.

Nova Scotia. *Debates*, February 22, 1965.

Ontario. Fair Tax Commission. *Fair Taxation in a Changing World: Highlights*. Toronto: University of Toronto Press, 1993.

————. *Legislature of Ontario Debates, Official Report—Daily Edition*. February 28, 1956; March 26, 1956; March 27, 1956; February 11, 1957; February 12, 1957; and March 28, 1957.

————. Ministry of the Environment and Ministry of Natural Resources. With Environment Canada. *Status Report, Spanish River—Harbour Area, Remedial Action Plan (RAP)*. June 1988.

————. Ministry of Agriculture, Food and Rural Affairs. "Buchanan announces Niagara tender fruit lands program." News Release, May 7, 1994.

————. Ministry of Natural Resources. L. A. Morse, author. *White Pine: Ontario Celebrates Its History*. 1984.

————. Ministry of Northern Development and Mines. *Mining Act Backgrounder: The Mining Land Tax*. Undated pamphlet.

————. Ministry of Northern Development and Mines. *Ontario's Mines and Minerals, Policy and Legislation: A Green Paper*. December 1988.

————. *Ontario Legislative Assembly Debates*. March 29, 1949; February 24, 1950; March 21, 1950; March 23, 1950.

————. Royal Commission Inquiry into Civil Rights, the Honourable James McRuer, Commissioner. *Report Number One*, Volume Three. 1968.

————. Task Force on the Ontario Environmental Bill of Rights, Richard Dicerni and Michael G. Cochrane, Co-chairs. *Report*. July 1992.

Ontario Forestry Association. *Forest People*. Number 2, 1993.

————. *Taxed to Death: A Report on the Impact of Cancellation of the Managed Forest Tax Rebate Program*. September 1994.

Owen, Bruce M., and Ronald Braeutigam. *The Regulation Game: Strategic Use of the Administrative Process*. Cambridge: Ballinger, 1978.

Pearse, Peter H. "Developing Property Rights as Instruments of Natural Resources Policy: The Case of the Fisheries." *Climate Change*, produced by the Organisation for Economic Co-operation and Development. Paris: OECD, 1992.

————. "Property Rights and the Development of Natural Resource Policies in Canada." *Canadian Public Policy* 14, no. 3 (1988): 307-20.

————. *Rising to the Challenge: A New Policy for Canada's Freshwater Fisheries*. Ottawa: Canadian Wildlife Federation, 1988.

————. "Scarcity of Natural Resources and the Implications for Sustainable Development." 1990.

Percy, David R. *The Framework of Water Rights Legislation in Canada*. Calgary: The Canadian Institute of Resources Law, 1988.

Peripoli, Bruno. "Forest policy misguided." *Eco-News*, Winter 1989/90, 7-8.

Political Economy Research Center. *PERC Reports* 7, no. 4 (December 1989).

Pollot, Mark L. *Grand Theft and Petit Larceny: Property Rights in America*. San Francisco: Pacific Research Institute for Public Policy, 1993.

Prosser, William. *Handbook of the Law of Torts*. 4th ed. St. Paul: West Publishing Co., 1971.

"Railway." *Encyclopaedia Britannica* 18: 1104-28. Chicago: William Benton, 1972.

Rankin, Murray. *An Environmental Bill of Rights for Ontario: Reflections and Recommendations. A Discussion Paper*. January 1991.

Reid, Ron. *Bringing Trust to Ontario: A Study on the Role of Nature Trusts, Phase I*. Federation of Ontario Naturalists, June 1988.

Reindeau, R. "Servicing the Modern City." In *Forging a Consensus*, edited by Victor Russell. Toronto: University of Toronto Press, 1984.

Risk, R. C. B. "The Law and the Economy in Mid-Nineteenth-Century Ontario: A Perspective." In *Essays in the History of Canadian Law*, edited by David H. Flaherty. Toronto: The University of Toronto Press and The Osgoode Society, 1981.

Rothbard, Murray. "Law, Property Rights, and Air Pollution." In *Economics and the Environment: A Reconciliation*, edited by Walter E. Block, 233-79. Vancouver: The Fraser Institute, 1990.

Rueggeberg, H. R., and A. Thompson. *Water Law and Policy Issues in Canada*. Vancouver: Westwater Research Centre, 1984.

Rust-D'Eye, George H. *Cabbagetown Remembered*. Erin: Boston Mills Press, 1984.

Sandberg, L. Anders, ed. *Trouble in the Woods: Forest Policy and Social Conflict in Nova Scotia and New Brunswick*. Fredericton: Acadiensis Press, 1992.

Saskatchewan Parks and Renewable Resources. *Fish & Wildlife Development Fund Activities 1989-1990*.

Scarman, Leslie. *English Law—The New Dimension*. London: Stevens & Sons, 1974.

Scott, Anthony. "Development of Property in the Fishery." *Marine Resource Economics* 5 (1988): 289-311.

———. "The Fishery: The Objectives of Sole Ownership." *The Journal of Political Economy* 63, no. 2 (April 1955): 116-24.

———. "Obstacles to Fishery Self-Government." *Marine Resource Economics* 8 (1993): 187-199.

Scott, Anthony, and Philip A. Neher. *Public Regulation of Commercial Fisheries*. The Economic Council of Canada, 1981.

Sharpe, Robert. *Injunctions and Specific Performance*. Toronto: Canada Law Book Limited, 1983.

Sinclair, Peter R. "Regulating the fisheries: quota controls and licensing policy." In *State Intervention and the Newfoundland Fisheries: Essays on Fisheries Policy and Social Structure*. Aldershot, Hants: Gower Publishing Co., 1987.

Smith, Adam. *An Inquiry into the Nature and Causes of the Wealth of Nations*, Book 4. New York: Collier, 1905. (First published in 1776.)

Smith, Fred. "Controlling the Environmental Threat to the Global Liberal Order." Paper presented to the Mont Pelerin Society Meeting in Christchurch, New Zealand, November 30, 1989.

Smith, Rodney T. "Water Reallocation Through Market Transactions v. Regulatory Fiat." Presentation to Waterscapes '91 conference in Saskatoon, Saskatchewan, June 7, 1991.

Stewart, Walter. *Paper Juggernaut: Big Government Gone Mad*. Toronto: McClelland and Stewart, 1979.

Stroup, Richard, and Jane Shaw. "The Free Market and the Environment." *The Public Interest*, no. 97 (Fall 1989): 30-43.

Sudbury Daily Star, "Camp Owners Get KVP Injunction." April 16, 1948.

———. "Court Dismisses Appeal by KVP in Pollution Case." November 23, 1948.

Sudbury Star, "Court Injunction Halts Races." September 10, 1970.

Sweeney, Richard James, Robert D. Tollison, and Thomas D. Willett. "Market Failure, the Common-Pool Problem, and Ocean Resource Exploitation." *The Journal of Law and Economics* 17, no. 1 (April 1974): 179-92.

Toronto Harbour Commission. *Toronto Harbour: The Passing Years*. 1985.

Toronto Star. Tyler, Tracey. "Court derails man's bid to stop subway noise." March 8, 1993.

Toronto Sun. Ruryk, Zen. "This land is your land?" March 15, 1994.

Trebilcock, Michael, and Ralph Winter. *The Impact of the Nuclear Liability Act on Safety Incentives in the Nuclear Power Industry*. Exhibit 967 in *Energy Probe et al*. v. *The Attorney General of Canada*. April 29, 1993.

Valley Farmers Forum. "Wetland designation devaluates property 90%" and "New wetlands regulations cuts off farmer's retirement plan." February 12, 1994.

Wall Street Journal. Anderson, Terry. "Wolves in the Marketplace." August 12, 1992.

————. Brannigan, Martha. "CAT Scan May Soon 'Map' Air Pollution." November 10, 1994.

————. Carlton, Jim. "Takings Cases Don't Always Favor Takers." November 10, 1992.

————. Eagle, Steven. "Private Property Rights vs. Public Works." March 2, 1994.

————. Freedman, Alix. "Power Lines Short-Circuit Sales, Homeowners Claim." December 8, 1993.

————. Fund, John. "Hayek's Heirs Contemplate Greener Pastures." September 9, 1991.

————. McCoy, Charles. "Cutting Costs: For Takeover Baron, Redwood Forests Are Just One More Deal." August 6, 1993.

————. Solomon, Lawrence. "Save the Forests—Sell the Trees." August 25, 1989. Excerpted in Dolan, Edwin G. and David E. Lindsey. *Economics*. 6th ed., 887-8. Chicago: The Dryden Press, 1991.

————. Taylor, Jeffrey, and Dave Kansas. "Environmentalists Vie for Right to Pollute." March 26, 1993.

————."Chicago Rules." October 13, 1993.

West, Bruce. *Toronto*. Toronto: Doubleday, 1979.

Wright, C. A., and A. M. Linden. *Canadian Tort Law: Cases, Notes & Materials*. 7th ed. Toronto: Butterworths, 1980.

"Yukon land donated." *Canadian Geographic*, November/December 1993, 15.

Index of Cases

Page and note references appear in italics after citations.

Walker v. *McKinnon Industries Ltd.*, [1949] 4 D.L.R. 739 (Ont. H.C.), aff'd [1950] 3 D.L.R. 159 (Ont. C.A.), aff'd [1951] 3 D.L.R. 577 (P.C.), *37n.16, 47-48, 51n.26, 123n.20, 249-51, 262n.54-263n.60*

Walter v. *Selfe* (1851), 4 De G. & S. 315, 20 L.J. Ch. 433, *47, 51n.25, 233-34, 259nn.1-5*

Warren v. *City of Gloversville*, 81 App. Div., 291, 293, 80 N.Y. Supp. 912, 913 (N.Y. Ct. App. 1903), *274-75, 277, 288n.27, 289n.28*

Watson v. *Jackson* (1914), 19 D.L.R. 733 (Ont. S.C.), *56, 66n.18, 278-79, 290nn.43,44*

Weston Paper Co. v. *Pope et al.*, 155 Ind. 394, 57 N.E. 719, 56 L.R.A. 899 (1900), *59, 67n.27, 270-71, 278, 288nn.14-19*

Whalen v. *Union Bag & Paper Co.*, 145 App. Div. 1, 129 N.Y. Supp. 391 (1911), 208 N.Y. 1, 5, 101 N.E. 805 (1913), *60, 67nn.28,29, 276-78, 289nn.35-40*

Wood v. *Sutcliffe* (1851), 2 Sim. (N.S.) 163, 61 E.R. 303, *123n.20*

Wood and Another v. *Waud and Others* (1849), 3 Exch. 748, 154 E.R. 1047, *64n.8, 123n.20*

Yates v. *Jack* (1866), L.R. 1 Ch. 295, *240, 260n.23*

John Young and Company v. *Bankier Distillery Company and Others*, [1893] A.C. 691 (P.C), *57, 66nn.20,21, 268-69, 275, 278, 280, 281, 285, 287n.8-288n.13*

Index